Collins

Cambridge IGCSE™

English as a Second Language

Susan Anstey, Alison Burch, Lucy Hobbs,
Avril Kirkham, Shubha Koshy,
Lorna Pepper and Emma Wilkinson

D1630845

STUDENT'S BOOK

William Collins' dream of knowledge for all began with the publication of his first book in 1819. A self-educated mill worker, he not only enriched millions of lives, but also founded a flourishing publishing house. Today, staying true to this spirit, Collins books are packed with inspiration, innovation and practical expertise. They place you at the centre of a world of possibility and give you exactly what you need to explore it.

Collins. Freedom to teach.

Published by Collins
An imprint of HarperCollins*Publishers*
The News Building
1 London Bridge Street
London
SE1 9GF

HarperCollins *Publishers*
Macken House
39/40 Mayor Street Upper
Dublin 1
D01 C9W8
Ireland

Browse the complete Collins catalogue at
www.collins.co.uk

10 9 8 7 6 5 4 3 2

ISBN 978-0-00-849309-7

British Library Cataloguing in Publication Data.
A Catalogue record for this publication is available from the British Library.

Authors: Susan Anstey, Alison Burch, Lucy Hobbs, Avril Kirkham, Shubha Koshy, Lorna Pepper and Emma Wilkinson
Additional content written by Celia Wigley, Lucy Cooper and Nicola Prentis
Publisher: Elaine Higgleton
Product manager: Joanna Ramsay
Project manager/Series editor: Celia Wigley
Development editor: Lucy Cooper
Proofreader: Denise Cowle
Cover designer: Gordon MacGilp
Illustrator: Ann Paganuzzi
Typesetter: Ken Vail Graphic Design
Production controller: Lyndsey Rogers
Printed in Italy by Grafica Veneta S.p.A

MIX
Paper from
responsible sources
FSC™ C007454

With thanks to our reviewers of the first edition: Catherine Errigton, Italy; Dean Roberts, UK; Rohan Roberts, UAE; Alan Schmidt, Czech Republic; Naghma Shaikh, India. And thanks to the students at the following schools for contributing answers to questions in Chapters 13–19 (facilitating teachers, to whom we are very grateful, in brackets): West Island School, Hong Kong (Shubha Koshy); The British School, Warsaw, Poland (Magdalena Halska); The Winchester School, Dubai, UAE (Rohan Roberts); The Riverside School, Prague, Czech Republic (Alan Schmidt); VIBGYOR High, Mumbai, India (Naghma Shaikh). With thanks to everyone who has provided feedback and shared insights from their own teaching, examining and understanding of the students studying for this qualification: Abhinandan Bhattacharya (JBCN International School Oshiwara), Samar Sabat & Rula Kandalaft (Rosary Sisters High School), Suzanne Sheha (Nile Egyptian School), Christine Mariou (PASCAL Private English School), Vanessa Mitchell (Collège du Léman), Sioban Parker, Susan Anstey, Avril Kirkham, Karen Harper, and Fiona Leney.

Third-party websites and resources referred to in this publication have not been endorsed by Cambridge Assessment International Education. Cambridge International recommends that teachers consider using a range of teaching and learning resources in preparing learners for assessment, based on their own professional judgement of their students' needs.

Exam-style questions and sample answers have been written by the authors. In examinations, the way marks are awarded may be different. References to assessment and/or assessment preparation are the publisher's interpretation of the syllabus requirements and may not fully reflect the approach of Cambridge Assessment International Education. The information in Chapters 13–19 is based on the Cambridge International syllabus (0510) for examination from 2024. You should always refer to the appropriate syllabus document for the year of your examination to confirm the details and for more information. The syllabus document is available on the Cambridge International website at www.cambridgeinternational.org.

Contents

Foreword

Dear students,

Welcome to the Collins Cambridge IGCSE™ English as a Second Language Student's Book! We hope it will enable you to take charge of your learning on your Cambridge IGCSE™ English as a Second Language course and to develop an independent, thoughtful approach to your English language studies. You are perhaps already fluent in one or more other languages, so we hope this book becomes an effective guide to the requirements of this fast-paced subject.

The skills and vocabulary covered in the book revolve around a number of interesting topics and world issues that will help you become much more fluent, clear and confident in your responses, both oral and written. It provides you with key skills in reading, writing, speaking and listening that will help make you a better communicator in all situations and give you a basis for further study in English. These skills include skimming and scanning, note-taking, summarising and shaping your writing for different audiences.

The Student's Book builds on your understanding of how languages work and offers you a variety of useful tips and strategies to improve the quality and accuracy of your spoken and written communication. Most importantly, this book gives you lots to think about and talk about while developing your reading, writing and listening skills in an international context. It uses a number of fun activities and current genres like emails, blogs, websites, news reports and magazine articles.

Each chapter begins with a set of fascinating 'Big pictures' and 'Thinking big' questions to get you thinking around the topic and working out what you already know about it. The questions may not necessarily relate to the questions later on in the chapter but they are an opportunity to start thinking about the new topic. You might discuss some of this in your first language, but make sure you record your responses in a handy journal or notebook to keep track of your growing knowledge and vocabulary in English. Once you have worked through a series of interactive reading, writing, speaking and listening tasks, you have the opportunity to work on a 'big task' with your classmates, which allows you to showcase your skills and vocabulary in a real-world context. You could set up an exciting competition around each task and get your friends and teachers to assess this.

You could use this book to cover a series of key skills which you wish to focus on, or as a topic-based textbook that you work through in class. It is helpful if you work with a friend or classmates to make the most of all aspects of the book, and not just the speaking and listening parts.

Good luck with your English studies and the language of global communication!

Shubha Koshy,

Hong Kong

How to use this book

Your Cambridge IGCSE English as a Second Language Student's Book is divided into two main sections.

Section 1: TOPICS AND SKILLS

The first section contains 12 chapters based on topics such as *technology*, *exploration* and *the environment*. Each of these chapters starts with a 'big picture' feature and ends with a 'big task' – you can find out more about these on the previous page. The chapter is then split into four parts, each focusing on one skill: reading, writing, speaking or listening. The skills you explore and practise are all relevant to the Cambridge IGCSE and IGCSE (9-1) English as a Second Language syllabuses (0510/0511/0991/0993) for examination from 2024.

Here are some of the features in these chapters:

- A list of the skills you will focus on is provided at the beginning of each section.

- A clear learning journey is shown using the same headings throughout: *Getting starting*, *Exploring the skills*, *Developing the skills* and *Going further*.

- 'Language boosters' help you to improve your understanding of English grammar and vocabulary.

- 'Glossary' boxes provide definitions of some of the more challenging items of vocabulary.

- The chapters end with a 'Check your progress' table where you can assess your learning and understand how to improve.

Section 2: EXAM PREPARATION

The second section of the Student's Book helps you develop the skills needed for formal assessment. You will have been building and practising your skills in reading, writing, listening and speaking in English in chapters 1–12 of this book and developing your ability to communicate effectively in English. Chapters 13–19 provide step-by-step advice on approaching different question types and help you to prepare for examinations, with example exam-style questions for you to practise your skills.

In the last section there are Sample answers to each of the exam-style questions in Chapters 13–19, together with our author's suggested marks and comments. Reading through these marks and comments will help you improve your answers and avoid common mistakes.

Listening exercises in both sections are supported by audio, so if you see this symbol 1.1 it means you should listen to the recording.

Contents map

Section 3: Speaking	Section 4: Listening	Big task
The importance of the internet • communicate your ideas clearly, accurately and effectively • keep a conversation going by developing ideas with details and examples.	**How technology is changing our lives** • identify relevant information • understand and select correct details and key question words • understand what is implied but not directly stated in a more formal conversation.	Give a presentation on the best technological inventions.
Polar exploration • research and organise ideas for giving a talk or presentation • plan an effective, individual opening for a talk or presentation.	**Underwater exploration** • recognise and understand facts when listening to short spoken texts • recognise and understand facts when listening to a longer and more difficult text • listen carefully and understand complicated instructions.	Prepare a presentation to win money for a chosen exploration project.
Health around the world • use a variety of structures when you are speaking • link ideas using a range of conjunctions • speak using abstract nouns and noun phrases to give variety to your sentences.	**Better health** • understand and pick out specific details when listening • predict the kind of information you will hear, including units of measurement • recognise high numbers when listening.	Create a website about young people's health.
How do we learn? • speak clearly using the most effective words to explain and describe • choose the correct vocabulary and level of formality for the listener.	**School and the real world** • select details from different kinds of spoken texts • use clues before you start listening to help you understand a text • understand what is implied but not directly stated in a conversation.	Research, plan and give a presentation on an ideal school.
Competition and the arts • build a conversation by asking and answering questions • be an active listener and add new ideas.	**Competition in business** • understand and pick out facts in short spoken and written texts • recognise and understand opinions in short spoken and written texts • recognise and understand fact and opinion in longer, more formal dialogues.	Write a talent show review.
Job interviews • pronounce words and speak clearly to be understood in a conversation • speak up confidently and clearly.	**Unusual jobs** • predict to help you understand and select details • select details to make notes or fill in forms when listening to a range of texts.	Write a job application and act out a job interview.
Pollution – slow poison? • express ideas clearly using the correct verb tenses • respond clearly, accurately and effectively to others, in conversation • communicate ideas clearly and confidently in a more formal talk.	**Where has all the wildlife gone?** • use key words and context to help predict content • understand what is implied but not directly stated during an interview.	Plan and give a multimedia presentation on local environmental issues.
Modern culture • use examples to support your opinions while speaking • include facts and expert opinions to support your point of view • use rhetorical questions to make your speaking effective.	**Disappearing ways of life** • understand and select relevant information in spoken texts • identify and understand opinions in a range of spoken texts • identify and understand conflicting opinions in an informal spoken text.	Write an article about a community whose culture and way of life are disappearing.
Problems with transport • use a variety of grammatical structures accurately and effectively when you speak • vary the tense of verbs you use according to the situation.	**Where will we go and how will we get there?** • understand connections and differences between related ideas • understand what is implied but not directly stated in a formal spoken text.	Design a leaflet for a new transport system and deliver a presentation.
Clothes and culture • use the right words when speaking about culture and clothing • use more specialised vocabulary appropriately.	**The price of fashion: who pays?** • listen effectively to fellow students • understand and select detailed information supplied by fellow students • understand what is implied but not directly stated in a conversation.	Organise a fashion show.
Television • disagree politely in a conversation • keep a conversation going by rephrasing what the previous speaker has said.	**Film** • understand and select facts in both formal and informal spoken texts • recognise and understand opinions and attitudes in a more formal dialogue.	Debate on how good for you screen time is.
Growing up • speak clearly and use the correct stress when speaking • vary your tone to interest your listener.	**Achievements of youth and old age** • recognise and understand ideas, opinions and attitudes • recognise connections between ideas.	Prepare a presentation about the different rights and responsibilities of young and old people.

THE BIG PICTURE

In this chapter you are going to think about technology and how it is changing the world we live in. You will:

- read about some of the technology we use
- think about the effects that it has on us
- research, think, talk and write about what you consider to be the greatest technological inventions of our times.

THINKING BIG

1 On your own, pick any two pictures from the collage that you find interesting.

- Look carefully at each picture and note down what you think each one is saying about technology.
- Make notes ready for a discussion.

2 In pairs:

- Explain to your partner why you chose these two pictures. Discuss your ideas and see how far you agree or disagree.
- Note down any interesting words or ideas from this conversation.

3 On your own, note answers to the following questions:

- What examples of technology have you used since you got out of bed this morning?
- Which of these items would you consider to be essential?
- Which of these items would you consider to be non-essential?
- How would you define technology? Write your own definition of what you consider to be 'technology'.

1
Technology

1.1 What is technology?

In this section you will learn to:

✓ skim and scan different kinds of texts for facts and details

✓ understand what is implied but not directly stated in an online article.

GETTING STARTED

1 What is technology and how is it used?

   a) As a class or in groups, share the ideas that you wrote about in 'Thinking big'.

   b) What were the earliest forms of technology and what did they help people to do?

   c) Discuss examples of technology that have changed in your lifetime and what they help you to do.

EXPLORING THE SKILLS

When there is too much text to read, or you are short of time, you do not need to read every single word on the page. Skimming and scanning are two techniques that will help you find quickly the information you need.

Skimming involves moving your eyes quickly over a text to get a general sense of it. It helps you get the 'gist' – the overall meaning – of the writing, without having to read it all carefully. You can then decide which parts you need to read more closely.

To find out quickly what a text is about:

- read the title first and then the subheadings

- look at any pictures to see what hints they give

- read the beginning and end of each paragraph

- let your eyes skim over the text and look out for key words.

2 Skim read the text on the next page to find out what it is about.

   Which of the following statements explains what the text is about?

   a) It gives the reasons why you should have computers.

   b) It tells you the bad things about computers.

   c) It tells you the history of computers.

   d) It is from a story about computers.

3 With a partner, discuss how you could tell which statement in task 2 was correct, and which it could not be.

A Computing then and now

A lot of things that are a **reality** in the 21st century might have seemed science fiction twenty years ago. The early computers invented in the middle of the 20th century were large and heavy and could only do basic **tasks**. Yet they became the **handheld devices** that we see everywhere today. On average, people check their phone every six minutes and we communicate through social networks with people we might never meet in person. We are seeing the beginning of driverless cars and the Internet of Things (IoT) – smart household devices that can be controlled remotely from a phone or send data to other machines. We are definitely part of an exciting Digital Age. Here are some of the highlights.

B 1958 Integrated circuit invented

Jack Kilby of Texas Instruments and Robert Noyce of Fairchild Semiconductor independently invent the integrated circuit – an electronic system essential for computers.

C 1968 The computer mouse makes its public appearance

The computer mouse is demonstrated at a computer conference in San Francisco. Its inventor, Douglas Engelbart of the Stanford Research Institute, receives the licence for the mouse 2 years later.

D 1977 Apple II is released

Electronics hobbyists Steve Jobs and Steve Wozniak release the Apple II, a desktop personal computer for the mass market.

E 1992 Personal Digital Assistant

Apple chairman John Sculley is the first person to use the phrase 'personal digital assistant' (PDA) to refer to handheld computers.

Adapted from 'Greatest Engineering Achievements of the 20th Century: Computers'

Once you have skimmed a text to get an overall sense of its meaning, you might need to find a specific detail. This is called **scanning** – looking over a text to find the exact information you want.

(4) Now scan the text above. Which paragraph A–E contains the answer to questions a–c below?

a) Who invented the integrated circuit?

b) When was the computer mouse first seen by the general public?

c) Which was the first personal computer?

TOP TIP

When you scanned for details, you probably used the subheadings to help you. You can also look for key words in the questions. For example, 'When?' will need a date or a time. 'Who?' will probably need a name. Underline these key 'question words' to help you narrow down what you are looking for.

GLOSSARY

reality	you say something is a reality when it is actually happening
task	an activity or piece of work you have to do
handheld	small and light enough to be used while you are holding it
device	machine or tool used for a specific task

READING SKILLS

11

DEVELOPING THE SKILLS

You can also use your skimming and scanning skills to find facts and details when looking at pictures in a text. For example, you can:

- look at what the pictures show
- look at any captions that go with the pictures
- see if the pictures have any labels explaining more about them.

5 Look at the online article opposite. Skim the article, looking also at the photos and headings, to answer the following questions.

a) Which two areas of smart home technology are talked about in the article?

b) List the things the technology can turn on.

Now scan for these details:

c) What will motion detectors do?

d) What will the facial recognition technology do?

GLOSSARY

motion detector technology that recognises when something moves

facial recognition the ability to recognise faces

GOING FURTHER

To understand the purpose of a text, we have to use our reading skills. Sometimes when reading we have to understand what is implied, or suggested, but not directly stated.

LANGUAGE BOOSTER When a meaning is **implied**, the writer does not say openly what he or she means, but the reader can work it out. For example, the meaning of a sign that says 'Do not walk on the grass!' is not implied, it is clearly stated. However, the meaning of a sign saying 'Thank you for keeping to the paved area' implies that the reader should not walk on the grass.

6 In pairs, look again at the last paragraph. Answer questions i) and ii).

i) *But the jewel in the crown of the smart home is smart security* means:

 A Smart security devices are expensive.
 B Smart security devices are colourful.
 C Smart security devices are the best.

ii) *Time will tell if this new technology actually brings peace of mind or not* means:

 A The technology will certainly makes us feel more relaxed.
 B The technology will give us more time to enjoy relaxing activities.
 C The technology may make us feel less relaxed.

These sentences give information in a subtle way. The writer expects you to read 'between the lines' and understand more than is actually written. For example, *But the jewel in the crown of the smart home is smart security* suggests that this is the best technology. So, the answer to **i)** is C.

Now read the whole article again and answer **iii)**

iii) Complete the sentence.

The main purpose of this text is …
- **A** to inform us about the latest gadgets.
- **B** to describe the gadgets in detail.
- **C** to persuade us to buy the gadgets.

Is your dream home a smart home?

You know what a smart phone is, but what about a smart home? The latest smart devices can turn lights, heating or music on even when you're not there. This technology can do more than just make your home more comfortable. Smart devices can also keep your home safe. Read on to find out more.

Smart comfort

Imagine never again coming home and opening the door to a cold, dark, silent house. Some smart locks can unlock your front door when they 'see' you, or other family members coming. And, via apps on your phone, you can programme smart devices to turn on lights, play your favourite music and make sure the house is warm by the time you get home. You can even programme the oven to have dinner ready.

Lights, heating, action!

Smart security

But the jewel in the crown of the smart home is smart security. Installing a device that connects your phone with a security camera is one simple way to know who's at your front door. But the latest technology provides a level of security that you might normally think of in connection with top-secret government buildings. Motion detectors will send a message to your phone if anything moves outside your house. And facial recognition technology can tell you if the movement comes from a stranger, someone you know, or just next door's cat. With your

Watch every room in your house from anywhere in the world

smartphone, you can even use the cameras from anywhere in the world to watch everyone inside your home while you're out. Time will tell if this new technology actually brings peace of mind or not.

The question is … will these new gadgets make our lives better or mean we spend even more time on our phones?

1.2 Smartphones on the brain

WRITING SKILLS IN FOCUS

In this section you will learn to:
✓ collect and organise ideas before writing to explain or inform
✓ communicate your ideas clearly and effectively through writing.

GETTING STARTED

(1) Research shows that people between the ages of 18 and 24 check their phones most often. On average people in this age group check their phones 74 times a day.

- How often do you check your phone?

- What did you last use your phone for?

TOP TIP

Cell phone is generally used in America and **mobile phone** is used in the UK and Australia. In spoken English people often drop the word 'phone' and say 'mobile' and 'cell'.

EXPLORING THE SKILLS

Whenever you write, you need to have a clear idea of what the purpose of your writing is. The purpose could be any of the following:

- to describe what something looks like

- to explain how something works

- to give information – facts and details about something.

For example, if you are giving someone information about smartphones, you would not need to include a description of your own feelings about mobiles. Just keep to the facts and be really clear.

(2) Imagine you have been asked to write a school magazine article about the advantages and disadvantages of smartphones. You have thought about this and produced the list of points on the next page.

In addition to thinking about the purpose of your writing, you should also think about the reader and format.

What is the purpose, who are the readers and what is the format of the writing outlined in Question 2?

Purpose: _____

Reader: _____

Format: _____

Smartphones

- Can learn vocabulary using your smartphone
- Unfortunately can be used to cheat in exams
- Some people can post unkind comments about other people which can be upsetting
- Can use for paying for things
- Some people can't stop checking their phones
- Lots of great apps, like those to keep fit and healthy
- Can set reminders/alarm so you don't forget things
- Can take photos
- Can take notes for studies
- Read the news
- Can video call friends and family all over the world
- Can listen to music and watch videos
- Can check and send messages to friends and family
- Adverts can show things, like very attractive models, that are not realistic

Before you write your magazine article, organise your list of points above into a concept map based on the advantages and disadvantages of smartphones. Make sure you have only ONE new idea per box. Add related ideas in smaller boxes linked to the main idea.

Copy the diagram below and add more points in the related boxes.

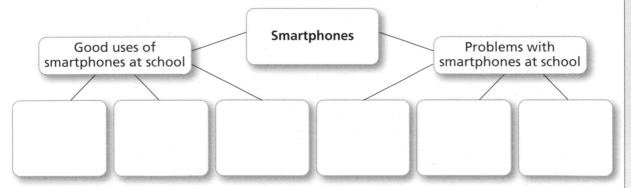

3 With a partner or in a group, talk each other through your concept map.

a) Talk to your partner or group about which of these points you agree with.

b) Note down:
- any interesting words that came up in your discussion
- the main points that were raised in your discussion.

DEVELOPING THE SKILLS

Remember that when you are explaining something to someone, you need to be very clear and keep to the facts.

(4) Imagine that your school or college needs to decide on its policy on smartphones. You have been asked to write a report for the management team. This report needs to explain:

- how smartphones are used by students during the school day
- the advantages and disadvantages of allowing smartphones at school.

At this point the management team is not asking for your opinion on what policy they should have – they want to know the current situation.

Draw a new concept map to organise your ideas. You might like to include the following headings in your boxes:

- How students use phones
- Possible advantages
- Possible disadvantages.

(5) Now write the report for your school or college management team. Use the plan on the next page to help you.

Remember: A report is a factual text and its purpose is to explain something and give information. Therefore, a report must only give information that is important to its reader. Sometimes you might be asked to write a report at school or at work.

Each paragraph must have a topic sentence that tells you what the rest of the paragraph will be about. Use ideas that you may have already discussed and develop these into paragraphs. Include only facts, not opinions, and use clear language.

Also think about your introduction and conclusion.

You could start like this:

As a student representative at our school, I have been asked to write a report about the use of smartphones by students at school.

Writing plan: Writing a report

Introduction:

(An opening paragraph to capture the reader's attention or introduce your purpose.)

Paragraph 1: Description of how phones are used by students at … school/college.

Topic sentence:

Paragraph 2: Advantages of using phones at school

Topic sentence:

Paragraph 3: Disadvantages of using phones at school

Topic sentence:

Conclusion:

(Summarise the main points presented. Be careful not to give any personal opinions.)

> **TOP TIP**
>
> Each paragraph must have a topic sentence that tells you what the rest of the paragraph will be about. The topic sentence is usually the first sentence of the paragraph. The supporting sentences after the topic sentence develop the main idea of the paragraph.

GOING FURTHER

6 Now write your report in full. Write about 200 words.
Remember to check the spelling and punctuation in your report.

1.3 The importance of the internet

In this section you will learn to:
✓ communicate your ideas clearly, accurately and effectively
✓ keep a conversation going by developing ideas with details and examples.

GETTING STARTED

Read the questions below and note down your answers. Then in pairs ask each other the questions.

(1) What sort of technology do you have in your home?

(2) What do you use the technology in your home for?

Try to develop a conversation from your partner's responses, for example:

Your partner: We have a virtual assistant in the kitchen.

You: How often do you use it?

EXPLORING THE SKILLS

Conversations are all about communicating your ideas clearly and appropriately. What makes for a good conversation in class?

It takes two to have a conversation, so both people need to:

● offer ideas

● listen carefully to the other person and respond properly

● avoid dominating the conversation

● find ways to keep the conversation going, for example by asking questions, sympathising, giving a personal example, asking for an opinion.

3 What do you use the internet for? Has the internet made our lives better? Read the following ideas.

I keep in touch with all my friends using social media.

I do research online.

I share videos via social media.

I post photos.

I listen to music online.

I watch TV and movies on demand.

People use filters so their photos look different from real life.

Some of my classes are online.

People can say unkind things on the internet.

You can get new music and movies as soon as they're released.

You can pretend to be someone else online.

You can talk to people all over the world on social media.

In pairs, discuss:

● Do you agree with them?

● How has the internet made our lives better?

● How has the internet made our lives worse?

If there are any words that you don't understand, discuss these with your partner and try to guess the meaning.

TOP TIP

If you come across a word you do not know, you can often guess its meaning from its context: in other words, from the ideas around it. For example, you may not know the word 'prestige', but if you hear it in the sentence: "According to some people, the latest smartphone increases prestige among friends and other schoolmates", you should be able to guess that it means something like 'respect and admiration'.

DEVELOPING THE SKILLS

Whether you are chatting to a friend or giving a formal talk to a group of people, and whether you are the speaker or the listener, you still have a responsibility to help communication. Think about eye contact, looking interested and asking questions at the right moment.

(4) You are going to have a conversation with your partner about whether the internet has made our lives better or worse. Think about what you will say, but also think about how you will respond to what your partner says. Read the communication checklist below which lists what you should do to respond properly to your partner. Have a conversation with your partner and try to keep the conversation going for longer.

Communication checklist	Conversation 1	Conversation 2	Conversation 3
Body language ● Do you look interested? ● Are you keeping your body language open? (no crossing arms or looking away) ● Are you leaning forward? ● Are you nodding? ● Are you smiling? ● Are you maintaining eye contact?			
Reactions ● 'Oh yes, I see.' ● 'How interesting!' ● 'Really?'			
Asking questions to keep the conversation going ● 'What do you think?' ● 'What about you?'			
Asking questions to understand ● 'When you say … do you mean … or … ?' ● 'Do you mean … ?'			

(5) When you have finished your conversation, with your partner go through the checklist again ticking the points you did.

(6) Join another pair and this time listen to their conversation ticking the points in the checklist that they do. Share your information with them. Change roles and let the other pair of students listen to your conversation. Share your information.

GOING FURTHER

When you are talking with another person, you have to be willing to keep the conversation going. We have already looked at some ways of doing this. Another way to keep a conversation going is to develop it, to move it on further, by giving examples and explaining them a little.

(7) Losing files on your computer can be very annoying. Have you heard of the 'cloud'? Read the advertisements on the next page and then, in pairs, discuss task 9.

Averting disaster

 Fileshare offers you **2GB** of free storage that you can increase to a full 16GB by recommending the service to others. Because Fileshare also **syncs** files to your other devices, it's a good place for your main work files.

 Storage+ offers a 60-day free trial and the cheapest pricing plan, Personal Premium, comes with 100GB of storage. If you pay more per month, you can get unlimited storage. Storage+ syncs all cloud storage in one place, and you can also access and update your folders through a browser or an android smartphone or tablet app, or Apple iPhone or iPad app.

GLOSSARY

GB (gigabyte)　　　　(in computing) one thousand and twenty-four megabytes

sync (synchronise)　to set up two or more devices so that any changes to the data on one device are also made to the other devices

8 An adult you know has had an IT disaster. Their home computer has crashed, losing all their important documents. They do not have any up-to-date backups, and you have decided to help them be more organised in the future. Prepare for a conversation where you will discuss their use of the computer and explain some ways they could back up their files.

Use the information above and the table below to make notes for your conversation.

Name of application	Storage capacity in GB	Synchronise options	Cost	Which is best?

9 Now, with your partner, take turns to role-play the conversation. When you are discussing the issue of backing up files, remember:

- if you are taking the role of the adult, ask questions and encourage the younger person
- if you are playing yourself, give examples and be ready to offer further details (you should have plenty to say after preparing the chart above).

1.4 How technology is changing our lives

In this section you will learn to:
✓ identify relevant information
✓ understand and select correct details and key question words
✓ understand what is implied but not directly stated in a more formal conversation.

GETTING STARTED

1 Think about some questions that you might ask your teachers, parents, carers or grandparents about technology in their youth. For example:

How did your grandparents communicate with friends, family and the rest of the world?

What equipment did your parents and grandparents use to listen to music?

What were some of the advantages and disadvantages of these methods?

2 Look at the pictures below. Considering each one in turn, discuss the following questions with your group.

a) What form of communication does the picture show? Describe it.

b) Which of these traditional methods of communication are still relevant? Why?

c) Under what circumstances might these methods of communication become relevant again?

EXPLORING THE SKILLS

Being a good listener is just as important as being a good speaker. There are many situations where you have to listen carefully to people talking and make sense of what they are saying in order to keep a conversation going or get information. There are different listening skills that you have to master, such as listening for gist. This means listening to understand the overall meaning of what is being said. Another skill is listening for detail where you are listening for specific information.

3 The questions below are general questions on the conversation that your teacher will play for you. The specific answer is not spoken, so you have to guess from the clues, or understand the gist (get a general overview). Remember to read the questions and think about what the words in the questions mean.

Listen to the conversation and quickly write down answers to the following. **1.1**

a) Where do you think the parents are as they speak?

b) Where do you think Edmond is at the start of the recording?

c) What are they talking about?

> **TOP TIP** If you are listening for detail, such as a name, number or object, you can ignore other information that does not sound like the information you are listening out for. This way you can get the information you need.

4 Listen to the recording for a second time to answer the following questions. This time you will be listening closely for details.

a) Why is Mrs Chan calling out to Edmond?

b) What does Mr Chan think is rude?

c) What are two of Edmond's excuses for being online?

d) Why does Mr Chan not believe him?

e) What is one of the comments on Edmond's report card?

f) What is Edmond's excuse for this?

g) What is for dinner at the Chan household?

DEVELOPING THE SKILLS

Remember to read the questions and make sure you understand them before you hear the recording for the first time. Underline any words in the question that will help you focus your mind and listen out for the answer.

5 Read through the questions below.

a) What is the problem with Edmond's performance at school? Give at least two concerns that Ms Burroughs has.

b) How much of the final English mark is made up by coursework?

c) What is happening in January?

d) What grades is Edmond getting now? What grades did he get in the past?

e) What is Mr Chan's complaint about the school's use of computers?

f) What are the suggestions offered by Ms Burroughs for Edmond's use of the internet at home? Which of them is the most extreme?

g) What are the benefits of the internet to teaching and learning, according to Ms Burroughs?

h) What has been agreed between the Chans and Ms Burroughs?

Now listen to the conversation between the Chans and Ms Burroughs, Edmond's English teacher. It is taking place during a parent–teacher meeting at the school. Then listen to the recording again to gather the information you need to answer the questions.

1.2

GOING FURTHER

Sometimes you have to listen extra carefully to work out what the speaker is thinking or feeling – what is being implied. We do not always say exactly what we mean, especially when we are in a sensitive situation. We do not want to be rude or upset people.

6 Most schools hold meetings where parents or carers meet with their children's teachers to discuss how they are getting on at school. Do you think parents and teachers speak differently at these meetings when the student is there, compared with when they stay at home? Spend a few minutes noting down your thoughts. Consider your own experiences of parent–teacher meetings, if you have been to any. Then match the list of 'teacher phrases' with what they might really mean (implied meaning).

Teacher phrase	Implied meaning
A I must admit I have some concerns about Edmond.	**1** Edmond has been lazy.
B Edmond is often distracted in class.	**2** Check on him regularly to make sure he is working.
C He needs to start working harder.	**3** If he doesn't start working harder, we will take more serious steps.
D This is a little dangerous for an exam course.	**4** I don't think Edmond is doing very well in general.
E Pop in to see how Edmond is getting on.	**5** He won't pass if he continues like this.
F If things don't improve, let's talk again.	**6** Edmond does not concentrate.

7 Now listen to the recording again.

a) What does Mrs Chan want to find out in this conversation?

b) What are the three individuals' attitudes to internet use by young people? Write one sentence about each of the following:

    i) Mr Chan

    ii) Mrs Chan

    iii) the teacher.

c) Find an example where you can tell what each person means, even though they are not saying it openly.

8 In groups of three, role-play Mr and Mrs Chan's conversation with Edmond after the parent–teacher meeting. What do you think his reactions might be?

Make sure you keep the parents true to their characters from what you have heard. You will be showing that you understand what is implied as you take on the personality of each character. You have more freedom with Edmond to decide how he might react.

The big task

You are about to organise and take part in an important competition called *Techno Greats*. In groups of four, you will choose the technological invention that has had the biggest effect on our lives. You will choose a technological invention from one of the following times:

- before the 20th century
- of the 20th century
- of the 21st century (so far).

Your group will present your decision as part of the competition, which will be judged.

In your presentation you must **explain**:

- who invented your chosen technology, where and why
- the purpose of the invention
- how it improved lives
- how it changed the way we work, live or entertain ourselves.

Each team has to research their invention and decide how they are going to present the information. Consider some of the following options:

- Bring in the object or invention, or a picture of it, to explain how it works/worked and what is/was special about it.
- Find posters, labelled diagrams and pictures.
- Create a short documentary explaining how the invention works/worked or what life would be like without this invention.

The judges must decide which presentation is strongest based on their choice of invention and their presentation.

Check your progress

Here are the Reading, Writing, Speaking and Listening skills you learned about in Chapter 1.

Use this table to decide how good you are at the different skills, and make a note of what you need to be able to do in order to move up a level.

READING
I can ...

- usually pick out the details I need from most kinds of texts
- usually understand what is implied but not directly stated

- pick out many details correctly from different kinds of texts
- understand some of what is implied but not directly stated when given some help

- pick out a few details correctly from straightforward texts
- understand how to skim read and scan a text

WRITING
I can ...

- organise most of my ideas clearly before I start writing
- write complicated information and detailed explanations clearly and with few mistakes
- use a good range of vocabulary precisely, including subject-specific words

- organise some of my ideas before I start writing
- write clear information and explanations, and only make mistakes when I try to use hard words or phrases
- use a reasonable range of vocabulary and sometimes try to use more subject-specific words

- understand how to collect ideas before I start writing
- write down simple ideas and explanations but make mistakes
- use a basic range of vocabulary to express some ideas

SPEAKING
I can ...

- express most of my ideas clearly, accurately and effectively
- interact with other people in a conversation and help move the conversation forward by developing and adding ideas

- express many ideas clearly
- respond at some length to other people in a conversation, giving details and examples

- express simple ideas so that they are understood
- respond to other people in a conversation and answer questions

LISTENING
I can ...

- understand most kinds of listening texts
- use the key words in questions to answer questions in full detail correctly
- usually understand what is implied but not directly stated

- understand different kinds of listening texts
- listen out for key words in questions to answer questions in some detail
- understand some of what is implied but not directly stated

- understand some listening texts
- understand how to listen out for key words in questions

THE BIG PICTURE

In this chapter you will:

- think about exploration, which is travelling to an unknown area to learn more about it

- consider how important it is for discovery, how exciting it can be and how it has shaped and changed our lives

- read, think, talk and write about the value of exploration and what has inspired explorers past and present

- discuss which areas remain to be explored in the future.

THINKING BIG

1 Choose two images that you find interesting. Decide which of the explorers looks the bravest and what makes you think that. Note down your ideas. Make notes ready for a discussion.

2 In pairs:

- Explain your choice of images to your partner. Say why you think they are interesting.

- Respond to your partner. Do you agree with your partner's explanation for why someone looks brave?

- Which expedition would you have most liked to go on? Explain why.

3 Discuss your choice with another pair.

2
Exploration

2.1 Explorers

In this section you will learn to:

✓ select relevant details from what you read in order to make notes.

GETTING STARTED

1 In pairs, brainstorm all the explorers you can think of. Then answer the following questions, writing short notes.

- Which explorers do you think have made the most dangerous journeys?

- What discoveries did they make?

- What dangers do you think they faced?

- What do you think the people back home thought about their travels?

2 Read the quotations below from explorers explaining their reasons for their expeditions. Some of these quotes are written in old-fashioned English so don't worry if you can't understand all the words. In pairs, discuss the following questions for each quote.

- What do you think the explorer was like?

- What do you think made them want to do these things?

❝*... some day I would go to the region of ice and snow and go on and on till I came to one of the poles of the Earth ...*❞

Ernest Shackleton, 1874–1922

❝*When I was but a little child, I had already a strong desire to see the world.*❞

Ida Pfeiffer, 1797–1858

❝*...should I meet with gold or spices in great quantity, I shall remain till I collect as much as possible.*❞

Christopher Columbus, 1451–1506

❝*Never, if possible, cover any road a second time.*❞

Ibn Battuta, 1303–1365

❝*All adventures, especially into new territory, are scary.*❞

Sally Ride, astronaut, 1951

Ida Pfeiffer

EXPLORING THE SKILLS

Often you only need to find the relevant details in a text in order to do a task. Remember:

- If you have to answer a question, read it carefully before reading the text.
- Read headings to help you understand what the text is about.
- Identify key words and information.
- Look for the relevant details in a text.

3 You are going to read a passage about a great Chinese explorer, Zheng He.

Read the text quickly and look at the picture. Which paragraph would you read to find out about the following?

- the ships used for the journeys
- the aims of the exploration
- where Zheng He went

Zheng He, the great Chinese explorer

The Chinese fleet

Six centuries ago a large **fleet** of Chinese ships sailed from China to Arabia and East Africa. The fleet consisted of up to 300 giant ships, surrounded by dozens of supply ships, water tankers, ships to transport horses, and patrol boats. There were more than 27 000 sailors and soldiers in the fleet.

Reasons for the journey

The Chinese fleet made these journeys to show the great power of the Chinese Ming **dynasty**. Loaded with Chinese silk, porcelain and lacquerware, the ships visited ports around the Indian Ocean, from East Africa to Indonesia, in order to trade. Here, Arab and African merchants exchanged the spices, ivory, medicines, rare woods and pearls which the Chinese imperial court wanted.

Details of Zheng He's voyages

Zheng He made a series of expeditions between the years 1405 and 1433. On his first trip in 1405, Zheng He visited Vietnam and reached the port of Calicut, India (which is now known as Kozhikode). On his return, he fought pirates.

Zheng He's fourth and most ambitious trip, in 1414, was to the Gulf. He brought back a giraffe from the Kingdom of Bengal as a gift to the emperor.

He then went to eastern Africa where he loaded lions, leopards, ostriches and zebras onto his ships. Back in China, officials bowed low when they saw these amazing animals.

GLOSSARY		
fleet	a large number of ships	
dynasty	series of rulers of a country who all belong to the same family	

DEVELOPING THE SKILLS

To identify the key points in a text it's a good idea to make notes. Note-taking is a very important skill, which you can use to record what you have read or listened to. This is particularly useful when you're doing research because you will need to read lots of different texts and you won't be able to remember all the information you have read.

In order to improve your note-taking skills, you need to practise finding specific information in a text.

First, you should skim-read the text to see how it is organised. You can look at the headings to help you. Then you can make notes.

4 Go to the second column in the passage on the previous page and read the text again. Copy and complete this table by taking notes.

Date of voyage	Where Zheng He went	Details of voyage

5 In pairs, discuss the following.

- Which journey would you like to have made? Explain why.

- Do you think the journeys showed the great power of the Chinese Ming dynasty? Explain your answer.

GOING FURTHER

Usually, notes are not sentences, just key words or short phrases. They do not contain descriptive details, emotional comments or opinions unless these are asked for. You can also leave out articles, like 'a' and 'the'.

For example, if the sentence in the text is:

I went to the North Pole by helicopter.

Your notes could be:

North Pole – helicopter

6 Many explorers in the past tried to get to the North Pole or South Pole – regions so remote and cold that they were very difficult to reach. Nowadays, it is possible for us all to visit such places.

After reading the text below, you will need to answer the following question:

What has made a trip to the North Pole possible for many people today?

a) Read the text and identify the information you will need in order to answer the question. Ignore details you do not need, such as personal opinions.

b) Make some brief notes.

Few places have stirred the hearts and minds of explorers more than the North Pole. I imagined the icy north as being a distant land. However, as I found out, it is now very accessible. This distant land can now be explored, thanks to modern transport, satellite and computer technology. This technology has really changed things and now there are lots of opportunities to go to the North Pole.

Before going on my trip I found out all I could about the North Pole using the internet. In the end I flew to Spitzbergen, an island off the north coast of Norway. I then took a ten day trip on board an ice cutter – that is a type of ship built specially to cut through ice. On the trip I stayed in a well-heated two-berth cabin. The ship was equipped with a helicopter, satellite maps and mobile phones. All of these items made the trip seem less hazardous and quite comfortable.

However, if the North Pole no longer seemed mysterious, it did not stop the beating of my heart as I experienced the once-in-a-lifetime thrill of standing on the top of the world looking around at the amazing Arctic landscape.

GLOSSARY		
	remote	far away and difficult to reach
	stir the hearts and minds	produce an emotional feeling
	accessible	easy to reach
	berth	a bed on a boat
	hazardous	dangerous
	thrill	excitement

7 In pairs, compare your notes. Talk about any similarities and differences you find. Discuss ways in which you might be able to improve your notes.

2.2 Space exploration

In this section you will learn to:
✓ collect and organise ideas
✓ write for or against a point of view
✓ include your own ideas when writing
✓ respond to ideas with a different opinion.

GETTING STARTED

(1) Look at the photos and take five minutes to note down your ideas about the following questions.

a) What do I know about space exploration?

b) What would I like to know about space exploration?

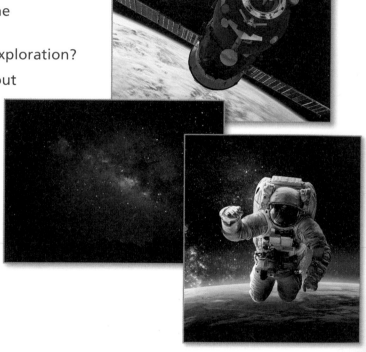

EXPLORING THE SKILLS

Before you start writing you need collect and organise your ideas.

One way of doing this is to use a **KWL** table. This helps to organise your ideas into:

- What do I KNOW?
- What do I WANT to know?
- What have I LEARNED?

What do I KNOW about space exploration?	What do I WANT to know about space exploration?	What have I LEARNED about space exploration?
There have been many space missions to Mars.	How much does space exploration cost? What…? When…? Where…? Why…? How…?	

(2) Copy the table and complete the first column.

3 In pairs, discuss what you know and what you would like to know about space exploration. Add your questions to the second column.

4 Now try and find answers to your questions. Decide together on good places to look for this information.

5 When collecting information, you need to decide what is relevant and what is not relevant. Which of the following sentences is not relevant to the topic of space exploration?

a) Many new inventions have resulted from space exploration, such as memory foam and scratch-resistant sunglasses.

b) Mobile phones rely on satellite technology.

c) At night I look up at the moon and stars.

d) Studies estimate that China's space programme costs around $9 billion a year.

6 Mind Maps® and mind webs can help you plan your writing. Think about the advantages and disadvantages of space exploration and make a mind map like the one below to note your ideas and questions. Discuss these ideas in groups.

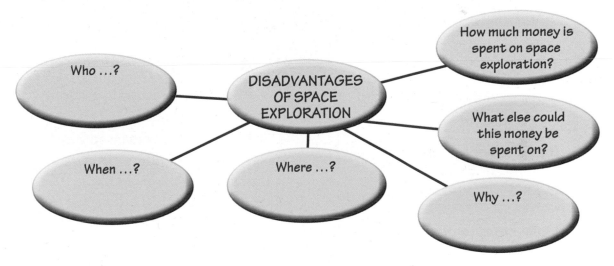

Who ...? DISADVANTAGES OF SPACE EXPLORATION How much money is spent on space exploration? When ...? Where ...? What else could this money be spent on? Why ...?

DEVELOPING THE SKILLS

7 The text on the next page talks about why we explore space.

Read the text and then, in pairs, ask each other:

- What are the advantages of space exploration?
- What are the disadvantages of space exploration?

USA SPACE EXPLORATION

Search [_____]

Home	News	Missions	Media	Resources

Why should we explore space? Why should so much money be spent on space exploration when it could be spent on so many other things?

Humans have been looking up at the stars for thousands of years. But we only developed the technology to travel into space in 1957 when the Soviets sent a satellite above the Earth. In 1961, they followed it with the first man in space. Then the Americans beat them to the moon in 1969. Since then, two spacecraft have landed on Mars and two more have passed Pluto and are still exploring further. But, apart from cool pictures of other planets, what benefits do we get from spending billions of dollars on the 'space race'?

Thanks to space exploration, we have increased how much scientists know about space, the Earth's atmosphere and how the planets were created. But daily life has also improved. Without space exploration, we would not have satellite TV or radio, GPS or the internet. In fact, the list of technological benefits includes microwave ovens, aeroplanes that fly better and create less noise and pollution, and help for patients with heart, skin and bone problems. In the future, we may solve some of Earth's problems by finding other planets to live on. Or, perhaps we will find ways to replace things we are running out of, like fuel.

On the other hand, perhaps humans will just destroy another area of natural beauty. Already, while there are 2000 active satellites travelling around the Earth, there are another 3000 dead ones. So far, humans have left 190 000kg of "space junk" on the moon. It's easy to see that humans benefit from space exploration, but does space benefit from us?

---

8 Write a speech for a debate on either the advantages or the disadvantages of space exploration.

- Decide whether you are arguing for the advantages or disadvantages of space exploration.

- Make notes to organise your ideas and plan your speech. Select the three most important points that you want to talk about.

- Plan your speech in five sections:

  Paragraph 1 – say whether you're arguing for the advantages or disadvantages of space exploration
  Paragraph 2 – state your first idea
  Paragraph 3 – state your second idea
  Paragraph 4 – state your third idea
  Paragraph 5 – summarise what you have said

- Use phrases from the Language booster box above to give your opinion

LANGUAGE BOOSTER Here are some useful phrases you can use to express your opinion.

I am certain that…

I am absolutely convinced that…

It is possible that…

I don't think we need to…

It is true that…

I would argue that…

I would like to suggest that…

GOING FURTHER

Often there are different views about an issue. You need to show that you have considered different opinions before you give your own view on the issue. Read the following text and identify the phrase used to introduce an opinion.

> *It is true that space exploration can cost billions of dollars; however, it is important to remember that the benefits to the world are also great.*

9 Read the text on the previous page again. What is the writer's point of view?

10 Read the sentences below. Respond to each one with another sentence which gives a different opinion, starting with 'However…' and then using one of the phrases in the Language booster on the previous page.

Example:

Space is the most exciting place left to explore.

However, I would like to suggest that it would be better to spend the money on solving problems on our own planet first.

a) Space exploration can bring peace to the world.

b) Space travel causes air pollution.

c) Many new inventions have resulted from space exploration.

d) Space travel is very dangerous.

11 Now complete the third column of your KWL table with the answers to your questions in the second column.

2.3 Polar exploration

In this section you will learn to:
✓ research and organise ideas for giving a talk or presentation
✓ plan an effective, individual opening for a talk or presentation.

1 The North Pole and the South Pole are the polar regions of our planet.

- Identify the North Pole and South Pole on the maps below
- Why do you think people want to explore these regions?
- What do you think are the challenges for polar explorers?

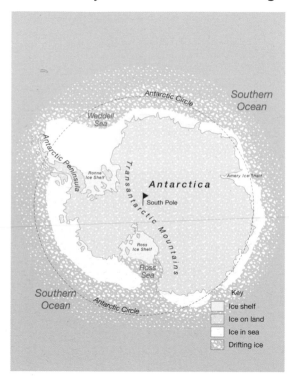

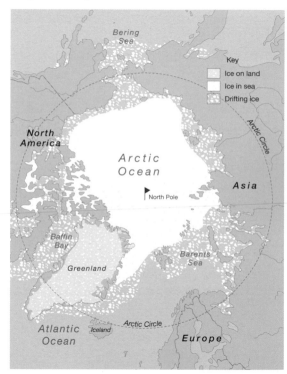

2 Below are some photos of the polar regions. Choose one photo and write notes answering the following questions.

- What do you think the photo shows?
- How does the photo make you feel?

EXPLORING THE SKILLS

When giving a talk, you need to express your ideas clearly to make sure your listeners understand. People find it hard to follow if you mix together lots of different ideas. To express your ideas clearly, you have to know what you are going to say. You need to organise your thoughts and words.

(3) In pairs, give a 30-second talk about the photo you chose.

Think about what you are going to say.

- First, say what you are going to talk about.

- Then say what the photo shows.

- Next say how the photo makes you feel.

- In your final sentence, thank your partner for listening.

(4) Colour coding can help you organise your ideas. Linking a colour to an idea makes it clearer.
Read the sentences below. In groups, decide on which coloured sheet of paper each one should go.

History of polar exploration

Reasons for polar exploration

Risks of polar exploration

Polar exploration and the environment

1) The first people to reach the South Pole in Antarctica were racing each other. The winning group, led by Roald Amundsen, reached the South Pole on December 15, 1911. But Robert Scott's group arrived on January 18, 1912. Scott and all of his team died on the way back.

2) Despite the freezing temperatures – as low as -90°C – there is a lot of wildlife in both the Arctic and the Antarctic. Many tourists visit to see whales and penguins, for example.

3) Global warming means that today it's possible to cross the North-West passage using large ships. So much ice has melted that the water is much deeper than it used to be.

4) Wearing socks made of the wrong material is very dangerous because they become wet and then freezing cold. This can cause a serious infection, called gangrene, in the toes.

ROALD AMUNDSEN
1872–1928

5) As polar ice melts, scientists are discovering new viruses, bacteria and plants that have been frozen for many thousands of years.

6) Nowadays a lot of scientists are interested in the polar regions. But, before them, traders explored the poles to find shorter ways to travel between Europe and East Asia.

7) There are deep cracks in the ice called 'crevasses'. Snow 'bridges' can form on top of the crevasses. This makes them hard to see and many people have died from falling into them.

8) It took more than 400 years to find a route for ships to pass through the Arctic. In 1903, the first person to sail through this North-West Passage was Roald Amundsen. He had to use a small boat because, in some places, the water was only one metre deep.

DEVELOPING THE SKILLS

5 Nowadays it is possible to visit Antarctica as a tourist. Read the following opinions and in pairs organise the comments into two groups

- advantages of tourism to Antarctica
- disadvantages of tourism to Antarctica

Don't include any comments which are not relevant.

I don't think they should let tourists travel in Antarctica. Let there be one place on Earth that's only for animals and nature! I know there are strict rules that stop tourists on Antarctic cruises from going too close to the animals. But I don't think that's enough. Animals like whales are curious. If they see ships and hear people, they come closer to see what's happening. Also, there might be accidents where animals are hurt by the ships. Or the ships might create problems for the fish or plants that bigger animals eat.

Some people think that the tourists that visit the Antarctic will learn how important it is to protect the environment. But people already have important wildlife right outside their front door and many of them do nothing to look after it. I live in a beautiful village in the countryside. Every summer, it's full of tourists. They leave rubbish everywhere and complain that they can't get good Wi-Fi for their smartphones. Most people work and live online and expect to have Wi-Fi everywhere they go. I'm sure Antarctic tourists aren't different! I don't think people will change the way they live because they have been on an Antarctic cruise. They will just take some great selfies with snow and penguins for social media. Nowadays there are such amazing wildlife documentaries that no-one needs to visit the Antarctic to learn about it. I've learned a lot about tigers in India from watching documentaries on TV.

Another reason I am against Antarctic tourism is that accidents can happen. If a cruise ship sinks or spills oil into the ocean, it can pollute the area for years. And the tourists themselves can bring in seeds on their shoes. These 'foreign' plants might change the local wildlife forever if they start growing there.

6 In pairs, take turns to play both parts in the following role-play:

Student A: You have just come back from a cruise around Antarctica. It was such an amazing experience that you want to encourage your friend to travel there too. Describe what you saw and why you would recommend the trip.

Student B: You don't think that tourists should travel to Antarctica. Give your reasons and explain why you don't want to go there yourself.

GOING FURTHER

Try using a strong opening when you give a talk or presentation so that it grabs your listeners' attention. Add ideas and stories of your own to make it more interesting.

DID YOU REMEMBER TO … ?

Successful openings for presentations often do one or more of the following:

✓ Greet the audience.
✓ State what the person is going to speak about.
✓ Use **rhetorical questions**.
✓ Use the personal pronoun 'we' to connect with the audience.
✓ Use facts and statistics.
✓ Use an anecdote (personal story).

 LANGUAGE BOOSTER — A **rhetorical question** is a question used for effect. It does not require an answer.

7 Read the following openings for two presentations.

- Which features from the 'Did you remember to … ?' are used in each opening?

- In pairs, discuss which features work the best. Say why.

> *Good morning everybody. We are here today to discuss the effect of tourism on the polar regions. Tourism to Antarctica has more than doubled over the past ten years. Which means that many more people have learned how beautiful these areas are and how important it is to save them from global warming. Take me for example: I've been on TWO polar cruises. I flew from America and then took a cruise ship. It was amazing BOTH times and I came back determined to do whatever I could to stop global warming.*

> *Did you know that tourism creates 8% of the gases that are responsible for global warming? As we all know, there is concern around the world regarding climate change. Statistics show that even if we reduce greenhouse gas emissions, more than a third of the world's glaciers will melt before the year 2100. But how can we help to prevent climate change and save the planet unless we reduce the amount we travel?*

8 Plan an opening paragraph for a presentation about either the advantages or the disadvantages of tourism in Antarctica.

- First, decide whether you're arguing for or against tourism in Antarctica.

- Look back at the information and opinions on previous pages to help with your ideas.

- Look again at the DID YOU REMEMBER? list above and include some of the features suggested.

- In groups, practise giving the openings of your presentations to each other.

2.4 Underwater exploration

LISTENING SKILLS IN FOCUS

In this section you will learn to:

✓ recognise and understand facts when listening to short spoken texts

✓ recognise and understand facts when listening to a longer and more difficult text

✓ listen carefully and understand complicated instructions.

GETTING STARTED

1 Did you know that a lot of the Earth's deep ocean remains unexplored? Look at the photos on this page and the next.

a) Think of five questions you would like to ask about underwater exploration.

b) In groups of four:

share and make a list of all your questions

sort the questions into themes or ideas.

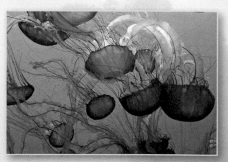

EXPLORING THE SKILLS

A fact is something that can be proved to be true, for example:
The Mariana Trench is the deepest part of the ocean.
It is useful to be able to select facts when you are listening to information.

2 Look at the two advertisements below, and then listen to each radio advertisement. What is each one advertising?

2.1

FRIDAY SALE!

Joe Diver Equipment

We are the underwater specialists.

2.2

DEEP BLUE DIVER TRAINING COURSES

Only $25 per hour for those aged 16 to 18.

3 You are now going to hear some phrases from the first advertisement again. Note down the letters (a), b), c), etc.) as you hear the facts.

2.3

a) We are the underwater specialists.

b) Well known for being really comfortable.

c) This special offer is our best price ever!

d) That's an amazing $13 saving.

e) And don't forget, there's free shipping with orders over $100.

4 Listen again to some phrases from the second advertisement. Note down the letters as you hear the facts.

2.4

a) We believe that all courses should be fun.

b) Our 'Discover scuba diving' course is for ages 16 and above.

c) An hour in the beautiful blue sea accompanied by your instructor.

d) Our prices are very reasonable.

e) If you are aged between 16 and 18, it is $25 per hour.

f) Prices include all equipment hire.

5 Which advertisement gives more facts than opinions?

DEVELOPING THE SKILLS

6 In pairs, look at the picture of an underwater robot submarine. Discuss with your partner.

a) What do you think it is exploring?

b) What are the lights for?

7 Listen twice to the interview and answer the questions about deep-sea exploring.

2.5

a) Where is the interview happening?

b) Why is deep-sea exploring exciting for Nadima?

c) What are hydrothermal vents?

d) What is Nadima doing on her next trips?

Sometimes we need to listen out for specific words to fill in gaps in a text. Read the text on the next page carefully before you listen to the recording to get an idea of the sort of information you should listen for. Afterwards, check that the answer makes sense – especially the grammar.

GLOSSARY		
	hydrothermal vent	underwater volcano
	bubbles	small balls of air or gas in a liquid
	sample	a small quantity of material to show what it's like
	mineral	a substance that is formed naturally in rocks

8 Listen again to the interview and then copy and complete the form below with the relevant details. Each answer will be between one and four words. 2.5

DEEP-SEA EXPLORATION

<u>**Where they're exploring today:**</u> Today they're exploring
.... km under the ocean.

<u>**Equipment used:**</u> The equipment used for deep sea
exploration is called an ....

<u>**Advantages of the robot submarine:**</u>

It can stand .... in the very deep sea.

It can dive much .... than humans can.

It is .... than deep-sea submarines that can
carry people.

<u>**How it works:**</u> The submarine is .... to a ship
on the sea. Someone on board the ship can look at a
.... and .... the vehicle where to go.

<u>**Recent discoveries:**</u>

Scientists have new ideas about how [life on earth] began.

Scientists have found plants and minerals to use for new
....

<u>**Uses for robot submarines:**</u>

Scientific research

Exploring sunken ....

Exploring deep sea ....

GOING FURTHER

You need to listen particularly carefully for facts and details when you are being given instructions.

9 In pairs, look at the instructions below for how to make a boat out of paper (origami).

10 Take turns to read aloud the instructions. The other person listens carefully and makes the boat. See if the person making the boat can do it without looking at the diagrams.

LANGUAGE BOOSTER

Instructions use the **imperative** form of the verb. This is the root of the verb, e.g. 'to fold' → 'fold' (root) → 'Fold the paper in half.'

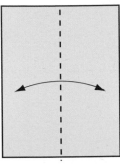

Start with a rectangular piece of paper. If you have coloured paper, it should be coloured side up. Fold in half, then open.

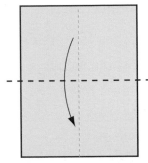

Fold in half downwards.

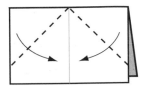

Bring the top corners in to the centre fold line.

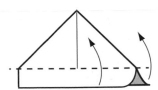

Fold the bottom flat edge upwards and do the same to the back. Crease well.

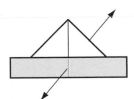

Pull the sides out and flatten.

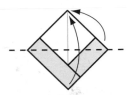

Fold the front layer up to the top and do the same at the back.

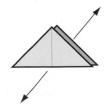

Pull the side apart and flatten.

Gently pull the top parts of the model outwards, making a boat shape.

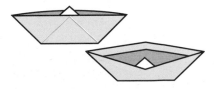

Flatten well to crease all folds. Then open out slightly, forming a boat shape.

11 Make up instructions to make something else out of paper.

The big task

Imagine that you live in a country that wants to invest a hundred million dollars in exploration. You are going to give a presentation to win the money for your chosen exploration project.

- Project A: exploring Antarctica for research purposes
- Project B: exploring for possible valuable shipwrecks in the sea
- Project C: exploring the planet Mars
- Project D: an exploration project of your choice

Work in groups of four. Three of you choose one of the projects each. You are going to put forward reasons to invest in that project. The fourth person will be the decision maker.

First, brainstorm for your presentation.
- In silence, write five questions you would like to explore about your chosen project.
- Join together with other people in your class who are working on the same project and combine your ideas. Make a concept map or web to note down your ideas.
- Decision makers, think of three questions you would like to ask each person about their project.
- Decision makers, join together and produce a list of questions you would like to ask each person about their project.

Now research more information for your presentation.
- Each person uses the internet or the library to find out more information.
- Skim the information. You cannot use all of it.
- Make notes of five facts that you think are interesting or you can use to support your project.
- Now report back to other people supporting your project. Share ideas. Decision makers do the same.

Next, organise your information.
- Organise the information into themes for reasons why the country should invest in your project. Use colour to help you.
- Use only your best ideas. Discard any facts or ideas that you don't need.

Now prepare the first draft of your presentation. Your presentation can only last two minutes.

Check your progress

Here are the Reading, Writing, Speaking and Listening skills you learned about in Chapter 2.

Use this table to decide how good you are at the different skills, and make a note of what you need to be able to do in order to move up a level.

READING
I can ...

- usually understand and pick out all the details I need to complete notes
- pick out many details correctly to complete notes
- pick out a few details correctly to complete notes

WRITING
I can ...

- organise most of my ideas clearly before writing for or against a point of view
- confidently include several of my own ideas or examples when writing to argue a point
- organise some of my ideas before I start writing for or against a point of view
- sometimes include a few of my own ideas or examples
- understand how to collect ideas before I start writing for or against a point of view
- make use of ideas given to me and try to include one or two of my own examples

SPEAKING
I can ...

- research efficiently and then organise a good range of relevant ideas for a talk or presentation
- prepare an effective opening for a talk using my own ideas
- research and then organise some relevant ideas for a talk or presentation
- plan a suitable opening for a talk, trying to use a few of my own ideas
- research and prepare some simple ideas for a talk or presentation
- try to prepare an opening for a talk using the ideas I have found or been given

LISTENING
I can ...

- understand most kinds of listening texts, including longer and more difficult ones, and can usually pick out all the facts I need
- listen thoughtfully and closely, and follow complicated instructions successfully
- understand different kinds of listening texts and pick out many of the facts I need
- listen very closely and follow quite complicated instructions with some success
- understand straightforward listening texts
- pick out some of the facts I need
- listen closely and follow straightforward instructions

THE BIG PICTURE

In this chapter you will:

- consider health – what it means to be healthy, and why it is important to stay as healthy as possible

- think about healthy food, and about exercise

- research, think, talk and write about the most important ways to stay healthy.

THINKING BIG

1 Look at the photos.

- Make notes about the different aspects of health shown in the photos.

- Which of the activities do you think are the healthiest?

- Which of these activities do you do? Which ones don't you do?

- Which things shown in the photos can cause health problems? Which ones can prevent problems?

- In your experience, are there any challenges to staying healthy? Describe these.

2 In pairs, look at the photos with your partner.

- Discuss what you know about each of the types of exercise or food shown.

- Ask your partner questions about what they like and dislike in the photos, and what they do to stay healthy.

3 On your own, jot down ideas about the following:

- What advantages and disadvantages can you think of for some of the activities shown?

- Do you think you are healthy? Why, or why not? What do you do that makes you healthy, or what could you do to improve?

- Why is it important to be healthy?

3
Health

3.1 Healthy eating

In this section you will learn to:

✓ select facts and details accurately from a written text
✓ understand the importance of units of measurement
✓ understand phrases about time
✓ use key question words to help find answers.

GETTING STARTED

1 Read the questions below and discuss your ideas with a partner.

- What is your favourite food?
- What kind of food is healthy?
- Is it easy to have a healthy diet?
- Do you think you have a healthy diet?

2 The diagram below shows advice for a healthy **diet**. Study the different **food groups**. How does this compare with what you discussed with your partner in task 1? How often do you eat food from these different groups?

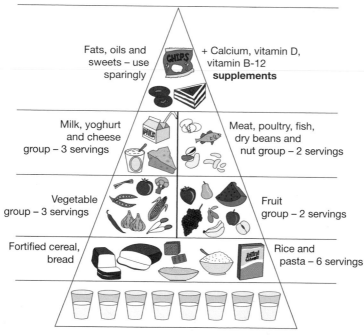

Water 8 servings

GLOSSARY		
diet	food that a person or animal regularly eats	
food groups	the groups into which different foods may be placed according to what they provide the body, such as carbohydrates or proteins	
supplement	a pill that you take or a special kind of food that you eat in order to improve your health	

EXPLORING THE SKILLS

When you read a text, you will often have to select the facts that contain the information you need. For instance, you may need to know numbers and measurements in order to follow instructions. Remember to include or check the units of measurement used – there is big difference between a teaspoon and a tablespoon of chilli powder!

3 Katie has shared the following recipe with her friends on a social media site. Read the recipe and the comments from Katie's friends. Do you think you would like this meal?

Moroccan chicken

Ingredients
1 tbsp of olive oil
1 × 1.5 kg chicken, cut into
  8 pieces
1 large onion, chopped
3 cloves of garlic, crushed
1 tbsp of fresh ginger
2 tsp of ground coriander
2 tsp of ground cumin
500g tomatoes, chopped

100ml chicken stock or water
4 tbsp of yogurt
Small bunch of coriander,
  chopped, and couscous
  to serve

Method
1. Heat 1 tablespoon of olive oil in a pan. Brown the chicken. Put the chicken to one side and fry the onion in the same pan until soft. Stir in the ginger, garlic, cumin and coriander, and cook for about a minute. Add the tomatoes, mix everything together well, reduce the heat, and cook for 15 minutes, stirring occasionally.
2. Boil the water or stock and add this liquid. Place the chicken pieces on top, season to taste, lower the heat, cover and simmer until the chicken is soft – it should take about 30 minutes.
3. Stir in the yogurt and serve with chopped coriander and couscous.

Hi everyone!
I thought I would share this amazing recipe with you. Please try it and tell me what you think. I'm looking forward to hearing from you.
Love Katie xxx

(A) Thanks Katie. I cooked the recipe last night and it's perfect. I've been running out of ideas for my customers and a meal from North Africa would really make a change. Will let you know what they think. Carly

(B) Hi Katie. I prepared this meal and gave it to my flatmates. They loved it, but I couldn't join in as I'm allergic to onions. I'm going to try the recipe without onions next time. Have a good weekend. Rosie

(C) Wow Katie! What an amazing taste! I'm vegetarian, so I made it with tofu instead of chicken. It worked very well. If you find any more recipes, please share them with me. Amy

4 Read the recipe and comments again and answer the questions. For questions e–g, tick the correct box.

  a) How much chicken do you need?

  b) How much chicken stock or water do you need?

  c) How many tomatoes do you need?

  d) How long do you cook the dish in the second stage?

  e) Who was unable to eat the meal? A ☐ B ☐ C ☐

  f) Who changed the ingredients? A ☐ B ☐ C ☐

  g) Who owns a restaurant? A ☐ B ☐ C ☐

LANGUAGE BOOSTER Abbreviations for measurements are often used in factual writing such as recipes:
g = gramme
kg = kilogramme
tsp = teaspoon
tbsp = tablespoon
ml = millilitre

(5) Underline the units of measurement in your answers to task 4. Check that you have chosen the correct kind of measurement. Add to your answers, writing out the measurements in full and in their abbreviated form, if there is one.

(6) Do you think this is a healthy recipe? Why? Look back at the food pyramid in task 2. Think about which food groups the recipe contains and which groups it doesn't.

DEVELOPING THE SKILLS

Information about timings is very important in texts like this. You can easily pick out numbers in a factual text, but also look out for words used with them, such as *about* or *up to* – these show that the times may not be exact.

(7) Underline the expressions in these phrases which show that the times and numbers are not exact.

a) I've been a vegetarian for about a year.

b) You can cook this dish for up to an hour in the oven at a low heat.

c) It doesn't take long to prepare, just five or six minutes.

d) This recipe will serve more than four people.

e) You don't need a lot of honey, only a few spoonfuls.

Read the sentences again. In pairs, write similar sentences using these expressions.

LANGUAGE BOOSTER Factual texts need to be very clear in presenting information and instructions. In the recipe there are some technical terms related to cooking, such as *brown*, *season* and *simmer*. Look up the meaning of these and other words from the recipe. Make a list of these words and their definitions.

GOING FURTHER

You may have to answer questions about longer texts. Read the questions first to find key words. These will give you clues about what you need to look out for. For example, if the question starts with 'When', you must look for a time or date. If a question asks 'Who?', you will look for the name of a person, and if it asks 'Where?', you will look for the name of a place.

8 Here are some questions. Read them carefully and underline the key question words. In pairs, discuss what sort of answer you might expect.

a) Where were the large, flat breads first baked?

b) When did people start to sell pizzas in Italy?

c) When did Queen Margherita go on a tour of Italy?

d) Who cooked her a special pizza?

e) Why did American and European soldiers eat pizza?

f) What happened when the soldiers went back to their countries?

9 Now read the text and answer the questions above.

Pizza is now an international dish. You may think that pizza is an Italian invention, but interestingly it was the early Greeks who first baked large, round, flat breads which they flavoured with oil, herbs and spices.

The idea came to Italy in the 18th century, when flat breads called 'pizzas' were sold on the streets. They didn't have anything on top of them like we expect today. They were cheap and tasty, and they were eaten by poorer people.

In about 1889, Queen Margherita of Italy went on a tour of her country. During her travels she saw many people eating this large, flat bread. She was curious and wanted to try one. She loved it, and invited Chef Rafaelle Esposito to come to the royal palace and make a selection of pizzas for her.

Rafaelle decided to make a special pizza for the queen. He put tomatoes, mozzarella cheese and fresh basil on it to show the colours of the Italian flag: red, white and green. This became the queen's favourite pizza and Pizza Margherita is now famous all over the world.

Pizza spread to America, France, England and Spain, but it didn't become popular until after World War II. Many American and European soldiers tasted it for the first time when they were in Italy during the war. When they returned home, it became a popular meal in their countries.

Adapted from 'History of Pizza'

③.2 Healthy body

In this section you will learn to:
- ✓ use a range of different kinds of sentences in your writing
- ✓ use simple, compound and complex sentences accurately
- ✓ include a range of appropriate linking devices and noun phrases to add detail and variety.

GETTING STARTED

1 Read the questions below and discuss them with a partner.

- What kind of exercise do you do?
- Do you exercise for fun, or because you want to be healthy?
- Why is it good to exercise?

2 Read the following comment from an article about exercise. Does this information surprise you? Discuss your ideas with a partner.

> 66 *Running can reduce the effects of ageing and give older people a new lease of life.* 99

EXPLORING THE SKILLS

Remember that a sentence contains a subject and a verb and it always starts with a capital letter and ends with a full stop, question mark or exclamation mark.

Using a clear and accurate sentence structure is a basic part of writing. It is important to be able to use different types of sentences. This gives your writing more effect and impact. Two of the main types of sentence are simple sentences and compound sentences.

Short sentences that contain one main idea are called **simple sentences**.
For example:

subject   **verb**

I cycled to school.

Simple sentences are useful for giving clear explanations and instructions. They can also add more drama to writing, or give emphasis to a particular point.

Read the following explanation from a book about running.

> You will do most of your running on an athletics track. At school, this may be marked out on grass. In stadiums, tracks are made of a special surface which provides grip. Outdoor tracks are 400m long. Different races have different starting points. These are marked out on the track.
>
> From 'Tell me about sport: Running'

This uses a series of simple sentences to present the information in a clear way.

 LANGUAGE BOOSTER We often use the verbs 'go', 'play' and 'do' when we talk about sports:
I *go* rock climbing.   I *play* ice hockey.   I *do* Pilates.
Can you think of more sports to add to each category?

Compound sentences contain two or more ideas that are equally important. These are joined together using conjunctions such as 'or', 'and' or 'but'. For example:

It was raining <u>and</u> we got wet.

Read another sentence from the same book.

❝ *You may not break a world record but you can record a personal best.* ❞

Here, the writer joins ideas with 'but' to explain the idea in more detail.

3 Read the text below. Decide whether each numbered sentence is simple or compound.

[1]Running is a good form of exercise. [2]It is cheap and easy to do. [3]You can run on your own or you can run with other people. [4]I usually run three times a week but sometimes I run more often. [5]It is a great way to get fit.

4 Choose a sport you know. Imagine you are writing for a young reader and write instructions explaining how to do it. Use a combination of simple and compound sentences for different effects.

- To explain the sport and how to do it, use simple sentences.
- To give more information about why the sport is good for you or why it is fun, use compound sentences.

TOP TIP 'Go' is often used with sports that end in '-ing' (e.g. running, swimming), and 'play' is often used with sports that use a ball (e.g. football, hockey, basketball).

DEVELOPING THE SKILLS

Using lots of simple sentences will get your ideas across but it may not be very interesting for the reader. Joining your ideas together in compound and complex sentences is a more fluent way to write and it is more interesting for the reader.

Complex sentences add further information, offer explanation, etc., using other conjunctions such as 'when', 'after' and 'because'. The extra information in a complex sentence does not make sense on its own or it sounds unfinished.

> I often go to the sports centre <u>because</u> I go swimming and see my friends there.

5 Read the following text and answer the questions below.

> My friend does karate. He trains three times a week. Sometimes he trains four times. He does it at the sports centre. He's in a team there. It makes him healthy. It is also fun.

a) Is the information easy to understand?

b) Is the text interesting to read?

Read another version of this text.

> My friend does karate and trains three or four times a week at the sports centre. It makes him healthy and it is also fun.

In this version, the connected ideas are joined together in compound sentences.

6 Now read another text and write a better version of it. Work with a partner. Decide which ideas are connected and could be linked together into compound or complex sentences. Use the conjunctions in the box.

> Football is a popular sport. Lots of people watch football. Lots of people play it. There are football teams in most towns. There are matches between different teams.

| and | when | but | after | or | because |

7 Now write your own paragraph about a sport you enjoy doing or watching, or one you know about. Use simple, compound and complex sentences to express your ideas in different ways as described above. Use compound and complex sentences to join and explain your ideas. Use simple sentences to add effect and impact.

GOING FURTHER

Another way to make your writing more interesting is by using noun phrases in your sentences. Look at the following examples.

We went on a bike ride.

We went on a five-kilometre, sunny bike ride along the river and into the woods.

The second sentence tells us more about the bike ride. The noun 'bike ride' has been extended to 'five-kilometre, sunny bike ride' by adding the 'five-kilometre' and 'sunny'. This is called a **noun phrase**. Now we know that the writer travelled five kilometres on the bike, on a sunny day and that he or she was next to a river.

Noun phrases are important in writing because they allow you to include lots of information in a few words. They make your writing more exact. They can also be used to help you persuade the reader.

8 Read the following sentences. Complete the gaps using the words in the box to make the sentences more interesting or persuasive.

| cold   three-kilometre   amazing   difficult   long |

a) I really enjoy going for _____ walks in the country.

b) Josef is going on a(n) _____ run on Saturday.

c) We had a(n) _____ journey back down the mountain, but we got home safely in the end.

d) They went for a swim in the _____ sea after the race.

e) Don't you think she's a(n) _____ athlete? She's set a new world record.

9 In pairs, discuss which sports you enjoy doing, and which sports you do not enjoy. Make notes about how you could describe the sports in interesting ways.

10 Now work individually to write a magazine article for young people about one of the sports you discussed. Remember to:

- use simple sentences to explain how the sport works and to give instructions

- use compound and complex sentences to join your ideas more fluently

- add information with noun phrases to persuade your reader that this is a good (or a bad!) sport.

3.3 Health around the world

In this section you will learn to:
- ✓ use a variety of structures when you are speaking
- ✓ link ideas using a range of conjunctions
- ✓ speak using abstract nouns and noun phrases to give variety to your sentences.

GETTING STARTED

1 Around the world, there are serious problems which have a bad effect on people's health. Read the questions below and discuss them with a partner.

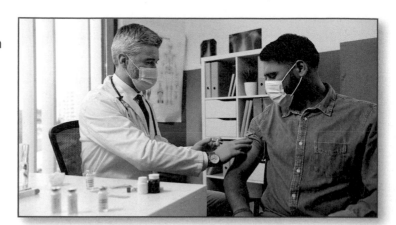

- What kinds of problems can have a bad effect on people's health around the world?

- What can be done to prevent these problems or reduce their effects?

EXPLORING THE SKILLS

You can use a range of sentence structures to add interest to your spoken communication just as you can to your written work.

> **GLOSSARY**
>
> **vaccine** — an injection given to people to stop them getting a disease

The conjunctions 'and', 'but', 'or' and 'so' can all be used to explain your ideas in more detail and to give your reasons. This is useful when you need to explain your ideas clearly and during discussions where you need to support your arguments.

Read the following sentences and the notes:

People say that medicine is very advanced, but not everyone has access to the best medical care. — 'but' is used to introduce an idea which is different from the first idea

Not everyone has access to clean water or is able to visit a doctor when they are ill. — 'or' is used to give more possibilities than the first idea

More vaccines are being used, so fewer people are becoming ill. — 'so' is used to show the result of the first idea

We need to improve education and access to modern medicine around the world. — 'and' is used to join similar ideas

These show how ideas can be joined or extended using a variety of conjunctions.

(2) In pairs, think of a topic related to an important health issue you know about. One person says the beginning of a sentence and the other person completes it, using conjunctions. The ending can agree or disagree with the first idea in the sentence.

For example:

    A   *It's important to do exercise ...*

    B   *... and eat the right food to stay healthy.*

Here are some sentences you could start with:

    You can do yoga ...

    I don't like sport, ...

    It's best not to eat a lot of chocolate ...

(3) Look at the photo on the opposite page. Think about the words you need to describe what you see. Refer to a dictionary to check on any vocabulary you need.

(4) Read the following comments:

> *I think people not eating a healthy diet is the biggest health problem at the moment. If people ate healthy food, it would save a lot of lives.*

> *For me, the most important issue is clean water. Dirty water can cause a lot of illness.*

With a partner, make notes about both of these comments. Try to think of at least three arguments to support each one. You could use some of the following phrases.

    I think that… I believe that… In my opinion, …
    I don't think that… I disagree with the idea...

(5) In your pairs, discuss which of these world health problems it is most important to solve. Choose a role and develop your notes from task 4. Try to use a mixture of simple and compound sentences.

(6) Record your conversation and listen to it. How did you develop your ideas using simple and compound sentences?

(7) In groups, discuss your ideas about the newspaper stories below. You can argue for another health issue if you think something else is more important.

Report back to the class on what your group thought.

> In 2019, the World Health Organization reported that one in three people around the world do not have access to safe drinking water.

> Millions of lives could be saved if the new vaccine is successful. It's important that it is available to everyone and isn't sold at a high price to make money for the company that developed it.

DEVELOPING THE SKILLS

When presenting your point of view in spoken form, you need to use compound sentences to give your reasons and make a persuasive argument – just as you do in persuasive writing.

8 Read the following comments and answer the questions.

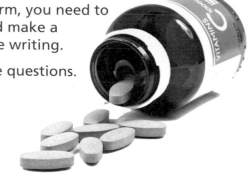

> *I think vitamin supplements are a good thing. You can eat anything you like and get the vitamins you need from tablets. It's easy to be healthy with supplements.*

> *In my opinion, having a healthy, happy mind is more important than what you do or what you eat. Your mind is the most important thing.*

a) Does the first person think that a healthy diet is important?

b) Does the second person think that physical activity is as important as how happy you are?

c) Do you agree with either of these opinions?

9 Imagine you are a young person discussing health with a parent or carer. Discuss what you think it means to be healthy. Work in pairs.

Student A: You are the teenager. You don't think it is important to have a healthy diet, and you don't understand why your mum or dad doesn't agree. You think it is more important to be happy. Think of reasons to support your point of view.

Student B: You are the parent or carer. You think it is more important to eat well and exercise. Think of reasons to support your point of view.

Spend a few minutes preparing your ideas individually. You can make notes to help you remember your main points.

10 Now do the role-play in pairs. Record your conversation and play it back to check that you have used a variety of sentence types.

DID YOU REMEMBER TO ... ?

When speaking:

✓ You can use simple sentences for more impact.

✓ Remember to use 'and', 'but', 'or' and 'so' to explain your ideas in more detail.

✓ Remember that it is quite normal in a conversation to have pauses, or to say 'er...' or 'um...' while you think.

GOING FURTHER

Having as wide a vocabulary as possible will help you express your ideas when speaking. In the writing section earlier in this chapter, we looked at using noun phrases. Here are some examples of noun phrases you could use when talking about health and diet:

> a balanced diet   fizzy drinks   clean water
> junk food   an active lifestyle   a healthy breakfast

11 Working with a partner, copy the table below and put the phrases above into it. Find more examples for each column from earlier in the chapter. Can you think of examples of your own to go in each column?

Phrases about food	Phrases about sport and exercise	Phrases about health and happiness
organic food	regular exercise	a positive state of mind

LANGUAGE BOOSTER You can now start to use abstract nouns (nouns that name things that cannot be touched) to add interest to what you say. Read the following definitions and match them to the words in the box.

a) the state of being excited
b) not having enough strength to complete a task
c) the quality of being very tired, or not having strong muscles
d) the physical energy that you have

> fatigue   excitement   weakness   strength

12 In pairs, take it in turns to use the abstract nouns in the Language booster in a sentence about health.

13 Work with a partner. Discuss your ideas about the following points.

- What is your preferred method of staying healthy – having a healthy diet or doing lots of exercise?

- Do you think it is easy to have a healthy diet?

- Is the lifestyle in your country generally healthy or unhealthy?

- What can happen if many people in a society are unhealthy? For example, if lots of people smoke or eat too much junk food, what effect does this have?

- Do people all over the world have the same concerns about health? If not, how do they differ?

3.4 Better health

In this section you will learn to:

✓ understand and pick out specific details when listening

✓ predict the kind of information you will hear, including units of measurement

✓ recognise high numbers when listening.

GETTING STARTED

1 Discuss the following questions with a partner.

- Do you have any habits that you know are unhealthy? For example, do you eat too much junk food, or do you play computer games a lot?

- If you do, how can you change these habits?

EXPLORING THE SKILLS

When you listen to people speaking or to an audio recording, you may have to listen for specific information such as numbers or units of measurement. It is useful to think in advance of what you might expect to hear. For example, if the question asks how much something costs, you can expect to hear an answer given in units of money, such as dollars.

2 Think of what units of measurement you might expect to hear in the following situations:

- buying apples in a market

- discussing distances for a journey

- a report on football results.

3 You are going to listen to a train announcement. Think about what units of measurement and other numbers you will need to listen for.

3.1

What units and numbers did you expect to hear? Were your guesses correct? Answer the questions:

a) Which platform is the train leaving from?

b) What time is it leaving?

c) How long is it until the train leaves?

obese	something found in foods such as fish, eggs, soya, which you need for healthy growth
diabetes	(adj.) containing less fat than other foods, diets, etc.
calorie	something found in food that is good for you, for example, a vitamin or mineral
low-fat	very overweight and therefore unhealthy
nutrient	a unit of measurement for the energy value of food
protein	a medical condition in which someone has too much sugar in their blood

4 Listen to a report about health. What is the problem discussed? **3.2**

5 Read the sentences below and think what word might go in each gap.

Number of obese people in Britain by 2030: _____.

This is _____ of adults and a _____ of children.

Cost to the NHS is currently _____.

A total of _____% of boys and _____% of girls aged

between _____ and _____ were obese in 2020.

Now listen again to the report about obesity and complete each sentence with the correct information.

DEVELOPING THE SKILLS

Before listening to a text, it is useful to think about the kind of information you might hear. This will help you select the relevant details to answer the questions.

6 You are going to hear a person talking about food groups. Before you listen, look back at the food pyramid in Section 3.1 and discuss in pairs what you know about each of the food groups.
Can you add any different food or food types to these lists?

Bread, cereal, rice, pasta	important for …
Fruit	important for …
Vegetables	important for …
Dairy	important for …
Meat, fish, beans, eggs, nuts	important for …

How is a vegan diet different?

(7) Make notes of the numbers you hear to complete the table below. **3.3**

Food group	Number of servings
Bread, cereal, rice, pasta	
Fruit	
Vegetables	
Dairy, plant-based alternatives	
Meat, fish, beans, eggs, nuts	

(8) Read the text below and complete the notes.

> I thought I ate quite healthy food, but I was surprised when I listened to information about the food pyramid. I only have one serving of vegetables and two of fruit a day – that isn't enough. I have four servings of food from the protein group, including meat and eggs, and that could be too much. I usually eat about seven servings of food from the bread and pasta group, so that's ok.

a) The writer should eat more _____.

b) She should eat less food from the _____.

c) She eats the right amount of _____.

(9) Read the text below. What does it say about the diet of young people in Britain? Discuss your ideas with a partner.

We know from research that rather than eating fruit and vegetables, the typical teenager these days lives on junk food, such as burgers and chips and snacks like chocolate, crisps and fizzy drinks. For some kids junk food is 30–40 per cent of their diet.

This food is cheap, popular and available everywhere. It can be bought on the way to school, after school and at lunchtimes.

What's more, the National Diet and Nutrition Survey found only nine per cent of teenagers ate the recommended servings of fruit and vegetables. And girls are worse than boys, often following diets and cutting out important food groups.

So what effect is this having? Now experts believe diet could play a big role in the moods of teenagers and rule-breaking.

And new research has shown that giving secondary school kids a supplement can improve their behaviour.

The study, conducted by Oxford University on 200 13- to 16-year-olds at a school in London with typically poor diets, found that taking a vitamin, mineral and fish oil pill led to reductions in bad behaviour in just 12 weeks.

The scientist Dr Jonathan Tammam says: 'This shows that nutrition can have a serious effect on the brain health and behaviour of our children, which should be considered a serious public health concern.'

Despite this, according to the survey, teenagers are the age group with the worst diets in the UK and fail to get basic vitamins and minerals needed for growth and good health.

'The situation is very serious because teenagers are preventing their brains getting the nutrients they need,' warns Professor John Stein, an expert on the effects of nutrition on the brain.

Adapted from 'Junk food and poor diet is blamed for blighting behaviour of Britain's teenagers' *Daily Record*

LANGUAGE BOOSTER Look at this list of nutrient groups from the text. Research why they are important for your body, and write three foods that are in these nutrient groups.

| carbs | dairy | vitamins | minerals |

10 Read the article again and answer the questions.

   a) According to the text, what do some teenagers eat too much of?

   b) What behaviours is bad diet causing?

   c) Why do experts think supplements are a good idea?

   d) Why is it important to have a healthy diet when you are a teenager?

11 Now listen to two friends discussing this article. Do they agree or disagree with it? Give reasons for your answers. 3.4

12 Working in groups, discuss whether you think you have a healthy diet. Give your reasons in the same way as the people in the dialogue did. Do more girls or boys eat well in your group?

GOING FURTHER

You may have to distinguish and understand high numbers when you are listening. It is important to learn how high numbers are spoken and how they are written in numerals.

13 Practise reading aloud the numbers in the table below with a partner.

Number	Word
1000	One thousand
10 000	Ten thousand
100 000	One hundred thousand
1 000 000	One million
10 000 000	Ten million
100 000 000	One hundred million
1 000 000 000	One billion

14 Listen to some sentences containing more high numbers. For each one, choose the correct answer. 3.5

   1 a) 120 400   **b)** 12 400   **c)** 1 240 000

   2 a) 1 560 110   **b)** 15 110   **c)** 150 110

   3 a) 3 075 000   **b)** 30 750   **c)** 3075

15 Write some high numbers of your own and think about how to say them. Swap your numbers with a partner and read out each other's numbers.

The big task

> You are going to create a website about health for young people in your school. The website should cover topics such as ways to stay healthy and why it is important to stay healthy.

1. Working in groups, talk about your ideas and make notes.

2. Remember that a website needs to have a clear structure. It usually has a home page, which introduces the topic and gives an overview. Think of this page as an introduction. You can then have different headings to organise your work into different areas, such as Food and Exercise. These would make up different pages of the website.

3. In your groups, decide who is going to provide information for each web page. You can work individually to research information and then discuss it as a group and decide what to include.

4. Remember to present your ideas using a variety of sentence types. Use simple sentences for clear instructions and compound and complex sentences for joining ideas and giving detail or reasons.

   Try to use noun phrases as well, to make your writing more interesting and persuasive, and include abstract nouns if possible.

5. When you present numbers and measurements to support your ideas, make sure you use the right abbreviations where necessary. Check that you know how to say any high numbers you are using.

6. Add photos to attract attention.

7. As a group, present your website to the rest of the class.

Check your progress

Here are the Reading, Writing, Speaking and Listening skills you learned about in Chapter 3.

Use this table to decide how good you are at the different skills, and make a note of what you need to be able to do in order to move up a level.

READING

I can …

usually understand and pick out all the details I need

make effective use of key question words to find all the information I need

often understand and pick out many of the details I need

make use of many key question words to find most of the information I need

sometimes understand and pick out a few of the details I need

recognise some key question words

WRITING

I can …

use simple, compound and complex sentences accurately and securely, and can vary my sentence structures for clarity and effect

use noun phrases securely and confidently to add variety

use simple and compound sentences accurately and securely, and try to use complex sentences to vary my sentence structures

sometimes use noun phrases to add variety

use simple sentences accurately, and try to use compound or complex sentences to vary my sentence structures

occasionally use simple noun phrases

SPEAKING

I can …

confidently use a good variety of structures when speaking

make confident use of abstract nouns and noun phrases to give accuracy and variety

use some variety of structures when speaking, though I may falter

use abstract nouns or noun phrases to add some variety

use a limited range of structures when speaking, and may hesitate or search for words

identify abstract nouns and noun phrases

LISTENING

I can …

understand and pick out exactly the details I need, including all numbers, when listening to longer and more complicated texts

confidently predict the type of information I need by understanding the clues in the questions

securely recognise and understand all numbers

understand and pick out many of the details I need, including most numbers, when listening to longer or more difficult texts

often predict the type of information I need by understanding the clues in the questions

sometimes understand and pick out some of the details I need, including some numbers, when listening to straightforward texts

sometimes predict the type of information I need by looking at the clues in the questions

THE BIG PICTURE

In this chapter you will:

- think about your amazing brain and the role it plays in your education, both formal and informal
- read about schools in ancient times and compare them with schools today
- think about schools in the future
- listen to others talk about education and what needs to change.

THINKING BIG

1 Look carefully at the photos about learning. Choose the photo that you like most. Explain to a partner why you've chosen it.

2 On your own, write a short response to the following questions using the photos to help with ideas.

- How do you learn to do something?
- How did you learn to read or write? Did someone teach you?
- Think about a time when you enjoyed learning something. How did it feel?
- Think about a time when learning was hard. What were the reasons?

3 In pairs:

- Discuss your responses with your partner. Which are the same as your partner's answers? Which are different?
- Decide in what ways your partner's learning experiences differ from yours.
- Note down any interesting ideas that emerge from your conversation.

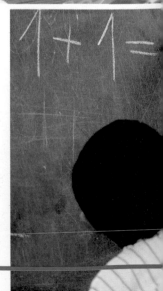

4
Education

4.1 How your amazing brain works

In this section you will learn to:

✓ select relevant details to answer questions

✓ identify and select relevant information from more difficult texts.

GETTING STARTED

1 Can you name any parts of the brain?

2 What makes the human brain so different from the brains of other mammals?

Note down some thoughts that might answer these questions before you proceed.

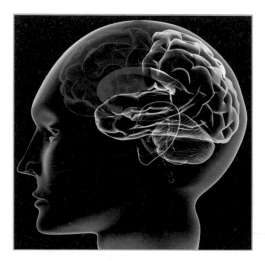

EXPLORING THE SKILLS

When you read for detail and information, you need to know exactly what you are looking for.

It can help to read the text in small sections. Stop and think what each section means before moving on to the next one. Then try to put the ideas into your own words.

If you have to answer questions, read them carefully and check that you understand them. Look up any words you don't know or try to guess their meaning from the context. This means looking at the other words in the same sentence in order to work out the meaning of words you don't know.

3 Read the following questions carefully and check that you understand them before reading the text that follows. Then answer the questions about the text.

a) What is the approximate weight of the human brain?

b) What is the brain largely made of?

c) Why does the brain not feel pain?

d) What helps us remember the alphabet?

e) What is remarkable about children who learn two languages before the age of five?

> **TOP TIP**
> Look for key words in questions. For example, 'Where?' will need a place. 'What?' will need a fact. 'Why?' will need a reason. Underline these key 'question words' to help you find what you are looking for.

EDUCATION

Brain facts

Did you know that the brain is made up of about 75% water and weighs around 3 pounds? Strangely, there are absolutely no pain receptors – nerve endings – in the brain. This means that although you may think you are experiencing pain in the brain, the brain itself can feel no pain.

Memory is formed by associations, so to promote memory when studying we should create associations – linking one idea with another. 'A for apple' is an example of an association that we learn early on in life when we begin to learn our ABC. We learn to link together the word 'apple' with the letter 'A' and probably a picture of an apple. This can be done in any language: children who learn letters, characters or symbols in their own language will make similar links and associations. Remarkably, children who learn two languages before the age of five have a different brain structure from children who learn only one language.

Adapted from 'Brain Facts' by Pamelia Brown

4 Look at the questions and the text again.

   a) Underline the words that appear in both the questions and the text.

   b) Underline the words in the text that you used in your answers.

   c) When you see the question words 'What' and 'Why', what information are you looking for?

DEVELOPING THE SKILLS

5 Read the article below twice, and then write five questions that can be answered by it.

How your brain works with languages

Neurobiologists have recently found that being bilingual has some advantages. Their research has shown that being able to speak and use more than one language before the age of five significantly improves a child's ability to concentrate and could delay or reduce the risks of illnesses like **senile dementia**.

In the past, and even today, some parents and teachers have felt that children who are exposed to more than one language could become very confused. They even believed that it could delay their **intellectual** growth! This is clearly incorrect as most bilingual children reach the same language targets as their monolingual classmates and don't show any evidence of being confused. On the contrary, the latest research shows that most bilingual students are able to focus better on their tasks and are less **distracted**. They are also able to pick out more easily the information that is most relevant to their task and ignore **irrelevant** material.

Some scientists feel that being bilingual increases the supply of oxygen and blood flow to the brain. This keeps nerve connections healthy and can help to delay or reduce diseases like senile dementia.

GLOSSARY		
	senile dementia	a mental illness that affects some old people and that causes them to become confused and to forget things
	intellectual	involving a person's ability to think and to understand ideas and information
	distracted	unable to concentrate, preoccupied
	irrelevant	not relevant

GOING FURTHER

Reading texts that are more difficult to understand can be more challenging. When you have to answer questions about them, you still need to identify the key words in the text.

6 Read the following texts of Howard Gardner's view on multiple intelligences and then answer the questions on the next page.

> **TOP TIP** Sometimes you may come across unfamiliar words. Do not be put off – keep reading and you may be able to work out the meaning from the rest of the sentence.

Multiple intelligences

The Theory of Multiple Intelligences (MI) was proposed by Howard Gardner, a professor at Harvard University, in 1983. According to this theory, intelligence is not a single thing that can be measured as a number such as an IQ. Instead, there are nine types of intelligence, which everyone has in a different and unique combination.

Existential
To exhibit a tendency to pose and ponder questions about life, death and ultimate realities

Verbal/Linguistic
The capacity to use language to express what's on your mind and to understand other people.

Intrapersonal
Having an understanding of yourself, of knowing who you are, what you can do, etc.

Logical/Mathematical
The ability to understand the underlying principles of some kind of system of cause and effect.

Interpersonal
The ability to understand other people.

Multiple intelligences

Visual/Spatial
The ability to present the spatial world internally in your mind.

Naturalist
The ability to tell the difference between living things as well as showing sensitivity to other features of the natural world.

Musical/Rhythmic
The capacity to think in music, to be able to hear patterns, recognise them and perhaps play with and move them around.

Bodily/Kinaesthetic
The capacity to use your whole or parts of your body, to solve a problem, make something or put on a production.

Multiple intelligences

Type of intelligence	What learners like to do
Linguistic (word smart)	Write articles, read books, tell stories, do word puzzles, learn rhymes, memorise facts, tell jokes, debate, learn song lyrics.
Mathematical-logical (logic smart)	Solve problems, do Sudoku, calculate quickly, play strategy games, reason things out, explore patterns and timelines, analyse statistics.
Spatial (picture smart)	Do art and design activities, draw, build and create models, read maps and charts easily, think in visuals, do jigsaw puzzles, make cartoons, charts, posters and floor plans, enjoy photography, art and design.
Bodily-kinaesthetic (body smart)	Move around, act things out, do hands-on learning, do craft, touch things to see how they work, dance, do sport and exercise.
Musical (music smart)	Sing and hum, remember melodies and rhythms, play instruments, keep time, rap, create jingles.
Intrapersonal (self smart)	Work alone, be independent, set ambitious personal goals, reflect and think, go after own interests, be individual at all times, keep diaries or journals, start independent research and inquiry projects.
Interpersonal (people smart)	Be with others and socialise, lead and organise groups, resolve conflicts, empathise with others, co-operate with others, organise and go to parties often.
Existential	Pose and ponder questions about life and death. Ask questions about who we are and our purpose in life. Read religious texts and philosophy in search of answers.
Naturalist (nature smart)	Learn about nature, love animals and birds, know about the natural world and how it works, show concern for the environment, enjoy being outdoors, can name plants and animals.

a) At which university did Dr Howard Gardner develop his Theory of Multiple Intelligences? In which year did he do this?

b) How many intelligences are listed here in total?

c) What other word describes people who are *body smart*?

d) What do those with a high naturalist intelligence like to do? What might their hobbies be?

e) What activities do *picture smart* people enjoy? Why?

f) If you like to play strategy games and explore patterns, which intelligence might you have more of?

g) Which intelligence encourages rewriting stories and learning poems?

h) List two qualities of those who have a high *interpersonal* intelligence.

i) What do those with high *existential* intelligence like to do?

(7) Read the descriptions of types of intelligence again and think about which of these describes you. There may be more than one.

4.2 Schools past and future

In this section you will learn to:

✓ use appropriate vocabulary accurately and effectively when writing to inform or explain

✓ use a wide range of vocabulary for variety and clarity.

GETTING STARTED

1 Think about the following ideas or discuss them with a partner. Note down your ideas.

- What kind of school do you go to today?
- What is the history of your school?
- What changes have there been to schools in your country over the past 100 years?

2 Now look at the photo of an old-fashioned school in England. Talk to your partner about what has changed, considering the following:

- what the school building looked like
- what people thought of girls going to school
- what was taught as part of the curriculum
- what the teachers were like
- what the students wore
- how they were punished for bad behaviour.

EXPLORING THE SKILLS

In order to write effectively about a particular topic, you need to build up a bank of vocabulary that is associated with that topic. Start gathering words now from your discussion.

Building an effective vocabulary is a bit like a game. You need to complete the process before you can 'win' and make the word your own.

Until this circle is complete, words can bounce into your brain and right out again without becoming a part of your vocabulary!

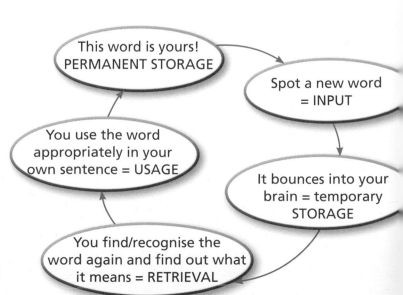

This word is yours! PERMANENT STORAGE

Spot a new word = INPUT

You use the word appropriately in your own sentence = USAGE

It bounces into your brain = temporary STORAGE

You find/recognise the word again and find out what it means = RETRIEVAL

3 Find out how accurately you can use words about education. How many of the words or phrases in the box below do you know the meaning of? How many can you use about yourself and your school?

- boarding school
- day school
- qualification
- school leaving certificate
- co-educational
- curricular activity
- coursework
- extracurricular activity
- optional subject
- public examination
- private tutor
- discipline
- attendance
- academic
- achievement
- vocational
- rote-learning
- corporal punishment
- term/semester
- interactive

4 You have been asked by your head teacher to write a friendly email to a new student who is about to join your school. The purpose of the email is to:

- welcome them to your city and school
- tell them what they need to buy before they join the school
- inform them of any key words that are used in your school, and any vocabulary they will need to know to get around the school. For example: Upper School Area = USA; LS = Life Skills; cafeteria = tuckshop/refectory/lunchroom.

DEVELOPING THE SKILLS

When you encounter a new word, look up its meaning and then 'place' it in relation to words you already know on that topic. Having a wide vocabulary that you really understand will help you write precisely to inform and explain.

5 Read about ancient Egyptian schools. Then answer the questions below.

Ancient Egyptian Schools

In ancient Egypt, wealthy families sent their sons to school by the age of four. Young girls, however, were not educated unless they were princesses or members of nobility, close to the pharaoh, the highest power in Egypt. A young boy's career was decided for him by his father, before he started school, and he was only educated in what would be useful to his future career. For example, if he was to become a potter, he would only learn how to make pots and pans. If he was to become a blacksmith, he would learn about metals and metal work. Being a scribe or a tax collector, which required reading and writing **hieroglyphics**, was highly valued. These professions paid well but the skills they required took several years to master. Young scribes had to spend long hours at their teacher's house copying out hieroglyphics on papyrus with a reed brush and ink. Mistakes on the papyrus, or even talking, could be severely punished.

a) Which group of Egyptian girls was allowed to have an education?

b) What was the name given to Egyptian script?

c) What was considered bad behaviour? How was a young scribe punished?

 GLOSSARY | **hieroglyphics** | symbols in the form of pictures which are used in some writing systems, for example those of ancient Egypt

6 Now read about ancient Indian schools and answer the questions that follow.

Ancient Indian Schools

In ancient India, schools were in **hermitages**, deep within the forests, run by very strict *Rishis* or *Gurus,* who were their teachers. These schools were given to the teachers by the king or the temples and everyone could go to school. Young men and women were sent to live with their teacher's family until they finished their education anywhere between the ages of 15 and 25. They slept on the floor and cooked their own food. Students began studying at dawn. They were taught to read, write, chant and memorise in **Sanskrit**. They studied many things including mathematics, grammar, yoga and the natural world. They were given homework and could ask questions but most often the teacher wanted them to find their own answers to difficult questions. Lessons consisted of lectures sitting at the teacher's feet followed by practical exploration and meditation in the forest. Service to the teacher had to be unquestioning at all times. Punishment for students could include **fasting**, **banishment** from lessons and unpleasant chores.

GLOSSARY		
hermitage	a quiet place where people live away from others
Sanskrit	an ancient Indian language
fasting	not eating any food or meals for a period of time, especially for religious reasons
banishment	being sent away and not allowed to return

a) What were ancient Indian teachers called?

b) Where were schools in ancient India located?

c) What was included in the curriculum? What language was it taught in?

d) Name two of the punishments students might be given.

7 Write a school magazine article describing and explaining what you have found out about schooling in ancient times and how it compares with the present day. Comment on what has changed and what has not. Include information on:

- what was studied
- learning styles
- teachers
- discipline.

Make sure you use the correct vocabulary.

LANGUAGE BOOSTER Your article might include some of the following 'compare and contrast' phrases to help comment on the different kinds of schooling:
similar to, different from, although, better, worse, however, not unlike, in contrast.

Asking 'Did you know…?' questions is another way of engaging the reader.

GOING FURTHER

Repeating the same words can sound boring. Using a range of **synonyms** correctly will help you to keep the reader's interest.

8 Copy and complete the table below, adding the **synonyms** in the word bank below to the correct row.

school		
student		
teacher		
vacation		
busy		

- learner
- college
- hard at work
- holiday
- tutor
- campus
- professor
- occupied
- break
- pupil

9 In pairs, discuss these questions:

a) Have you noticed any changes in schools since you started school? What are they?

b) Have you noticed any changes in the way you're taught and the way you learn? If so, what are they?

c) Imagine that $50 million is going to be spent to transform your school. What kind of a school would you like to have?

10 Write a short report describing your ideas for a school of the future. You can suggest changes to:

- school buildings and classrooms
- the library
- the cafeteria
- how classes are taught.

TOP TIP

Use headings and subheadings to make your report easier to read.

Give a reason for each of your suggestions.

Use a variety of synonyms and accurate vocabulary.

4.3 How do we learn?

In this section you will learn to:
✓ speak clearly using the most effective words to explain and describe
✓ choose the correct vocabulary and level of formality for the listener.

GETTING STARTED

1. Note down everything that comes to mind when you think back to your primary school.

   - What was the name of your favourite primary school teacher?

   - What do you remember about their classroom?

   - What was your first day of school like?

   - What are your earliest memories of school?

   - Think about your five senses. What smells, sounds or sights do you remember most?

2. In pairs, share your information and ask some questions about your partner's primary school experience.

EXPLORING THE SKILLS

When you were talking together about your experiences, you will have noticed that the wider your vocabulary, the more able you were to describe a person or a situation accurately and vividly. Just as when you are writing, the most accurate choice of noun, verb, adjective or adverb will make your speaking more effective.

LANGUAGE BOOSTER

The main parts of speech are nouns, verbs, adjectives and adverbs. As you widen your vocabulary, you should be aware of what part of speech a word is

noun – a word that refers to a person, thing or idea, for example, *teacher*, *classroom*, *education*

verb – a word that expresses an action or a state, for example, *to study*, *to be*

adjective – a word that describes a noun, for example, *short*, *clever*

adverb – a word that adds information about an action, for example, to study *hard*, to walk *slowly*

key words in questions – words that help you find information in a text, for example, *why* (a reason*)*, *where* (a place), *what* (a fact), *when* (a date or time), *who* (a name).

3 Now read the text about Mrs D'Souza. Some words have been underlined. Copy the table below. Identify what type of word each one is and add it to the correct column in the table. Some have already been added as examples.

> Mrs D'Souza was a <u>fabulous</u> <u>teacher</u>. She was <u>tall</u> and <u>dark-skinned</u> with <u>thick</u>, <u>curly</u> <u>black</u> <u>hair</u> that <u>was</u> <u>securely</u> <u>fastened</u> by a <u>net</u>. She <u>wore</u> <u>beautiful</u> <u>print</u> <u>dresses</u> and <u>high-heeled</u> <u>shoes</u> that <u>clicked</u> on the <u>tiled</u> <u>floors</u> of the classroom. She <u>smelled</u> of <u>roses</u> and <u>perfume</u>. She was <u>always</u> <u>ready</u> to <u>comfort</u> little first-year children who <u>were</u> <u>crying</u> as they said goodbye to their parents.

Noun	Adjective	Verb	Adverb
teacher	fabulous	was … fastened	securely

4 Make a few notes about one of your first teachers. Then tell your partner about the teacher, trying to use the best adjectives and verbs that you can to describe what the person was like.

DEVELOPING THE SKILLS

Remember that in order to communicate well your vocabulary must be as descriptive and precise as possible.

5 You will now hear from a young woman about how the brain learns. Listen to the extract twice.

a) The first time, note down only key vocabulary.

b) The next time you listen, take notes. Think about:

- how emotions affect our learning
- what food and water the brain needs
- physical conditions that affect the brain
- the best conditions for learning.

GLOSSARY

neurons	nerve cells
neural pathways	routes along which messages from the nerves travel
dehydrated	lacking water in the body
curious	wanting to learn or know something

6 In groups, share your notes. Add any information you missed and highlight any key words that were new to you all.

(7) Using your notes, discuss the questions below with a partner.

- Do emotions affect your learning? Do you notice a difference in your learning if you're happy, sad or anxious?

- Talk about a time when you were happy and relaxed while you were learning something. How well did you learn? What did you learn?

TOP TIP Remember to use a combination of information using key words and advice like: *The brain needs a lot of water. Make sure you drink water regularly while you are working or studying.*

- Do you have a balanced and healthy diet that supports your brain in its learning? What could you do to improve this?

- Do you take 'brain breaks', where you do some physical exercise or move around?

(8) In your group, gather together the information you know about the best conditions for learning. Make a note of the key words you would use if you were giving a talk to a class of younger students. What do you think would be essential for younger students to know?

(9) Use the key words to help you deliver a two-minute talk to your partner.

GOING FURTHER

Just as when you are writing, when you speak about a topic it is important to use vocabulary that is appropriate to the listener. For example, you need to think about how formal you should be. When you are chatting to your friends, your language will be very informal. When you prepared your talk for younger students, you probably made an effort to use language that you thought they would understand. Perhaps you explained some technical or scientific points.

However, a talk for teachers would sound very different from a talk designed for students. Think about the level of formality and vocabulary used in the following:

Talk to teachers: *Emotions can impact greatly on the way we learn. Stress and anxiety can inhibit learning.*

Talk to students: *Feelings can affect the way we learn. Worry and stress can prevent us from learning so well.*

The student version is less technical and more informal than the teacher version.

(10) You are now going to listen to an audio clip about **Mind Maps®**. Mind maps are similar to concept maps but include much more detail. As you listen, think about who the speaker may be speaking to. In pairs discuss the following questions:

- Do you think she's speaking to young children, older students, or business people? Why?

- What features of the talk may not be suitable for a) a younger audience or b) a formal presentation?

- If you were explaining Mind Maps to a friend, you might use less formal language than this speaker uses. Identify three phrases or sentences that you might change and discuss how you might change them.

For example, the speaker says:

A Mind Map can be drawn by hand or created digitally using a software program. Digital Mind Maps have the advantage of being able to be made in minutes and are quick and easy to edit.

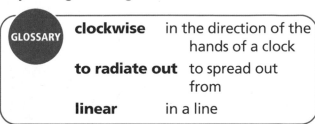

GLOSSARY	**clockwise**	in the direction of the hands of a clock
	to radiate out	to spread out from
	linear	in a line

You might change this and say to a friend:

You can draw a Mind Map by hand but there's a really good app which you could use instead which makes it much quicker.

(11) Using what you have heard, work with a partner to prepare two separate talks: one for teachers and another for younger students. Both talks must include:

- basic information on mind mapping

- how mind mapping improves memory and creativity

- the benefits of mind mapping to teaching or learning in the classroom

- a demonstration of how to create a mind map.

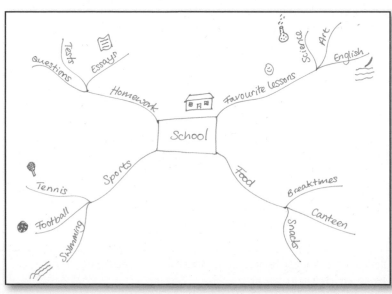

(12) Give your talks to the class. Did you all manage to show the difference between a talk aimed at teachers and one aimed at younger students? What were these differences?

4.4 School and the real world

In this section you will learn to:
✓ select details from different kinds of spoken texts
✓ use clues before you start listening to help you understand a text
✓ understand what is implied but not directly stated in a conversation.

GETTING STARTED

1 Think about which aspects of the school curriculum are going to be necessary once you leave school. Do one of the following and make notes.

a) Ask your parents or another adult what they do in their jobs on a daily basis. Which of these skills did they learn at school?

b) Pick a job or a career that you would like to have in the future. What skills and knowledge will you need to do that job?

2 Make a table like the one below to list **skills** and **knowledge** that you are acquiring at school and investigate their real-world uses. Fill in the last gap and then add some more rows with your own ideas.

Skill/knowledge from school	Use in real world	Career that requires this
Organisation: handing in work on time, keeping a diary	Meetings, deadlines, projects	All careers!
Understanding chemical symbols	Reading labels, buying vitamins	Biologist, teacher of biology, medical professional
Reading maps	Getting directions	

GLOSSARY

skill something you learn *how* to do, for example, riding a bike or driving a car

knowledge information that you learn, for example, the periodic table, mathematical equations, the stages of a river

EXPLORING THE SKILLS

It will help you to understand spoken text if you can get some idea of the context – that is, where the people are, or the reason why they are there. You may be given some information before you listen to an extract. This will help you start to focus on the sort of things the speakers will be talking about. If you are not given much information, try listening out carefully for clues. For example:

Who – who is speaking? There could be several speakers. Listen for different voices.

Role – what do the participants in the extract do? What is their job or profession?

Context – where or when is the conversation happening? What do you think has just happened or is going to happen?

Point of view or **opinion** – this is harder to listen for. It tells you what the speaker feels or thinks about the issue being talked about.

Keep these pre-listening tips in mind during the following task.

> **TOP TIP**
>
> You can predict that you are going to hear vocabulary to do with education and learning. This will help you understand what is going to be said.
>
> Remember to read the questions through carefully before the recording is played, perhaps underlining key words which will help you pick out the answers.

3 You are going to hear about a child **prodigy** called Adora Svitak. She is a young woman who has published books and spoken at conferences and who runs her own blog and teacher-training series. 4.3

Listen carefully to the information and then answer the questions below.

1. At what age did Adora begin teaching?
2. What is Adora's view of technology in the classroom?
3. What does Adora think adults can learn from children?
4. What was Adora's first book called?
5. What was Adora's favourite subject at school?
6. What does Adora like doing in her spare time?

> **GLOSSARY** **prodigy** a person with some marvellous talent

DEVELOPING THE SKILLS

Here is another chance for you to practise your pre-listening skills. Remind yourself of the tips on the previous page and remember to use the clues. Read the questions and look out for the key question words before you listen.

4 Listen to three senior school students talking about the ideas of Alvin Toffler, author of a book called *Future Shock*. One of the students, Zara, has just watched an online clip of Toffler speaking about his concerns regarding public education in the USA. Zara shares her thoughts on the talk with two of her friends, Jeremy and Anna.

Alvin Toffler

> **GLOSSARY**
>
> **radical changes**   important and big changes
> **obsolete**   no longer in use, out of date

a) How is Jeremy feeling?

b) Which parts of her schooling does Anna enjoy?

c) How old was Alvin Toffler when the video was made? Why does his age surprise the other students?

d) What did Toffler think was the purpose of public education in the 18th and 19th centuries in the USA or UK?

e) What are the similarities between the old factory and the current school?

f) What does Jeremy want to do in the future? Who would he like to learn from?

g) Name two roles that teachers could have in the new education system.

h) Why does Jeremy want to stay up late?

i) Why is Anna unsure about working with younger students in art classes?

j) Describe two features of Toffler's 24-hour school.

5 With a partner, discuss the answers you gave in task 4. Talk about the following questions from your own viewpoint:

   a) Which aspects of your current schooling do you think are like working in a factory?

   b) Which aspects of current schooling do you think are useful and practical?

   c) Which aspects of your schooling do you think are not very useful to your generation and should be changed?

   Your discussion could include topics such as:

   the school, timetable, curriculum, organisation, rules, classrooms, use of computers, teaching methods

> **TOP TIP**
> During your discussion, stop your partner to ask clarifying questions and check your understanding of what they are saying. A polite way to interrupt them might be:
>
> *'Could I stop you there for a second? Do you mean… or… ?'*
>
> *'Could you please say that again? I think I missed that.'*
>
> *'I am not sure I understand what you mean by… . Could you rephrase that or explain it to me?'*

GOING FURTHER

You sometimes have to listen 'between the lines' to understand what someone implies but does not say directly. Notice how a speaker might make a comment or ask a simple question when they want to guide your thoughts in a particular direction, without being obvious.

As you answer the next set of questions, you will find that sometimes you have to use clues to answer the questions, and not just select details from what the person says.

6 Listen again to Jeremy, Anna and Zara talking about present and future schooling. Can you read between the lines? **4.4**

   a) What is Jeremy's current attitude to school? Has it always been this way?

   b) What kind of a relationship do you think Anna has with her grandmother?

   c) Which phrase tells you that Anna is quite fond of school? Does she want to shut down schools?

   d) Why do Anna and Jeremy disagree slightly on the idea of a 24-hour school?

   e) Name two things that you learn about Jeremy from this conversation.

The big task

In groups of three or four, you are going to research, plan and give a presentation on your ideal school. Imagine that this is a school of the future, the kind of school you would want your children to go to or would like to go to yourself. Make sure you think about accurate vocabulary to describe the school and its technological wonders.

1 You must research and include the following in your presentation:

- the name of the school and its aims/philosophy – logo or badge optional

- the school building, where it is located and how it works – classrooms, hall, cafeteria, toilets, library

- the curriculum – what is taught, how, when and why

- the teachers – how they teach, their attitude to teaching and learning

- the rules and culture of the school – uniforms, assemblies, timings, organisation, punishments

- links to the world outside school – how these will be achieved.

2 Think about how you will present this school to your classmates and teacher. You could use one or more of the following:

- a role-play or drama with music

- a short film/audio recording

- a photo story

- a day in the life of your school

- a slide presentation with a voiceover.

3 Once you have done your presentation, write it up as a newspaper article that outlines the importance of funding and creating this school for your local community.

Check your progress

Here are the Reading, Writing, Speaking and Listening skills you learned about in Chapter 4.

Use this table to decide how good you are at the different skills, and make a note of what you need to be able to do in order to move up a level.

READING I can …	WRITING I can …
usually understand and pick out all the details I need from texts	use a good range of vocabulary effectively and confidently when writing to inform or explain and can express quite complex ideas
often understand and then pick out many of the details I need from texts	use some variety of vocabulary when writing to inform or explain and can express straightforward ideas clearly
sometimes pick out a few of the details I need from texts	use a limited range of basic vocabulary effectively when writing to inform or explain and can express simple ideas so that they can be understood

SPEAKING I can …	LISTENING I can …
usually find the most effective words to explain or describe something usually choose exactly the right level of formality	pick out exactly the details I need when listening to texts, including complex ones, using the clues in the questions to help usually understand what is implied but not directly stated in a formal talk
sometimes find the right words to explain or describe something sometimes find the right level of formality	pick out many of the details I need when listening to texts, using the clues in the questions to help understand some of what is implied but not directly stated in a formal talk
use a limited range of vocabulary, and may hesitate or search for the right words to explain or describe something understand the need to find the right level of formality, but find it hard to adapt	sometimes understand and pick out some of the details I need when listening to straightforward texts sometimes use the clues in the questions to help me answer straightforward questions understand straightforward formal talks

THE BIG PICTURE

In this chapter you will:

- think about competition both in nature and in the human world

- read and talk about competition in nature where animals fight for resources

- think and write about what drives us to compete against each other and to want to win in competitions ranging from sports to business.

THINKING BIG

1 On your own, look at the pictures and think about any competitions you have entered or would like to enter.

2 In pairs, rank the following statements from 'most true' to 'least true' in your opinion. People enter competitions:

- to prove they are the best
- to gain the admiration of others
- to get the prize/reward
- to increase their confidence
- to make money
- to show they are better than other people
- because they enjoy the game/business/ sport/subject
- to push themselves to their limits
- to perform better.

3 When do you think competition is unhealthy?

5

Competition

5.1 Competition in nature

In this section you will learn to:
✓ use text features to pick out key points, facts and details
✓ take notes on related details in a text.

GETTING STARTED

1 Look at the following photos. Think about what the animals or plants are competing for in each photo.

2 In pairs, make a list of resources (things they need) that animals compete for in nature.

3 Now write down three questions or topics you would like to know more about to do with competition in nature.

EXPLORING THE SKILLS

When you are reading any text, you should use all its features to help you understand it. The following can help you to find the information or detail you need quickly:

- headings
- fact boxes.
- photos and illustrations

4 Skim read the text opposite. In pairs, discuss where in the text you would look for the following. Identify the features in the text that helped you find these details:

- what a shark looks like
- shark attacks on people
- where sharks live
- how big a shark is.
- how sharks find food

5 Now read the text carefully and answer the following questions.

a) Where do sharks live?

b) What happens when a shark's tooth falls out?

c) How do sharks hunt? Give **two** details.

d) Why can sharks swim fast? Why might this be an advantage?

e) Do you think another animal would attack the shark? Give **one** reason for your answer.

f) Write two sentences to describe what a shark looks like. Use at least three adjectives.

g) What's the author's opinion on sharks? How do you know this?

h) You are on a beach in South Africa and your friend refuses to go into the water because he/she is afraid of a shark attack. What would you tell them?

> **TOP TIP**
>
> **Non-fiction** texts often use fact boxes to highlight key information.

> **GLOSSARY**
>
> **predator** an animal that kills and eats other animals
>
> **food chain** a series of living things which are linked to each other because each thing eats the one next to it in the series
>
> **apex** the top or the highest point

THE GREAT WHITE SHARK

Fact box
Length: Up to 6 m
Weight: 3350 kg
Speed: Up to 59 km/h

Habitat
The great white shark lives in cool coastal waters all over the world but can swim very long distances across oceans and is capable of swimming 19 300 kilometres in nine months.

Skeleton
Sharks have skeletons made of a strong material, which can bend more easily and is lighter than bone, which means this fierce predator can swim at up to 35 mph.

Hunting
The great white shark does not compete for food. It has no natural enemies, is at the top of the food chain and is therefore an apex predator. It hunts alone and usually eats dolphins, seals and sea lions, which it typically attacks from below. However, great white sharks will eat whatever they find.

Teeth and jaws
The great white has long rows of teeth that are continually replaced when old ones fall out. It can grow up to 20 000 teeth in a lifetime. Both its upper and lower jaws move, and this makes them more powerful than the jaws of any other creature in the world.

Great white's reputation
Great whites, and sharks in general, have a bad reputation. But the statistics do not support its man-eater reputation. In fact, fewer than 50 people are attacked annually by great whites and only 10% of the attacks result in deaths.

DEVELOPING THE SKILLS

Different texts use different features for different reasons. In addition to the list in 'Exploring the skills', non-fiction texts often use:

- captions
- bold/capital letters
- bulleted lists
- maps
- quotations
- navigation bars.

6) Read the text opposite about killer whales and answer the questions.

   a) Which text features listed above does the text use?

   b) What type of text is it?

   c) Where would you expect to read it?

   d) Compared with the text about sharks on the previous page, which is easier to read? Give one reason for your choice.

   e) Which text is the more informative? Give one reason for your choice.

   f) Which text includes a quotation? Why do you think it is used?

7) Look again at the text about killer whales. Where would you look or click on the page if:

   a) you only spoke French

   b) you wanted to join an expedition

   c) you wanted to read a blog about an expedition

   d) you wanted to watch a video of an expedition?

8) Summarise in one sentence what you will do on the expedition.

9) How does the author of the fact box feel about orcas?

GOING FURTHER

In order to improve your note-taking skills, you need to practise finding and organising related details in a text.

10) You have been asked to write a short text explaining why either the great white shark or the killer whale is such a good hunter. Look back at the text about your chosen animal. Then copy and complete the table below with the relevant details.

Skeleton/size	Hunting	Teeth/jaws

GLOSSARY	outdoor pursuit	an activity you do outside, for example, diving, biking, canoeing
	clicks and whistles	sounds whales make to communicate
	migration	moving from one place to another
	pod	a group of whales
	prey	an animal hunted and killed for food by another animal
	protected status	classification as an animal that by law may not be harmed or killed

Ocean Adventures and Conservation

Whale, coral reef and seabird conservation and study expeditions
Outdoor pursuits with a difference!

Home   Trip calendar   Video   Whale-watching   Scuba-diving   Seabird watching   Blogs

'Experience of a lifetime!'

This conservation work expedition will take you off the coast of Iceland to study orcas, or killer whales. You will photograph whales and record them as part of a long-term scientific survey.

You will listen to and make recordings of whale **clicks and whistles**. All this is an effort to find out a whale's life history and its **migration** patterns across the oceans.

Expedition contribution: $2500
Dates: 2–11 April,
14–23 April,
26 April–5 May

**Choose a trip and
BOOK NOW!**

Fact box

- Orcas typically measure 6–8 m but can be up to 10 m in length and usually weigh 6–10 tonnes (6000–10 000 kg).
- They usually have 40–50 teeth.
- Orcas often live and hunt in **pods**: a group of whales works together to surround **prey**, pushing it into a small area before attacking.
- The orca is an apex predator because it has no predators other than humans. Unfortunately, whales are still hunted even though they now have **protected status**.

5.2 Competition in sport

In this section you will learn to:
✓ use paragraphs correctly
✓ link ideas to write a smooth-flowing paragraph
✓ use a variety of connectives to join ideas within writing.

GETTING STARTED

Humans also seem to enjoy competing against each other. It may not be competing for food or light like animals or plants, but for many other reasons. Sport is one area where people enjoy seeing who will win.

1 In pairs:

- Talk about any sports, games and activities that you play. At what level do you play?

- Brainstorm all the sports you know. Then list them under two headings, for example:

Team sports	Individual sports
Football	Gymnastics

Discuss your headings.

- Note down any interesting words or ideas from your conversation.

2 As a class, list five of the biggest sporting events in the world. Now rank them. Which event is the most important?

3 On your own:

- Look at the photos and at the list of words in the table below. Add three words or phrases of your own that you use often when talking about competition in sport.

cross the finishing line	
score points	
win the cup	

- Next, choose four of the words or phrases. Write sentences using these.

EXPLORING THE SKILLS

A **paragraph** is a group of sentences which discuss one main idea.

- Paragraphs break up the text and make it easier to read.

- They organise information into meaningful chunks.

- A new paragraph usually introduces a new idea.

- Often there are one or two supporting details in a paragraph, which give more information about the main idea.

A **topic sentence** captures the entire meaning of a paragraph or a group of paragraphs. It often appears at the start of a paragraph.

 Haile Gebrselassie is known as one of the greatest long-distance runners. In his career he broke 15 world records, won gold medals and set new standards in long-distance running. Haile Gebrselassie, an Ethiopian, had to run 10 kilometres daily to go to school and this laid the foundation for his running career.

topic sentence

supporting facts

4 Silently read the newspaper article below.

5 In pairs, identify the following in each paragraph:

- where each new paragraph starts
- the main idea
- the topic sentence
- the supporting facts or details.

THE HIGHS AND LOWS OF WOMEN'S FOOTBALL

Women's football is becoming increasingly popular at all levels. Figures show 29 million girls and women play football, and FIFA hopes to see that number rise to 60 million by 2026.

International women's football is fairly new. The first women's international tournament was held in China in June 1988, 61 years after the first men's World Cup. That event led to China holding the first FIFA Women's World Cup™ three years later. At first, matches only lasted 80 minutes instead of 90 and there was a lack of international media attention. Although the US team won, watched by 65 000 people at the Guangdong Stadium, many Americans had no idea their women's team was even playing!

By 2019, the women's game had grown and was starting to be recognised internationally.

The Women's World Cup in France was broadcast in 205 territories, with a global audience of 1.12 billion.

The American team is the most successful women's team to date. In 2019, it won the World Cup for the fourth time while the audience in the stadium shouted 'Equal pay! Equal pay!' They were angry because the female team earned just $4 million for its victory while the men's team earned $8 million for losing in the first round in 2014. In fact, the US men's football – or soccer as it is known in America – team has never won yet earns more money than the women. However, thanks to new broadcasting deals women's football now reaches a bigger audience than before. This also means that more money will go into investing in women's football.

DEVELOPING THE SKILLS

To write well you need to join different ideas together smoothly. **Conjunctions** or **connectives** join sentences together. Some examples are 'and', 'but', 'so', 'although', 'because,' 'in spite of' and 'besides'.

6 Combine the sentences below to make one paragraph using conjunctions from the box.

as	but	in spite of	which	because	although

Most people agree that the 2010 World Cup was a resounding success. It was held in South Africa. The winner of the tournament was Spain.

Many commentators agree that South Africa was also the winner.

South Africa showed that Africa can host a tournament as big as the World Cup. The weather was cold. The welcome from South Africans was warm. The welcome was friendly. South Africa was defeated in the first round of the tournament. The tournament turned out to be a huge success.

Connectives not only link ideas within a paragraph, they also link one paragraph to the next.

7 In pairs:

- Identify the connectives in the reading passage 'The highs and lows of women's football' on the previous page.

- Make a list of all the connectives you found and any others you know and complete the table, inserting the connectives in the correct column.

Sequence order	Time order	Cause and effect	Contrast	Add information
At first	In the morning	As a result	in contrast	Moreover

GOING FURTHER

Summarising a text means that you are explaining an idea or ideas in a shortened form. You take the most important points from a text and rewrite them in your own words. This is a useful skill in particular when you are writing an essay. For example, you might read lots of different information and then need to summarise it to include it in your essay.

A good **summary** includes the main points/ideas, uses your own words and is ordered logically.

8 First, re-read your ideas from task 5 for the main points of each paragraph in 'The highs and lows of women's football' article. Then read the summary of the article below and answer the questions.

a) Which of the features listed on the previous page does it use?

b) Identify the connectives.

c) What ideas or sentences from the original article does it include?

d) Find two details from the original article that are not in the summary.

e) Do you think it summarises the main points? Give your opinion.

> Rising numbers of women and girls are watching the world's favourite game – football. The numbers might be as high as 60 million by 2026. Although the women's game began international competitions 61 years later than the men's, it was reaching audiences of 1.12 billion by 2019. Surprisingly, in spite of performing much better than the men's team, the US women's team are paid less.

9 Write a short report of a recent sports competition at your school/college or in your local area. Start with a topic sentence. For example:

> The Inter-regional School Football Championships were the most exciting event in this year's school sports calendar.

TOP TIP   Re-read your report and check you have:
- included a topic sentence and supporting facts or details
- used connectives.

5.3 Competition and the arts

In this section you will learn to:
✓ build a conversation by asking and answering questions
✓ be an active listener and add new ideas.

GETTING STARTED

1 In pairs, discuss the following:

- What do you know about the *Got Talent* show?
- What type of performances are allowed?
- Would you like to audition for the *Got Talent* show? If yes, why? If no, why not?
- Why do you think people want to appear on such TV shows?

EXPLORING THE SKILLS

Asking questions is a very useful way of building a conversation. You can use questions to:

- open a conversation
- ask a question back
- change the direction of a conversation
- request information or opinions
- develop an idea
- ask someone to repeat something.

When replying to questions, try to avoid short answers. Build the conversation using examples. The best way of giving examples is to provide answers to questions without them being asked, especially if you are given 'closed' questions, such as, 'Did you watch *Vietnam's Got Talent*?' For example:

Answer: 'Oh yes. I watch every week. ——— answers question: 'When'
I saw the violinist yesterday while ——— answers questions: 'What', 'When'
I was visiting my grandmother. and 'Where'
I didn't think she was very good.
What did you think?' ——— asks question back

2 Two friends are discussing *China's Got Talent*. Read the dialogue below and identify the questions.

Li:	Did you see *China's Got Talent* yesterday?
Bao:	Oh yes. I'm **addicted**. I watch it every week.
Li:	Oh, I missed it last night. What happened?
Bao:	The 20 girls on a bicycle **act** got **knocked out**, but, well, I didn't think they should win anyway. So, who do you think is going to win?

Li: Well, I quite like the young girl pianist. I particularly liked it when she mixed in a jazz section with a classical piece. But, the panel of judges don't seem to like her performances very much. They always complain that she doesn't have much **personality**. Although I didn't approve of the way the judges talked to her the other day. Did you see that?

Bao: Yes, that was shocking: they were so cruel that the girl was almost in tears. But I'm not sure a pianist should win anyway. You know everybody plays the piano nowadays. For instance, I heard the other day on the radio that between 25 and 40 million children are learning the piano now in China. And I'm not sure she's that special, although I did hear she practises for over 12 hours a day.

Li: Wow – that's a lot! So what do you think about the violinist?

Bao: Hmm. Not sure. Don't you think he's too **ambitious** and self-important? Obviously, it's never easy to play at that level and it's a bit unfair to judge him on the strength of his attitude rather than his performance, but he is so **determined** to succeed.

GLOSSARY		
	addicted	liking something very much
	act (noun)	one of several short performances in a show
	knocked out	being defeated in a competition, so that you take no more part in it
	personality	if someone has personality, they have a strong and lively character
	ambitious	having a strong desire to be successful, rich or powerful
	determined	having made a decision to do something and not letting anything stop you

3 Re-read 'Exploring the skills'. In pairs, discuss the purpose of each question in the dialogue above. Then copy the table below and complete the first two columns to show how each question is used.

Question	Type of question and how it is used	Examples given in answer
1 Did you see *China's Got Talent* yesterday?	To open the conversation. The question assumes that the friend also watches the TV show.	I watch it every week.
2		

4 Next, re-read the answers to each question. Then complete the third column of the table with **one** example or way that the speaker gives more information.

5 In pairs, practise reading the dialogue aloud, taking turns to read the different parts. Discuss who you think is guiding or controlling the conversation.

DEVELOPING THE SKILLS

Did you know you can build a conversation using different types of questions?

> Type 1 is the **What** question, asking for information:
>
> What did you see/hear?

> Type 2 asks for **an opinion or response** to what you saw or heard:
>
> What did you like/not like (most)? How did it make you feel?

> Type 3 question is the **Why** question and asks for reasons for the opinions expressed:
>
> Why do you think this?

Often when we want to build a conversation, we need to give an example. You can use these phrases to introduce the example:

> *For example*   *For instance*
>
> *To give you an example*   *Let me illustrate*

To develop a conversation from your example/opinion, it is useful to support it by adding the reason why. This broadens the discussion to more general matters.

For example:

> *The* Got Talent *contest is a waste of time.*
>
> *For instance, we all sit down on a Saturday evening to watch when we could be using that time to practise an instrument! I think all of us get more fulfilment actively playing an instrument than passively watching someone else play.*

6 In pairs, identify the phrase that introduces an example in the conversation in task 2. What happens to the conversation afterwards? Discuss how the example works in the conversation.

7 Give an example to support each of the following statements. Do not forget to give reasons why, to back up your example.

- The *Got Talent* contest encourages us all to sing or dance or play an instrument.

- The *Got Talent* contest has made young people obsessed with fame and money.

8 In pairs, have your own conversation about the *Got Talent* contest in your country. If you have not seen the programme, then use one that is popular in your country. Start the conversation like this:

> *Have you been watching the* Got Talent *contest?*

GOING FURTHER

The aim of a conversation is often to appreciate what your partner says by actively listening and taking turns. You can help develop the conversation even more by adding new ideas. You can do this, first by listening carefully and then by:

- showing that you have listened to their point (even if you have a different opinion) by rephrasing what your partner has said

- then giving your opinion

- then asking a question back.

For example:

> I didn't approve of the way the judges talked to the pianist the other day. ——— rephrasing what your partner has said
>
> Yes – I agree that was shocking. ——— agreeing The judges were so cruel that the girl was almost in tears. But I'm not sure a pianist should win anyway. ——— giving your opinion You know everybody plays the piano nowadays. What do you think? ——— asking a question back

9 Choose one of the topics listed in the box on the right. Tell your partner about the topic, giving examples and reasons for your opinion.

Your partner should listen very carefully because they must repeat back to you what you have said.

> **Topics**
> - The latest film on the market
> - The last competition you entered
> - The latest video game on the market

10 Now your partner chooses a second topic listed in the box. Listen carefully to what they say about it. Then follow the three steps in 'Going further'.

11 In pairs, you are going to have a conversation of no more than ten minutes. The aim is to keep the conversation going. Each choose one of the following themes. Write a list of five questions you want to ask your partner about their chosen topic.

> **TOP TIP** Don't forget to listen actively to what your partner says.

- listening to music
- painting
- playing an instrument
- films
- video games.

5.4 Competition in business

In this section you will learn to:
✓ understand and pick out facts in short spoken and written texts
✓ recognise and understand opinions in short spoken and written texts
✓ recognise and understand facts and opinion in longer, more formal dialogues.

GETTING STARTED

Businesses usually want to sell you things or ideas. They are competing for your money and your time in order to become the market leader.

1 In pairs, discuss and decide who the market leader in your country is for:

- footwear
- computers
- cars
- fast food.

2 Discuss and give a definition of 'market leader'.

3 Now discuss which of the following competes better for your time and your money.

- Buying a book from the local bookshop or buying the same book on the internet.
- Downloading songs by your favourite band or going to the cinema to see the latest movie.
- Saving some money to buy a new mobile phone or going to a festival.
- Working overtime on Friday evening to earn double wages or staying in and watching TV.

4 Discuss and agree on a definition of 'competition' in business. Write it down. Compare your definition with another pair.

EXPLORING THE SKILLS

When you say something is a fact, or fact, you mean that it is true or correct. You can prove that it's true. Your opinion about something, on the other hand, is what you think or believe about it. An opinion is a belief or judgement which may not be based on fact. Your opinion is not necessarily the truth, but it might be.

For instance, someone might point to a phone and say the following three statements:

'This is a phone.' – fact

'This is a great phone.' – opinion, this is what the speaker believes

'This is the best phone.' – opinion or belief, this is what the speaker believes, but this phone is only 'the best' if you compare it against all the other phones. 'The best' is a superlative so this phrase is used when you are comparing things.

Knowing the difference between what is fact and what is opinion or belief is important. Some people might be trying to persuade you to do something, so they might state opinions as facts in order to convince you. It is important for you to think about the speaker's purpose and choice of language. This is particularly important when reading or listening to advertisements.

5) Skim the advertisement opposite for a new smartphone package. In pairs:

   a) Identify the opinions in the advertisement.

   b) Decide if you think the phone is free. Give reasons for your answer.

   c) Discuss if you think it is the 'best offer yet'. Give reasons for your answer.

   d) Note down ideas about why companies advertise their products.

> **Great savings on the latest mobile phone deals**
>
> # Free ZTC 3000
>
> ✪ Only $37 monthly subscription*
>
> ✪ Unlimited minutes
>
> ✪ Unlimited texts
>
> ✪ A massive 1GB of data usage
>
> * 24-month tie in
>
> *It's the best offer yet!*

DEVELOPING THE SKILLS

When advertising, companies are competing for your money, so they will try to persuade you that their product is the best. The people in the ads rarely introduce their opinions with 'I believe …' or 'I think …' but will often try to convince you of their opinions by:

- mixing facts with opinions
- telling you why they think something is useful/beautiful/good, etc.

6) Now listen to an influencer talking about a new range of shower gels.   **5.1**

   a) Why is she so excited about this range in particular?

   b) What does she do to make people want to buy it?

   c) Do you think we have to agree it's a pretty sweet deal?

7 Listen again. Write the letters **a)** to **i)** in your notebook and identify the facts and opinions by writing F next to facts and O next to opinions, as listed below.

a) The packaging is so beautiful.

b) All the packing uses 98% recycled plastics.

c) It's 100% cruelty-free.

d) … [Cruelty-free] is really important.

e) It's got way more bubbles than most shower gels.

f) It's perfect for me because I love jasmine.

g) It's too early for them now we're only in March.

h) It smells even better than the real thing.

i) It's a pretty sweet deal.

GOING FURTHER

Numbers and percentages often indicate that something is a fact.

8 Later, you are going to listen to an interview about the history of mobile phones. Before you do, discuss the following in pairs.

a) What do you know about the history of mobile phones?

b) Look at the photo of one of the first mobile phones. How have mobile phones changed since then?

c) Do you think you will get more facts or more opinions in this interview? Why do you think that?

9 These are all words you will hear in the listening passage. Match each word on the left to its definition.

a) antenna

b) estimation

c) forecast

d) grow like wildfire

e) handset

f) predictive texting

g) vibrate function

h) wildly incorrect

A technology that makes typing on a mobile phone easier by suggesting words the user may wish to insert

B telephone mouthpiece and earpiece in a single unit

C setting that makes a mobile phone shake slightly instead of ringing to warn you someone is calling/texting

D very wrong

E spread very quickly

F guess

G predict

H long thin device that sends and receives radio signals

10 Listen to the passage a first time and answer the following question. 5.2

What has happened to the popularity of mobile phones?

11 Listen again and copy and complete the following table to chart the history of mobile phones.

Date	What happened
1985	First mobile phone appeared that did not have a battery the size of a briefcase
1996	
2000	
2001	
2003	
2007	
2024	

12 Listen again to the last paragraph and complete this table, which lists the percentage of people who own a mobile phone in different countries. Write what kind of phone the percentage refers to.
S = smartphone, M = regular mobile phone, A = any kind of phone

5.3

Percentage / Type of phone	Country	Percentage / Type of phone	Country
71% / S	the USA		Singapore
	the UK		Saudi Arabia
	China		Hong Kong, China
	India		

13 Read the following text (it starts from Dr Suhuyini's second speech in the listening passage). Identify two opinions.

> **DR SUHUYINI:** Mobile phones have got smaller and lighter and because of this the popularity of mobile phones has grown like wildfire.
>
> **INTERVIEWER:** What numbers are you talking about?
>
> **DR SUHUYINI:** Well, in the 1980s one mobile phone company forecast a world market of 900 000 phones by the year 2000. But they got it really wrong – their estimation was wildly incorrect. By 1998 more mobile phones were sold worldwide than cars and PCs combined. Today, about 1.2 million mobile phones are sold every three days.

14 On your own, write notes on the three most important features for you in a mobile phone. When and why do you use them? Why are they important?

15 In pairs, discuss what is important to you in a mobile phone and why.

16 As a whole class, discuss:
- Why do you think mobile phones spread 'like wildfire'?
- Why do you think the features of a mobile phone keep changing?
- Do you think a new feature on a phone is always a benefit?
- What does this say about your society?

The big task

You are the reporter for your school magazine and have been asked to write a review of the annual school talent show, which was also recorded for a local TV channel.

1 On your own, brainstorm what type of acts you think will appear in your school's talent show. Think about:

- dance
- solo singing
- groups/bands
- music/instruments
- circus/novelty acts.

2 Now decide:

- which acts performed
- what happened on the night
- who you/the audience liked best/least how the contest made you feel
- what the winner's reactions were
- what this means for the school.

3 Write a first draft of your review.

4 Now go back and check your review. Add a title (make sure the title is less than five words). Check:

- spelling
- that you have at least one fact
- that you have at least one opinion.

5 Write a final copy of your review.

6 Hold a class competition and vote for the best review of the talent show. Before you decide, think about how you will mark the reviews. For example, will you give more marks for:

- an interesting review
- accurate English
- good presentation skills?

Check your progress

Here are the Reading, Writing, Speaking and Listening skills you learned about in Chapter 5.

Use this table to decide how good you are at the different skills, and make a note of what you need to be able to do in order to move up a level.

READING	WRITING
I can …	**I can …**
confidently use text features to understand and then pick out most of the key points usually pick out all the related details I need from a text I have to summarise	use paragraphs correctly and confidently when writing link quite complex ideas together, using a variety of connectives, to form smooth-flowing paragraphs in a summary regularly use a variety of connectives to help me write an effective summary
use text features to understand and then pick out key points pick out many of the related details I need from a text I have to summarise	sometimes use paragraphs when writing sometimes link my ideas, using connectives, to form a smooth-flowing paragraph in a summary
sometimes use text features to understand and then pick out key points pick out the basic related details I need from a text I have to summarise	make limited use of paragraphs when writing sometimes join a few ideas together, using some basic connectives, to form paragraphs in a summary

SPEAKING	LISTENING
I can …	**I can …**
build a conversation with confidence, by taking my turn at asking and answering questions be an effective listener and often add my own new ideas	understand and then pick out exactly the facts I need when listening to short informal dialogues usually recognise and understand opinions expressed in informal and formal speech
help build a conversation by responding well to questions be a competent listener and sometimes add a few of my own ideas	understand and then pick out many of the facts I need when listening to short informal dialogues sometimes recognise and understand opinions expressed in informal and formal speech
join in a conversation by giving short answers to questions be a fair listener and try to respond to other people's ideas	sometimes understand and pick out some of the facts I need when listening to short informal dialogues understand straightforward informal and formal speech

THE BIG PICTURE

In this chapter you will:

- think about work – the different kinds of work people do
- consider the kind of work you would like to do
- research, talk and write about ways to find work and to succeed at work.

THINKING BIG

1 Look at the photos. On your own, note down ideas about the following:

- What different kinds of work are shown in the photos?
- Which of these jobs do you think is the most interesting?
- What would be the rewards and drawbacks of each job?
- Which of these jobs would you like to do? Which ones wouldn't you like to do?

2 In pairs, look at the photos. Talk together about what you know about each of these jobs and the different types and places of work pictured. Ask your partner questions about what they would like and dislike about the work shown in the photos.

3 Discuss your choice with another pair.

- What is the most important thing about work for you – to make money, to do something you enjoy, to help others?
- What do you think would be the advantages and disadvantages of travelling a lot for your work? Would you prefer to work locally? Why?
- Do you prefer to work in a group of people or on your own? Explain your reasons.

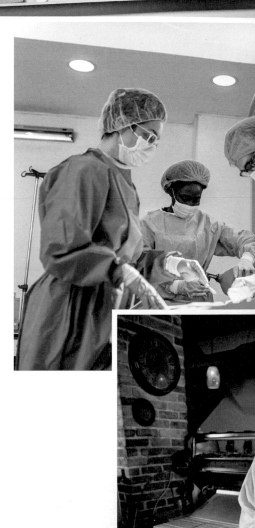

6
Work

6.1 Finding the right job for you

In this section you will learn to:
✓ select facts from a range of texts which also contain personal opinions
✓ recognise the language used to introduce facts and personal opinions.

GETTING STARTED

1 Before you can decide what kind of work you would like to do, you have to develop some awareness of what kind of person you are. Read the questions below and discuss your ideas with a partner. Make a note of your answers.

- What skills do you have – what kind of things are you good at doing? Are you good at working with computers or at communicating with other people?

- What do you enjoy doing? Do you enjoy working indoors or outdoors? Do you like working on your own or with other people?

EXPLORING THE SKILLS

As you already know from earlier chapters, it is useful to be able to pick out descriptive information, opinions and facts when you are reading texts. A **fact** is something that you can prove is true. For example, in the extracts on the next page, the facts about Leila are:

- She's 21.
- She works for herself.
- She set up her business a year ago.

The **opinions** are:

- Leila works too hard. (This is the writer's opinion.)
- Leila is happy. (This is Leila's own opinion.)

2 Read the descriptions of four different types of work personalities below. Then read the descriptions on the next page. In pairs, match each person to the correct type, and identify the facts that reveal this.

Creative: has lots of ideas and is always thinking of new products.

Managerial: is good at organising people and processes.

Technical: enjoys seeing how things work and being involved in the technical details.

Independent: can see what needs to be done and will take risks to make it happen.

Leila, 21, works for herself. She set up her own business a year ago and it is very successful. It is sometimes difficult, but she enjoys making decisions. I think she works too hard, but she says she's happy!

Rashid, 19, is great at working with people, and he seems to really understand what people are good at. He often has to organise meetings and projects. Some people think he talks a lot, though!

Kaya, 22, is a web designer. She often comes up with new ways to present information when no one else can think of any ideas. At school, her teachers thought she didn't work hard, but now everyone can see how talented she is.

Imran, 20, prefers to work alone. He enjoys making things work and repairing them when they do not work. He knows a lot about the machinery he works on. I find him a bit quiet, though.

(3) Read the personality types again and decide which type of worker you would be. Explain your choice. Think about your answers to the questions in task 1 and use facts about yourself to support your answer.

DEVELOPING THE SKILLS

In a text there are often signs in the language that show whether something is a fact or a personal opinion. Opinions are often given in personalised language, with phrases such as 'for me' and 'I find'. Facts may be given as numbers, showing an exact amount of something that can be counted and proved.

(4) Look at the extract below from a survey about work. This combines facts and opinions. It tells us that 750 boys and 600 girls want to run their own business. This is a fact shown by the statistics in the graph. What opinions can you find?

1. Do you want to run your own business?

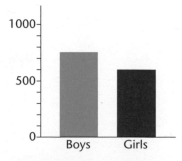

Number of people who want to run their own business

2. What is important for you about work?

"For me, it is the chance to make a difference. I want to work as a doctor, because I believe that the most important thing is to be able to help people who are ill or injured."
Marco, Rome

"I'd like to be a journalist and write stories and interview interesting people. I think travelling to new places is really exciting, and I also feel that sharing information is essential."
Yoshi, Tokyo

Here is more information from the survey you looked at on the previous page.

Young people and work

We interviewed lots of different young people for our survey on 'Young people and work'. Some of the people were still at school and others had just started work. This report shows the information we collected.

3. Would you prefer to work inside or outside?

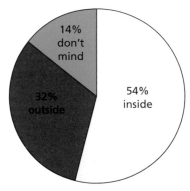

4. Do you want to go straight to work or go to college or university first?

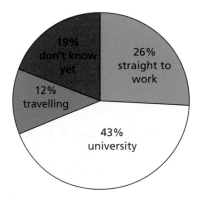

5. Where would you like to work?

66*Definitely in an office – I like to be indoors with my own desk and computer.*99 **Eric, Nigeria**

66*I think I'd like to work outdoors – I enjoy being outside and I think it would be more relaxing and interesting than being inside all day.*99
Domingo, Mexico

66*I'd like to travel with work – I wouldn't like to be in the same place all the time – that could get boring.*99 **Emilia, Brazil**

6. Where would you like to be in 20 years' time?

I'd like to be running my own company. I know exactly what I want to do and I'm really keen to work for myself.

Ruben, Switzerland

I'd rather not be working at that point – I want to be looking after my family.

Ana, Guatemala

I hope to have a good job in a big company – I'd like to be in charge of a small team of people but I don't think I'd like to be the CEO – it would be very stressful!

Hannah, London

5 Read the survey again and find the relevant facts to answer these questions.

a) What percentage of people in the survey do not mind whether they work inside or outside?

b) What percentage of people in the survey want to go to university immediately after school?

c) What do 12% of the people in the survey want to do before they go to work?

6 Now answer the questions below. Are the answers facts or opinions?

   a) Why does Eric want to work indoors?

   b) What two words does Domingo use to describe an outdoor job?

   c) What does Ana want to be doing in 20 years' time?

   d) What does Hannah think it would be like to be in charge of a large company?

7 With a partner, discuss how you would answer questions 3 to 6 of the survey. Share your ideas first and then make notes.

GOING FURTHER

If a text contains both facts and opinions, you will have to study it very carefully to interpret the information it contains. Look out for language clues and think about whether what it says can be proved, or whether it is the opinion of the writer.

8 Read the following text, then copy and complete the flowchart below.

> Many young people are nervous about leaving school and starting work. If you are lucky, there will be several options. The three main options open to young people are further education, training for a specific job, or starting work straight away.
>
> If you go into further education, you can specialise in a particular area. You might have to spend money on the course, but at the end you might get a better job because of it. However, many people feel that it is better to start earning money as soon as possible, rather than continuing studying.
>
> Training on the job is a useful alternative. You are taught a lot of useful skills while you earn some money. I believe this is an excellent way to achieve your goals.
>
> Finally, you could get a job straight away. There is often a lot of competition for jobs, so you will have to be prepared to try hard. Some people who try this option think that you often can't get the job you really want unless you have extra training or qualifications.

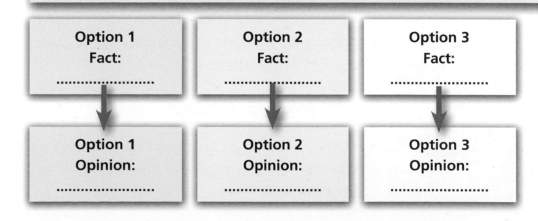

Option 1 Fact:	Option 2 Fact:	Option 3 Fact: ....
Option 1 Opinion:	Option 2 Opinion:	Option 3 Opinion: ....

6.2 Job applications

In this section you will learn to:

✓ use the appropriate tone and style when you are writing a letter or a magazine article.

GETTING STARTED

1 In pairs, discuss which type of communication you think is best for each situation.

a) You want to tell all your friends about what you did at the weekend.

b) You want to contact one friend quickly to arrange a meeting time.

c) You want to apply for a job.

d) You want to contact someone you haven't met to ask for information.

> **A** text message **B** formal letter **C** informal email **D** formal email

EXPLORING THE SKILLS

Just like your speech, your writing style also needs to suit different situations and different people. You will use different styles of writing and language when you write to a friend and when you write to someone you don't know. You might use different vocabulary, as well as different sentence structures and punctuation.

2 Read this letter from Murad to Samir. Is it written in a formal or an informal style? Discuss your ideas in pairs and find phrases to support your opinion.

Hi Samir,

How are things? I hope you had a great holiday. Did you go to the beach a lot? I've been working this summer in a restaurant. It was really hard work, because it's very busy. I was rushed off my feet!

At first I didn't like it, but since the first week I haven't looked back. It gave me the chance to save some money and make some new friends.

What have you been up to? Write soon and tell me what you've been up to!

Murad

P.S. My sister hasn't had a good summer break – she broke her leg three weeks ago! She fell off her bike and she's really fed up!

Here the writer uses informal language for writing to a friend. Murad starts:

> *Hi Samir,*
> *How are things?*

But to a teacher, you might start with:

> *Dear Mrs Rodia,*
> *I hope you are well.*

This is an example of how you can adjust your tone to suit your audience.

(3) You may come across **idioms** in informal writing. Beware, as they may not mean what they seem to mean! For example, in Murad's letter:

'I was rushed off my feet!' means that Murad was very busy. You can guess this from the context, as Murad talks about hard work and the restaurant being busy.

She's really fed up! means that Murat's sister is very unhappy. You can guess this because she hasn't had a good summer as she broke her leg.

DEVELOPING THE SKILLS

When you are writing, consider whether it is for a formal or an informal audience, and adjust your **tone** and **style** accordingly.

(4) Read the following letter. Is this a good letter of application?

Dear Mr Santorum

   Hi – I hope you're ok. I saw your advert, and I'd like to apply for the job. I'd love to work in a music shop and I think I'd be great at it. I love listening to music and playing the guitar – I could do it all day! I've got loads of young friends, too, so they'd all come in and buy things.

Can't wait to hear from you!
   Lissa Carlos

Discuss with a partner how Lissa's letter could be improved. You could group your answers under the headings 'Vocabulary', 'Content' and 'Tone'.

(5) Now read the following letter. Discuss in pairs how it is different from the previous letter.

Dear Mr Santorum,

I recently saw your advertisement in the newspaper for the position of part-time sales assistant in your shop selling musical instruments, and I would like to apply for this position. I am seventeen years old and I am a student at Newton College.

I feel I would be a good candidate for the job. I have experience of working in a shop, as I worked in a clothes shop last summer. I am also very keen on music, so I could bring a great deal of relevant knowledge to the role.

I would be very happy to come for an interview to discuss this. I am available to start work immediately.

Yours sincerely,
Mia Henley

---

6 Many ideas can be expressed using either formal or informal vocabulary. Notice how each pair of phrases below have the same meaning, but the way they've been used in these letters gives them a different tone.

In the context of these letters, which column of phrases sounds less formal and which sounds more formal?

job	position, role
loads of	many/much
I love …	I am very keen on

LANGUAGE BOOSTER

- In informal writing, it is acceptable to use **contracted** (shortened) forms:

  I've worked = I have worked

  I'd prefer = I would prefer

  In formal letters and other kinds of formal writing, contracted forms are not usually used.

- Notice how Lissa uses informal **punctuation** by using dashes to separate her ideas. In formal writing, it is better to use complete separate sentences. She also uses exclamation marks to add emphasis to certain words, phrases and ideas. This is a common technique in informal writing.

- Notice the clear **paragraph structure** in Mia's more formal letter.
  Paragraph 1 introduces the writer, explaining why she is writing and where she saw the advert.
  Paragraph 2 gives more detail about why she would be suitable for the job.
  Paragraph 3 gives her availability and offers to come in for an interview.

TOP TIP

To start a formal letter, you use 'Dear', with the person's name. If you don't know the name of the person to whom you are writing, use Sir/Madam.

To end a formal letter, if you have addressed the person by their name, use 'Yours sincerely'. If you used 'Dear Sir/Madam,' use 'Yours faithfully'.

7 Now read the job advert and write a letter of application.

> **Vacancy:** part-time waiter or waitress required for pizza restaurant. Must have relevant experience and be able to work on Saturdays. Write to Giuseppe Blanco, Napoli Pizzeria

---

DID YOU REMEMBER TO … ?

Remember to:

✓ Start the letter in the correct way.

✓ Use the appropriate tone and vocabulary for a formal letter.

✓ Include information relevant to the advert.

✓ Use a clear paragraph structure.

WORK

GOING FURTHER

When you are writing, consider who will be reading it and adjust your tone to fit. This means using appropriate language and structures.

8 Read the descriptions a) to d) and match them to the writing A to D:

a) a letter thanking your grandma for a present

b) a letter thanking your supervisor for their help on your work placement

c) a letter asking for information about a job

d) a text to a friend about your new job.

A
> Hi Nina!
> You'll never guess what – I've got a job in that great clothes shop!

C
> Dear Sir/Madam
> I was interested to read about the position of assistant on the news desk, and I would be grateful for more information.

B
> Dear Mr Khan,
> I would like to take this opportunity to thank you for your advice last week.

D
> Dear Grandma,
> Thank you so much for the present you sent to me – I love it.

9 Imagine you are writing an account of your work experience for the school magazine. Your readers are parents and other students. Which of the introductions below do you think would be the most suitable?

A *I've just spent three weeks doing work experience at the hospital in town. It was great – I was rushed off my feet, though!*

B *I have recently spent three weeks on a work placement at the local hospital. It was an interesting and very enjoyable experience.*

C *Have you ever considered the work placement scheme? I've just come to the end of a three-week placement at our local hospital, and I'd recommend it to anyone.*

> **TOP TIP**
>
> Think about:
> - how full forms and contracted forms are used
> - the tone of the vocabulary:
>   – which is most sophisticated
>   – which engages the reader best
>   – which describes the experience in the most detailed and informative way.

10 On your own, write a magazine article about a work placement experience you have had, or you can invent one. Remember to adjust your language to suit your audience.

(6.3) Job interviews

In this section you will learn to:
✓ pronounce words and speak clearly to be understood in a conversation
✓ speak up confidently and clearly.

GETTING STARTED

Remember that speech is an essential way to convey information. If speech isn't clear, information will be passed on incorrectly or not at all.

(1) Look at this picture.

- How do you think the person being interviewed feels?

- How would you feel in this situation? Why?

Note down your ideas.

EXPLORING THE SKILLS

In order to be understood in a conversation, it is important to pronounce words correctly and speak as clearly as possible.

(2) Listen to some extracts of speech. Are they easy or difficult to understand?

(3) Listen again. What is the problem in each situation?

(4) What problems could be caused in each situation by misunderstanding?

(5) Have you ever had a similar experience, in English or in your own language, where it was difficult to hear what a person was saying? What problems did it cause you?

6 You are going to practise talking clearly in different situations. Make notes about the following, but don't write down every word you are going to say:

a) information about your date of birth, your age and your address

b) times of a train or bus journey, and where stops are made – you can make this up using information from where you live

c) food you like to eat in a restaurant or café.

7 Now work in pairs. Sit with your back to your partner so that you cannot see each other. You could move your chairs apart if there is room.

Take turns to give each other the information you made notes about above. Your partner writes down what they hear.

8 Compare the information your partner wrote down with what you said. Discuss what you found easy and difficult about each other's speech.

> I could understand your numbers very clearly.

> I couldn't hear the name of the place where the bus would stop.

DEVELOPING THE SKILLS

In formal situations, you may find that you don't pronounce words as clearly as you would like. If you are slightly nervous, you may speak more quickly than usual.

9 Read the questions below and discuss them, in pairs.

a) Have you ever had a job interview? If you have, what was it like? If you haven't, what do you think it would be like?

b) If you feel nervous in a situation such as a job interview, what do you do?

10 Listen to the openings of two job interviews. Then, in pairs, choose words from the box, or any others you think are suitable, to describe how the candidates are feeling.

| nervous confident embarrassed happy shy calm |

11 Listen again to a short extract from each of the interviews.

In pairs, role-play a similar interview. In one version, the candidate should be nervous. In the other version, the candidate should be confident. Record your conversations, and then listen to them. Did you succeed in sounding nervous or confident?

12 Read the following questions and decide whether they would be asked by the interviewer or the job candidate.

a) Could you tell me about your experience?

b) Could you tell me more about the position?

c) Will I be able to do any training for the position?

d) Why do you think you would be suitable for the job?

In pairs, discuss your ideas, speaking clearly and thinking about your pronunciation.

> **TOP TIP**
> When you are speaking confidently, it is normal to run some words together. For example, when one word ends with a consonant ('with') and the next word starts with a vowel ('animals') these are naturally linked in speech: '*I'd like to work with ‿animals.*'
>
> However, it is also important to pronounce each word clearly, so it can be easily understood.

13 With your partner, read aloud the following answers to two of the interview questions. Again, think about your pronunciation and speak clearly. Which one do you think is the best answer to each question?

Question a) answers

I haven't got much experience, but I learn quickly.

I've never done anything like this before.

I've got a lot of relevant experience – I've worked in an office for six months and I've completed a course at college.

Question d) answers

I don't know really, but it sounds fun.

I believe I have useful skills and I am very keen to learn.

I get on with people, and I'm good at most things.

14 In pairs, make notes about all of the answers in task 13. Discuss why each one is suitable or not. Think about the language used and the ideas expressed.

> **TOP TIP** It is always a good idea to explain what you say with examples. Instead of saying *'I'm good at organising things'*, you could say, *'I'm good at organising things – I have been in charge of the school committee for a year, and also run a website for students.'*

15 You will now listen to a job interview. As you listen, think about whether the person will get the job. 🎧 6.4

16 Listen to the interview again. What does the candidate say about:

    a) his grades from college

    b) his skills

    c) what he enjoys at work?

GOING FURTHER

Recording yourself speaking is good practice for any situation where you might be nervous or stressed or have to speak clearly and confidently. Listening to yourself will show you where and how you can improve your pronunciation and clarity of speech.

17 You are now going to work in pairs to prepare role-plays for a job interview, taking turns to be the interviewer and the candidate.

Record your work, both as you prepare your ideas and after you have practised. Listen to how clearly you speak, and see if you can improve this each time you do the role-play.

Individually:

a) Choose a job from the box below, or think of a different one.

> waitress   shop assistant   assistant in a sports centre

b) Make a note of the skills that would be useful for the job you have chosen.

In pairs:

c) Think of questions that you might be asked in an interview for each job you have chosen.

d) Consider how you would answer these questions. Share ideas about how you could give examples to support what you say.

18 Now prepare each role-play together. Think of how you will start and end the interview. Decide on at least three questions and answers for each job. Remember to think about using the appropriate tone and language for a job interview.

19 Record yourselves as you carry out each role-play. Then listen to it. Are you surprised by what you hear? Can you think of ways to improve it?

6.4 Unusual jobs

In this section you will learn to:
✓ predict to help you understand and select details
✓ select details to make notes or fill in forms when listening to a range of texts.

GETTING STARTED

1 Discuss the following questions with a partner.

- Can you think of any unusual jobs?
  Compare ideas and make notes.

- What are the advantages and disadvantages
  of unusual jobs over jobs that you consider
  to be 'normal'?

EXPLORING THE SKILLS

When you are listening to longer texts, you may have to pick out specific
details. It is helpful to predict the kind of information you might hear. If
you are making notes, be clear which headings you will use; if you are
going to fill in a form, read through it to see what information it asks
for. This will help you to listen out for the information you need.

2 Read this introduction to an interview with a woman who has a very
unusual job – a shark personality profiler!

Interviewer: *Hi Mandy – well, this is a job I've never heard of before!
Can you tell me about it?*

Mandy: *Hello. Yes, well I work in Australia with sharks. My job is to
put tags on them to see how they behave, how often they feed and
where they go – that sort of thing.*

3 In pairs, discuss what you might hear in the rest of the interview.
What other questions might the interviewer ask? For example, the
interviewer might ask how long Mandy has done this job. In this
case, you might hear her reply with a number of months or years.

4 Listen to the rest of the interview. Were any of your predictions in
task 3 correct?

6.5

5 Listen again and note down the information you hear about the following:

    a) what Mandy likes about the job

    b) what you need to be able to do for this job

    c) why an animal might attack you.

DEVELOPING THE SKILLS

If you are given a form to fill in, you can work out what to listen for. Read through it and consider the information you will need to fill in the gaps, such as names, ages and places. Make sure you listen carefully for these. The information you put in the form must make sense. Unless you are asked for full sentences, just write a word or short phrase.

6 You are going to hear more interviews about unusual jobs.

    Look at the pictures. Listen and match each one to a speaker.

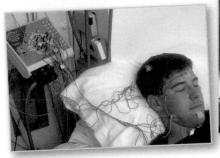

7 Read the following cards and think about the kind of detail you will need to pick out to fill in the gaps.

1.	2.	3.
Name of person: Kamila	Name of person: Max	Name of person: Jannah
Name of job:	Name of job:	Name of job:
How long person has done the job:	How long person has done the job:	How long person has done the job:
Where do they work?	Where do they work?	Where do they work?
Overall feeling about the job:	Overall feeling about the job:	Overall feeling about the job:

8 Listen again and copy and complete the cards.

9 Discuss these questions in pairs.

    a) What do you think are the advantages and drawbacks of each job?

    b) Which ones do you think are the most and least interesting? Why?

    c) Which one of these jobs, if any, would you like to do?

10 Read the article. Which city is the next big city for new businesses?

Work in the digital era

DESPITE SOME DIFFICULT years, London is still the biggest digital 'hub' in Europe. The city is home to some of the world's most famous companies and **start-up entrepreneurs**. Many of them had small offices in Shoreditch in East London, the famous entrepreneur spot also known as the 'Silicon Roundabout'. But, as some of these companies have grown bigger, they have changed location to other parts of London. When a small start-up with six staff becomes successful enough to employ 75 people, it needs more space but also better internet connection and to be closer to its clients in the City. London is not the only city in Europe that attracts start-ups. Berlin, Paris, Amsterdam and Barcelona are also important digital hubs. But, with costs going up, other cities are starting to catch up. Tallinn in Estonia has recently appeared on the start-up scene. One of the reasons for this is the Estonian government's E-residency scheme. This allows people from anywhere in the world to easily start an Estonian company online, without ever living in the country. Of course, successful start-ups also need **investors**. While London is still a major source of **funding** money for new start-ups, Estonia promises plenty of opportunities to help find investors.

11 Find the five words written in bold in the article above and write them in a list. Then match them to the definitions below.

a) people who start a new business

b) the centre of a place or activity

c) people who make money by lending money to new businesses

d) a new business

e) the money that helps a business get bigger

12 These words are also connected to digital start-ups. You'll hear them in the next exercise. Match them to their definitions.

a) database	**1** a person who buys things
b) trend	**2** something that is produced and sold
c) consumer	**3** an opinion about how good something is
d) product	**4** a computer programme
e) review	**5** a collection of data that you can use and add information to
f) software	**6** a change in what is popular

13 Listen to this report about one of the start-up businesses in Shoreditch.

 6.7

a) Which industry does this new business work in?

b) Is Julia an entrepreneur or an investor? How do you know?

14 Listen again and copy and complete the form with notes about the new business.

Name of business: _____
Where Julia is from: _____
Julia's age: _____
Ages of people involved: _____
The industry Julia works in: _____
Her software searches the internet for:
1: information about _____ and _____
2: what _____ are saying
3: product _____

15 Listen once more. Discuss the following questions with a partner.

a) In what way does this business rely on the internet?

b) Do you think this kind of business would have been possible 20 years ago? Explain your reasons.

GOING FURTHER

It is important to read through questions before completing a task so that you know what to listen out for. You can use prediction techniques to help you with longer and more complex texts.

16 Read the questions below and think about what information you can expect to hear.

a) Where does Edith work now?

b) What did she do first?

c) What did she decide to do?

d) Where did she move to after this?

e) Why was she able to do voluntary work?

f) Did she enjoy the conservation project?

g) What does she need in order to do her job?

17 In pairs, discuss the questions and compare your predictions.

18 Now listen to a journalist talking about how her career has changed as the internet has developed. 6.8

19 Now listen again and answer the questions in task 16.

LANGUAGE BOOSTER Match the words to the definitions.

a) voluntary work

b) part-time work

c) full-time work

d) flexible work

e) self-employed

1 work that you do all week, at regular hours

2 work that you do without getting paid for it

3 work that you do for part of the week or for a shorter day than most people do

4 work that can be done at different times during the week

5 earning a living from one's own business

The big task

In this chapter you have looked at different kinds of work. Now you are going to think about what would be your ideal job and how you would go about getting it.

1 In pairs, discuss your future – what would be an ideal job?
Note down some ideas about the work you would like to do.
- Why does it appeal to you?
- What skills and qualities does this job need that you have?
- Where can you do this job?

2 Do some research to find out more about your ideal job. Record your findings individually. Prepare a short fact sheet with information about the job, for example:

My ideal job: architect

An architect is a person who designs houses and other buildings. To be an architect you have to study at university for several years. You also have to complete training courses.

You need to be good at design and technology, and have good mathematical skills. It is important to be creative, but you also have to get on well with the people you are working with.

Architects often work in big companies, but you can be self-employed.

3 Look at this job advert and note the details about what the job involves and what kind of person should apply.

> **Wanted:** *young architect to join busy city-centre company. Must have relevant degree and training. Good design, technology and mathematical skills essential. Applicants should be creative and have good people skills. Write to Serena Matayo, Block 6B, High Street.*

4 Now imagine that you are writing a letter of application for this job. Think about how you can respond to each of the points in the advert. Make notes about your relevant skills and experience. Remember to use the correct level of formality for the job application letter.

5 Prepare your letter. Remember to use the correct style and register for a formal letter, and use the letter-writing conventions from this unit.

6 In pairs, act out an interview for this job you've applied for. The interviewer should think of five questions to ask the candidate based on their letter. Remember to speak clearly and confidently in an interview situation. Record yourselves to see how you sound.

Check your progress

Here are the Reading, Writing, Speaking and Listening skills you learned about in Chapter 6.

Use this table to decide how good you are at the different skills, and make a note of what you need to be able to do in order to move up a level.

READING
I can …

- confidently distinguish between facts and opinions in complex texts
- consistently recognise and understand the language used to introduce facts and opinions

- distinguish between facts and opinions in straightforward texts
- often recognise and understand the language used to introduce facts and opinions

- distinguish between facts and opinions in simple texts
- sometimes recognise the language used to introduce facts and straightforward opinions

WRITING
I can …

- consistently and confidently use the appropriate tone and style when writing a letter or magazine article

- sometimes use the appropriate tone and style when writing a letter or magazine article

- write a simple letter or magazine article, but tend to use the same tone and style without adapting it to reader and purpose

SPEAKING
I can …

- express quite complex ideas effectively
- consistently speak with confidence and clarity

- express most of my ideas so that they are understood
- speak clearly and with some confidence, so that I am generally understood

- express simple ideas, though may need support from my listener
- attempt to speak clearly, but may hesitate or search for words

LISTENING
I can …

- pick out exactly the details I need to make notes or complete forms
- consistently use prediction to help me understand and successfully find the right information

- pick out many of the details I need to make notes or complete forms
- sometimes use prediction to help me understand and find the right information

- pick out a few of the details I need to make notes or complete forms
- try to use prediction to help me understand and find the right information, but have limited success

THE BIG PICTURE

Think about this quote by Carl Sagan, a famous astronomer:

'The Earth is the only world known so far to harbour life. There is nowhere else, at least in the near future, to which our species could migrate. Visit, yes. Settle, not yet. Like it or not, for the moment the Earth is where we make our stand.'

Carl Sagan wrote this in 1994. Do you think this is still true? You are going to discuss this in this chapter.

THINKING BIG

1 On your own:

- Look at the photos opposite. Which show environmental issues and what issues might they represent? Which issue is most important to your part of the world?

- Now look at each photo more carefully. Write down the issue(s) represented by each one. Are some of them linked to each other? Are there other ways you could group these images?

- Number the photos in order of their importance as global issues, where 1 is the most important/urgent.

2 In pairs:

- Compare your order with your partner's. Are there some surprising differences? Are there some similarities?

- Explain why you think some global issues are more urgent and important than others.

3 In groups:

- See if you can agree on the three global issues we need to tackle most urgently.

- Brainstorm some of the things we could do as individuals about these issues.

7
Environment and wildlife

7.1 Our carbon footprint

In this section you will learn to:
- ✓ find and select facts and details in factual information
- ✓ understand what is implied but not directly stated in a piece of text.

GETTING STARTED

1. There is a lot of debate about what is actually happening to our planet. What have you heard? Consider the following topics and make notes.

   a) Wildlife species are disappearing rapidly.

   b) We are running out of freshwater sources.

   c) Pollution is a serious issue.

   d) Global warming is taking place as a result of CO_2 emissions.

EXPLORING THE SKILLS

Factual informational texts appear frequently in newspapers and magazines and you will come across them in school subjects, such as geography, in the world of work and in further study.

When you are reading factual informational texts that contain diagrams or charts, read the title first to try to work out the topic. Then look at the diagram to see what it shows and how this relates to the informational text. If numbers are included, look at these and how they are arranged. If you see a number with a percentage sign, this means that the total of all the numbers adds up to 100.

2. Read the definition of carbon footprint on the opposite page. What kinds of things might increase your carbon footprint?

3. Read about a typical person's carbon footprint and discuss these questions in pairs.

   a) Which sections of the pie chart do you think we might have more control over?

   b) How do you think your own carbon footprint might be different from or similar to the pie chart?

A typical person's carbon footprint

This shows the main activities that make up the total of a typical person's carbon footprint in some more economically developed countries. The blue sections represent direct contributions to CO_2 emissions, while the yellow sections represent indirect contributions to CO_2 emissions.

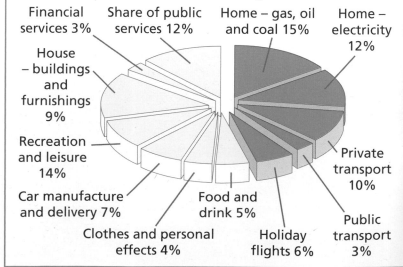

Financial services 3% • Share of public services 12% • Home – gas, oil and coal 15% • Home – electricity 12% • House – buildings and furnishings 9% • Recreation and leisure 14% • Car manufacture and delivery 7% • Clothes and personal effects 4% • Food and drink 5% • Holiday flights 6% • Private transport 10% • Public transport 3%

4 Read about global warming and greenhouse gases.
Then answer the questions that follow.

The Greenhouse Effect

Do you know what a greenhouse is? It's a glass building in which you grow plants that need to be protected from bad weather. The glass helps maintain a regular temperature and it can get very warm inside a greenhouse when the sun is shining. The greenhouse effect is the term used to describe the problem caused by increased quantities of gases such as carbon dioxide in the air. These gases trap the heat from the sun, and cause a gradual rise in the temperature of the Earth's atmosphere. This is called 'global warming'. Global warming can have an extremely bad effect on the Earth's weather, which can also have a harmful effect on wildlife, plants and humans. Greenhouse gas emissions are continuing to rise which is making matters even worse.

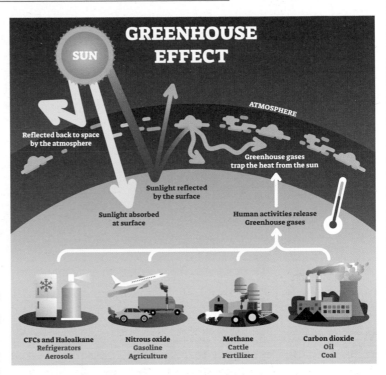

GREENHOUSE EFFECT

SUN

ATMOSPHERE

Reflected back to space by the atmosphere

Greenhouse gases trap the heat from the sun

Sunlight reflected by the surface

Sunlight absorbed at surface

Human activities release Greenhouse gases

CFCs and Haloalkane
Refrigerators
Aerosols

Nitrous oxide
Gasoline
Agriculture

Methane
Cattle
Fertilizer

Carbon dioxide
Oil
Coal

GLOSSARY	**carbon footprint**	the amount of carbon dioxide or carbon compounds released into the atmosphere by the activities of an individual, company or country
	CO_2	carbon dioxide
	emission	the release of something, such as a gas, into the air (verb = emit)
	atmosphere	the layer of air or gases surrounding a planet

a) What example of greenhouse gas emissions does the article give?

b) What is global warming?

c) What is negatively affected by greenhouse gas emissions?

TOP TIP Make sure you use the correct units or percentages when you are answering questions on graphs and pie charts. For example:

Private transport accounts for 10% of a person's carbon footprint.

In 2019, carbon dioxide emissions stood at 28 000 million metric tons.

DEVELOPING THE SKILLS

Sometimes the informational text will be accompanied by a bar chart. In bar charts, read what the x axis (the line along the bottom) represents and what the y axis (the line going up the side represents). Check to see if there is a key which shows what each colour represents.

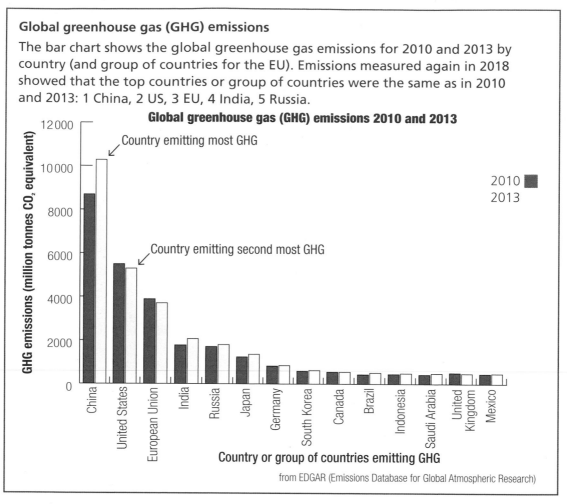

Global greenhouse gas (GHG) emissions

The bar chart shows the global greenhouse gas emissions for 2010 and 2013 by country (and group of countries for the EU). Emissions measured again in 2018 showed that the top countries or group of countries were the same as in 2010 and 2013: 1 China, 2 US, 3 EU, 4 India, 5 Russia.

from EDGAR (Emissions Database for Global Atmospheric Research)

Nowadays we get a lot of our information online. Sometimes adverts are made to look like informational texts online, so you might think you are reading information, but you are actually reading about something that someone wants to promote. When we research a topic or read a factual informational text online, we need to think about the following:

- Who has written the information? Can the site be trusted?
- When was the information written? Is there a date on the article?
- Why have they written this article? What is the purpose? Is the site independent? Or is the site trying to sell or promote something or a particular idea?

5. Do some online research into the causes of climate change. Then answer these questions.

   a) What information did you find out? Write down three things you found out.

   b) What websites did you use?

   c) Can you trust the websites? How do you know?

When reading factual informational texts:

✓ Read the title first.

✓ Work out how the diagram relates to the text.

✓ Check whether there is a key with the diagram.

If these texts are online:

✓ Check the author/site. Can they be trusted?

✓ Check when the article was written. Is there a date?

✓ Check the purpose of the site. Is it trying to sell or promote something?

GOING FURTHER

Writers do not always say things directly. Often we have to work out a writer's thoughts, feelings or attitudes and understand what is implied.

6 Read the article below in which a journalist thinks about his use of paper and its impact on the environment.

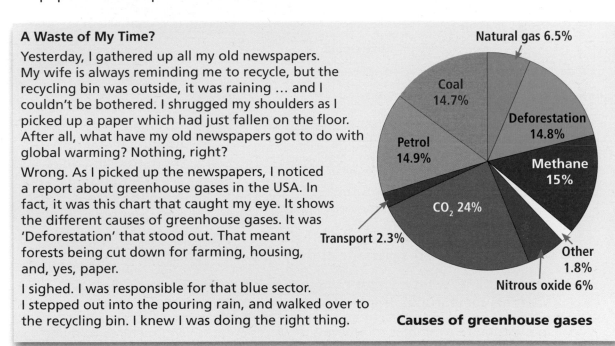

A Waste of My Time?

Yesterday, I gathered up all my old newspapers. My wife is always reminding me to recycle, but the recycling bin was outside, it was raining … and I couldn't be bothered. I shrugged my shoulders as I picked up a paper which had just fallen on the floor. After all, what have my old newspapers got to do with global warming? Nothing, right?

Wrong. As I picked up the newspapers, I noticed a report about greenhouse gases in the USA. In fact, it was this chart that caught my eye. It shows the different causes of greenhouse gases. It was 'Deforestation' that stood out. That meant forests being cut down for farming, housing, and, yes, paper.

I sighed. I was responsible for that blue sector. I stepped out into the pouring rain, and walked over to the recycling bin. I knew I was doing the right thing.

Natural gas 6.5%
Coal 14.7%
Deforestation 14.8%
Petrol 14.9%
Methane 15%
CO_2 24%
Transport 2.3%
Other 1.8%
Nitrous oxide 6%

Causes of greenhouse gases

Which of these statements best describes the writer's attitude at the start of the article?

- He always recycles and has to remind his wife, who forgets.

- He usually recycles things but does so out of habit, not because he really understands why.

- He is really committed to recycling, even when it is raining.

7 What does 'I shrugged my shoulders' suggest about the writer's attitude to recycling? What single word in the text signals his change of attitude when he sees the chart?

7.2 Water – the most precious resource

In this section you will learn to:
- ✓ use details to develop ideas when writing descriptions
- ✓ make descriptive writing convincing using the five senses.

GETTING STARTED

Fresh water is liquid silver,
More precious than a king's palaces,
More dazzling than a sultan's jewels.
Thousands tread dust for days to seek it,
Yet others waste and lose it.
'Our planet's full of water!' they say.
I say, 'Try to drink it then.'

Mike Gould

Read this short poem on your own.

1 Think about these questions. Make notes and then share your ideas with a partner.

> **TOP TIP**
> When you describe a personal experience, use the five senses of *sight*, *touch*, *sound*, *smell* and *taste* to help the reader enter your world.

a) Are there any words or phrases you don't understand? Have a guess at their meaning. If your partner does not know either, use a dictionary to help.

b) What do you think the message or the point of the poem is?

c) In the first line, what is water compared to? Why do you think the poet chose this comparison? This kind of 'picture in words' is called an image.

d) Find two more examples of where the writer creates vivid pictures to make his point. Explain why he makes these comparisons.

e) Be really honest and describe *your own* attitude to water and how much you use/waste?

f) With a partner, discuss which of the five senses the poet uses in his poem.

EXPLORING THE SKILLS

To make your point clearly, you need to use details to develop your descriptions. Adding adjectives, adverbs, facts and images can really make your writing come alive and engage the reader. For example:

We have a problem with water. **We have plenty of it, but it's the wrong kind.** ——— develops and builds on opening sentence

*Did you know that **about 70% of our planet is covered in water, but** only **about 3% is fresh water**? Just consider that as you let **sparkling, clear water escape** from your tap as you clean your teeth.*

facts add detail and make comparisons

well-chosen adjective makes us sound careless

vivid picture in words (an 'image') that brings facts to life

2 Now look at this sentence about water usage.

We need huge amounts of water for all our everyday needs.

You are going to take this topic sentence and develop it into a full paragraph.

a) First, add an example or explanation that develops what is said here. It could be about what our everyday needs are.
We need huge amounts of water for all our everyday needs. Just think about...

b) Now build the paragraph by adding new sentences, using the facts below. You may need to use connectives ('and', 'or', 'but', 'in addition', 'because') to turn these facts into sentences and join ideas together.
  - Recommended daily requirement for cleaning, bathing, cooking, sewage, drinking = approx. 50–100 litres per person.
  - 2.6 billion people only have access to about 5 litres of water per day.

c) Finally, make your writing come alive. For example, add a vivid image (a 'picture in words') which gives an idea of what it is like searching for water each day. You could start:
For many, the best sight in the world is...

DEVELOPING THE SKILLS

Including five-sense descriptions and accurate vocabulary can help you make your writing even more convincing.

A student is writing an article about his childhood memories. He is describing his first swimming lesson.

I remember going to the pool. I stood by it with all the other kids until the teacher told us to go in. I sat down on the edge. Suddenly, someone splashed me. It was horrible.

There is much more information the student could have added here. For example:
- more detail on how he behaved (did he sit down 'quickly', 'happily'?) and what he did
- what the pool was like (indoor, outdoor, modern, old)
- descriptions of the other students/teacher.

3 With a partner, think about the five senses. Write down what you think the child above could see, touch, smell, hear and even taste.

See	
Hear	children laughing, water slapping the sides of the pool
Smell	
Touch	
Taste	

4 Now rewrite the text, adding further detail.

- You can change or alter the text but it must still be about a boy's first swim.
- Write a minimum of 75 words.

5 A student was given a task in which she had to imagine life in the future in a world which is short of water. Beforehand, she was given some basic information on:

- the effects of lack of fresh water on health
- our overuse and waste of water
- the contamination of fresh water supplies, such as industrial waste in rivers.

As you read, identify where in the text she has used:

- facts and examples but also added her own original details or extra content
- vivid imagery or powerful verbs to reveal her feelings or views about the situation.

Today, in 2065, I live in a world without water. I am 15 years old, but I look 50, my skin is starting to crack and look dry like a desert road. My muscles are weak and I lack energy. My family and I can only think about water: finding or buying it, conserving it or storing it, dreaming and thinking about it. My father's job? He is lucky – he works in a desalination plant, converting salt water to fresh, but he doesn't get any extra favours or water.

I demand that my father talks about the past – a time when everyone had water. He tells me about beautiful, green trees in the city parks, full of bright, juicy leaves, and how he could enjoy relaxing, warm baths, or cool, fresh showers, whenever he wanted them. Back then, he was told that drinking about 8–10 glasses of water a day was ideal for a healthy lifestyle. Now, we're lucky if we get one glass, which I treat as if it were the finest meal on Earth. But he also tells me how companies and countries allowed poisonous chemicals to pollute rivers and lakes. When he was a boy, 2 million tons of sewage and human waste was thrown into water.

I often beg him to tell me why he and his friends didn't do more if they knew this. Why did they leave us with this dreadful result? He has no answer.

verb suggests strong feeling

adjectives

factual info backs up statement about companies

GOING FURTHER

One of the techniques the writer used was to 'zoom in' from the general to the specific or a 'close-up'. For example:

> *beautiful, green trees* **(general)** – *full of bright, juicy leaves* **(specific/close up)**

(6) Which is the general description in the line below, and which is the close-up detail?

> *I describe the beauty of the forests, the winding rivers, the scent of evening rain on blossom.*

LANGUAGE BOOSTER Adding vivid adjectives to well-chosen nouns to make noun phrases is a great way to add detail. For example, we can tell more about the writer's views on the opposite page when she adds the adjectives, 'relaxing' and 'warm' to 'bath' to make *relaxing, warm bath*.

(7) Imagine the writer steps outside and describes her village or town, and how a shortage of fresh water has affected it. Complete this paragraph by adding 'close-ups' to the general description. Remember to make use of the five senses to help you think of the details to include.

> *As I step outside my door, I see the wide field in front of me, with …*

(8) Now, write a newspaper article of 150–200 words about the importance of water. Describe:

- how precious fresh water is

- any water problems in your part of the world

- what steps you are taking to save water.

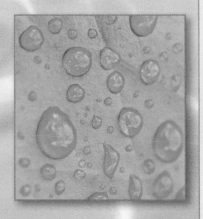

You can use any of the factual information in this unit, but you must add your own ideas, and make your readers think of water as a fantastic, life-giving resource.

DID YOU REMEMBER TO … ?

Use the information in the unit, but add your own ideas and examples.

✓ Include vivid descriptions of fresh water – how it feels.

✓ Use five-sense descriptions to let the reader 'into your world'.

7.3 Pollution – slow poison?

In this section you will learn to:

✓ express your ideas clearly using the correct verb tenses

✓ respond clearly, accurately and effectively to others in conversation

✓ communicate your ideas clearly and confidently in a more formal talk.

GETTING STARTED

1 Think about the following questions in pairs. Make notes on any interesting ideas.

- What are the sources of air, sea, water and land pollution around you?

- What issues or problems does pollution cause in your daily life?

- Who or what is responsible for this pollution?

- Who can do something about it? What should be done about it?

- What can you do about it?

2 Now quickly note your thoughts on pollution in your city or region. Don't worry about whether all the details are correct or not. If you have questions, note those down as well.

EXPLORING THE SKILLS

The sentences below are in the simple present tense (e.g. *leads*, *creates*) or the present continuous tense (e.g. *is shrinking*, *are becoming*). This is because they are referring to facts that are considered current or true over a long period of time.

a) The burning of fossil fuels *leads to* serious air pollution and also creates more greenhouse gases in our environment. (simple present tense)

b) The level of water underground is *shrinking* in many parts of the world. (present continuous tense)

c) Our freshwater sources *are becoming* too polluted for fish and other species to survive. (present continuous tense)

3 In your pairs, tell each other three facts that you have recently learned in science or geography. Write down each other's facts. What tenses are you using?

4 Tell each other three facts about what is happening in the room where you are at this moment. Write down each other's facts. What tenses are you using?

LANGUAGE BOOSTER The first verb in every sentence *must* agree with the subject (the person or thing doing the action) of the sentence.

The **simple present tense** is used to describe routines, facts, likes and dislikes or attitudes and opinions.

The verb 'to play'		
Subject	**Verb that agrees**	**Example**
I/you/we/they	Verb with no 's' ending	I play, they play
he/she/it	Verb with 's' ending	he plays, she plays, it plays
The verb 'to be'		
Subject	**Verb that agrees**	**Example**
I	An exception: 'am' is a special form of the verb 'to be' which only agrees with 'I'	I am
you/we/they	are	you are, we are, they are
he/she/it	is	he is, she is, it is

The **present continuous tense** is used to describe events as they are happening or that are still happening. It is usually constructed using the verb 'to be' and another verb with an '-ing' ending.

Subject	**Part of 'to be' that agrees**	**Example**
I	am	I am playing
you/we/they	are	you are playing, we are playing, they are playing
he/she/it	is	he is playing, she is playing

5 With your partner, play this explanation word game:

- Taking turns, use the verbs in the box and the labels on the diagram below to describe what is going on.

- Think about when you will use the simple present tense and when you will use the present continuous tense.

- Give a point to your partner for each tense that they use correctly.

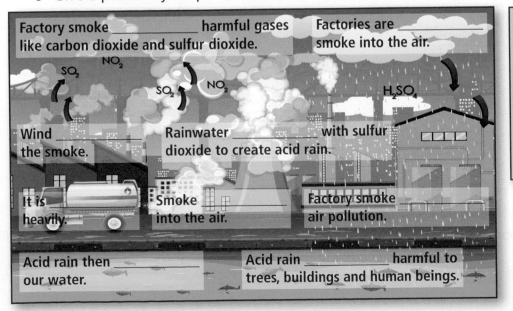

Factory smoke _____ harmful gases like carbon dioxide and sulfur dioxide.

Factories are _____ smoke into the air.

SO_2 NO_2

SO_2 NO_2

H_2SO_4

Wind _____ the smoke.

Rainwater _____ with sulfur dioxide to create acid rain.

It is _____ heavily.

Smoke _____ into the air.

Factory smoke _____ air pollution.

Acid rain then _____ our water.

Acid rain _____ harmful to trees, buildings and human beings.

contain
release
pollute
rise
cause
rain
mix
be
spread

DEVELOPING THE SKILLS

When you are discussing a topic with a partner or in a group, you need to listen and then respond clearly, accurately and appropriately, even if the situation is quite informal.

6 Read these extracts about air pollution. If there are any words you do not know, discuss them with your partner and see if you can work them out from the rest of the sentence. Only use a dictionary if really needed. Make a note of any new words.

The air we breathe

Air pollution is a severe problem – one that we ignore at the risk of our health and our economy.

Lung cancer is now the most common cancer in the industrialised world, and heart disease is the second-biggest cause of death in some places. **Smog** hangs heavy over many industrialised cities, where children grow up with asthma and other **respiratory** illnesses. Every year, cities lose billions of dollars due to health costs and losses in production.

These problems all go back to air pollution, whose consequences are long-term, sometimes **fatal** and almost always impact the public.

Much of the time, air pollution is invisible, but its effects are not. Millions of people around the world are breathing dirty air – with terrible health consequences, from respiratory disease to strokes, lung cancer, and heart disease.

Although economies are growing rapidly, it is often at the price of people's health and happiness.

From Greenpeace

A silent killer

Air pollution is a world-wide problem. Carbon monoxide is a colourless, odourless, poisonous gas produced by the incomplete burning of carbon in fuels, mainly by cars and trucks and also by forest fires and the burning of agricultural waste. In the USA, about 77% of carbon monoxide comes from transportation sources. In cities, as much as 95% of all CO emissions may come from automobile **exhaust**, according to the EPA.

Adapted from 'Carbon Monoxide' from *Environmental Science in the 21st Century* by Robert Stewart

GLOSSARY

smog	a type of air pollution caused when fog in the atmosphere combines with smoke to form a brown haze, which irritates the eyes and lungs
respiratory	relating to breathing
fatal	causing death
exhaust	waste gases, including carbon monoxide, which are emitted from a car or machine when it is in use

LANGUAGE BOOSTER

In the article 'The air we breathe' the author uses two phrases, one in the first paragraph and one in the last.

We ignore air pollution at the risk of our health and our economy.

Although economies are growing rapidly, it is often at the price of people's health and happiness.

at the risk of   at the price of

- If you do something at the risk of something unpleasant happening, you do it even though you know that the unpleasant thing might happen as a result.

- If you get something you want at a/the price of something, you get it but something unpleasant happens as a result.

7 In groups of two or three, talk together about air pollution in your part of the world. You can talk about your home countries, or the country where you live now if it is not the same.

- What causes the pollution?

- What is being done about it?

- Are there health consequences for people in your city or region?

GOING FURTHER

Now you will work together to give a talk in a more formal situation. You can feel confident that you have plenty of ideas and will know which tenses to use. You have gained a clear understanding of various types of pollution and the problems that air pollution in particular can cause.

TOP TIP

In order to give a speech that flows well and naturally, you need to spend some time planning together and making sure that your sections link well together. Also, be clear about your facts and key words, and check what each other is saying is clear.

8 In your group, prepare a six-minute talk about air pollution. Include:

- the dangers it causes to our health and happiness

- what could be done about it.

Your audience will be your classmates and teacher. Make sure each of you speaks for about two minutes.

- Try to ensure that your talk flows naturally and that each person's speech connects to the other's.

- You could use connective clauses like:

As Sarah pointed out when she introduced air pollution, the health hazards are often hidden...

or

If we know that smog causes respiratory illnesses, then we need to

7.4 Where has all our wildlife gone?

In this section you will learn to:

✓ use key words and context to predict content

✓ understand what is implied but not directly stated during an interview.

GETTING STARTED

(1) You have already seen the effect that human activities may have on our **habitats** and on pollution levels. What does this mean for wildlife and the many animal and plant species that share the planet with us?

(2) In pairs, discuss:

- Which animal or plant species have recently been considered **endangered** in your region?

- Which wild animals, birds or plants were you used to having around you when you were a young child? Are they still around? Will they be around in the future?

EXPLORING THE SKILLS

In Chapter 4 you learned about using what you read before you start listening to a spoken text in order to answer questions about it. You can develop this skill even further.

- Read the questions provided before you hear the extract so that you know what you are listening for.

- Identify any key words in the question, apart from the question words like 'where' or 'how many'. Take this question as an example:

  'Who is responsible for the death of so many tigers?'

  The word *who* tells you that your answer is likely to be the name of a person or a group of people. You know that you will need to listen out for the words *death* and *tigers*, because you can guess that you are likely to hear the answer close to these words. To help focus your mind, underline the key words in the question before you start listening to the text.

- Sometimes, you will have to be extra alert and listen out for words or phrases which mean the same, or something close to the same, as the key word in the question.

  Suppose you have been asked the question:

  Give two ways in which mankind has been responsible for the drop in numbers of wildlife.

You might decide to underline 'mankind', 'responsible' and 'drop in numbers'.

Then you hear the speaker say:

> The numbers of birds, animals, marine and freshwater creatures have declined by almost one third, according to the conservation organisation the World Wide Fund for Nature. They say that most of the blame for this terrible situation lies with human beings. Mankind has been responsible for this drop in numbers – through habitat destruction and pollution.

When you hear the key words you will know that the answer is likely to be given soon, and indeed it is: 'habitat destruction and pollution'.

Here is another, more tricky question:

> Who, according to the World Wide Fund for Nature, has caused a decline in the numbers of wild animals?

You might decide to underline the key words 'caused', 'decline in numbers' and 'animals'.

The answer is more difficult to find, because you have to understand that 'has been responsible for' means the same as 'caused by' and also that 'this drop in numbers' means the same as 'decline in numbers'. Only then can you understand that the answer is 'mankind'.

3 Here are some more questions. Remember to read them carefully and underline key words before the recording is played to you.

7.1

a) What is the problem the World Wide Fund for Nature is concerned about?

b) In what year did countries in Europe make a promise to prevent the **extinction** of certain animals?

c) Why do wildlife organisations fear that the situation might get even worse in years to come?

4 Next, a journalist tells us some facts and figures about **conservation**. Listen to what he has to say about this and answer the questions below.

7.2

a) What kind of animals are named on the IUCN Red List?

b) How many species are on the IUCN Red List?

c) What proportion of the world's birds are in danger of disappearing forever?

d) What percentage of the world's coral reefs are endangered?

e) Over the last five centuries, how many species of animal have been made extinct because of humans?

GLOSSARY		
	extinction	no living animals left
	endangered	at risk of extinction
	habitat	the natural environment in which an animal or plant normally lives and grows
	conservation	the action of keeping and protecting something
	jeopardy	danger of harm

DEVELOPING THE SKILLS

Often, after you have identified the key words in the question, you will have to listen out for words or phrases which mean the same thing. To help you do this confidently, you will need to have as wide a vocabulary as possible.

You are now going to explore your understanding of key words associated with wildlife and conservation. You might hear some of these words in the interview you will listen to in the next exercise.

5 Copy the table and put a tick or a cross in the second and third columns. Next, highlight any words that you might need to look up.

Then, in pairs, see if you can teach each other some of these words.

Key words	Seen/heard it before	Can spell it	Meaning/definition
conservationist			
activist			
co-exist			
dedicate			
remote			
carnivore			
predator			
protective			
deforestation			
be in conflict with			
destruction			

> **TOP TIP**
> Remember to underline the key words first. You can discuss with a partner which words you have identified and compare your ideas.

6 You are about to hear an interview with Prerna Bindra, a wildlife conservationist and writer. She has won awards for her work in the conservation of wildlife in India, particularly the tiger.

Listen to the first part of the interview and answer the questions below.

You will listen to the recording twice. After the first listening, check your answers and prepare to fill in any gaps. 7.3

a) What kind of house did Prerna live in as a child in India?

b) What kind of bird laid its eggs just outside Prerna's home?

c) What kind of animal can be found only in Gir National Park?

d) What were Prerna's two great loves as a child?

e) What career did Prerna take up as a result of these two great interests?

With your partner, compare your answers and discuss whether you identified the best key words.

Prerna Bindra

GOING FURTHER

Sometimes you have to understand what people mean from what is implied but not actually said. You have to pick up on the clues.

7 Choose the answer which best completes the sentence – A, B or C **7.4** – as you listen to the second part of the interview with Prerna.

i) India is:

    A the most popular country in the world to visit.

    B the country with the biggest population in the world.

    C the world's second most densely populated country.

ii) Village people might kill tigers because:

    A the tigers have killed the villagers' cattle.

    B the tigers' furs make good coats for the villagers.

    C killing tigers is popular with tourists.

iii) In the past, people:

    A thought that tigers were signs of good luck and fertility.

    B did not respect the tigers that lived near their homes.

    C thought that tigers would trample down the crops in the fields.

iv) Many years ago, elephants:

    A were given poison by the local people.

    B were never given huge spaces to live their lives freely.

    C were loved by people and even worshipped as a god.

v) The speaker, Prerna, believes that people and wild animals like tigers:

    A can live happily together in the same area.

    B can live together happily so long as people are educated.

    C can live happily side by side but not in the same space.

vi) The speaker, Prerna, thinks young people:

    A should never take up a career in wildlife conservation because it is too hard.

    B should think about a career in wildlife conservation because it is always a good laugh.

    C could take up a career in wildlife conservation if they enjoy a challenge.

vii) The speaker, Prerna is:

    A enthusiastic.

    B easily depressed.

    C desperate.

viii) Prerna's message to young people is:

    A there are many ways you can work for conservation.

    B study hard at college and look after yourself first.

    C they are too young to help with nature conservation.

The big task

In groups of three or four, you are going to plan and give a presentation of the most urgent environmental or wildlife concerns for your local city or region. In order to do this, you might want to consider one of the big issues you have been studying and how this relates to your local city, town or environment.

1 Using the information in this chapter as prompts, do your own research and identify local sources of information. The issue you choose could be one of the following:

- global warming and our carbon footprint
- the water crisis
- pollution – air, water or land
- disappearing wildlife.

2 Invite junior students at your school or your partner school to view your presentation. Your presentation should:

- describe the problem and explain why or how it came to be this way
- explain what some of the solutions might be
- suggest how listeners could get involved.

3 Think about how you will organise your presentation. Make sure you explain any real objects or exhibits. In order to grab their attention, here are a few suggestions.

- Include a multimedia presentation – a mixture of reading, viewing, listening and presentations. You could even include a short play as part of your presentation.
- Use visuals or big pictures to grab attention, but be prepared to explain the science and the geography behind these.
- Think about bringing in real evidence from your city or region to prove your points – this could include photographs and facts and statistics about land, water, sea or air pollution in your city, sewage, the difficult situation for wildlife or disappearing green areas.
- Arrange, if possible, to interview local experts or teachers at your school to find out their thoughts on your chosen issue.
- Suggest actions you can take as individuals, as students and as a school to help tackle the issue locally.
- Invite suggestions from your audience to 'act local and think global'.

Check your progress

Here are the Reading, Writing, Speaking and Listening skills you learned about in Chapter 7.

Use this table to decide how good you are at the different skills, and make a note of what you need to be able to do in order to move up a level.

READING

I can …

- confidently understand and pick out the details I need in texts which contain graphs and charts
- usually understand what is implied but not directly stated

- sometimes understand and pick out the details I need in texts which contain graphs and charts
- understand some of what is implied but not directly stated

- pick out a few details I need from straightforward texts which contain graphs and charts
- attempt to understand what is implied but not directly stated, but with limited success

WRITING

I can …

- consistently and confidently use details to develop ideas when writing descriptions
- make descriptions convincing by referring to the five senses appropriately

- use details to develop ideas a little when writing descriptions
- sometimes make descriptions convincing by referring to the five senses

- include one or two details when writing descriptions
- attempt to make descriptions convincing by referring to one or more of the five senses

SPEAKING

I can …

- express quite complex ideas effectively, using correct verb tenses consistently
- respond with confidence and clarity to others in conversations

- express most of my ideas so that they are understood, using mostly correct verb tenses
- often respond clearly to others in conversations

- express simple ideas, but will make errors in verb tenses
- attempt to respond in conversations, but do not appear confident and I may not always be completely understood

LISTENING

I can …

- pick out exactly the details I need by using key words
- consistently understand and answer multiple-choice questions by using key words
- usually understand what is implied but not directly stated

- pick out many of the details I need by using key words
- often understand and answer multiple-choice questions by using key words
- understand some of what is implied but not directly stated

- pick out a few of the details I need by looking for key words
- sometimes understand and answer straightforward multiple-choice questions by looking for key words
- attempt to understand what is implied but not directly stated, but with limited success

THE BIG PICTURE

In this chapter you will:

- write and talk about what you understand by 'culture'
- read about ways of life in different countries, how celebrations are an expression of culture and how cultural objects and art influence the societies in which we live
- discuss which cultures are being changed by the modern world.

THINKING BIG

1 In pairs, look at the photos.

- Make notes on what is shown in each photo.
- Guess which society or nation each one is linked to.
- Write one question you would like to ask about each of the photos.

2 In groups, make a list of things that make your culture (where you live now) special. Think about the following areas:

- arts
- celebrations
- different ethnic groups
- food
- lifestyle
- religions
- sports.

3 In pairs, compare your lists. Discuss any differences as a class.

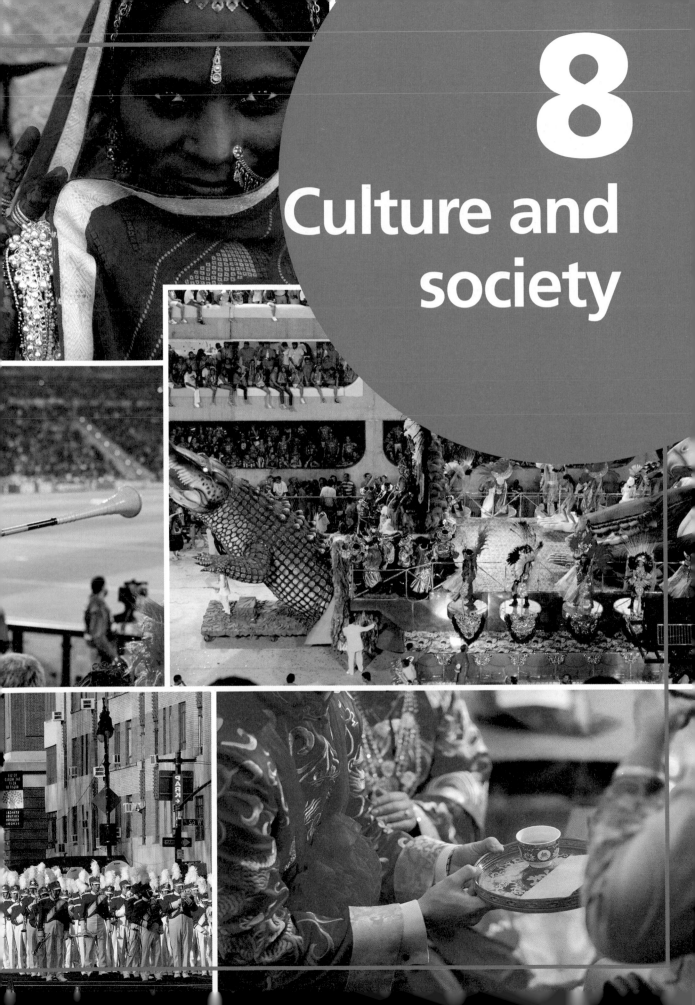

8

Culture and society

8.1 Art and culture

In this section you will learn to:
✓ understand and select information
✓ identify the overall viewpoint and understand the main points in a text
✓ make notes to summarise a text.

GETTING STARTED

People usually think of 'the arts' as an expression of the **culture** of a particular place. But what really counts as art?

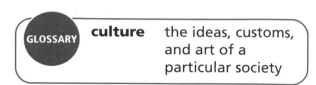

GLOSSARY **culture** the ideas, customs, and art of a particular society

1) Which of the following do you think count as art?

a) carpet weaving **c)** photography **e)** hip hop

b) calligraphy **d)** ballet **f)** pottery

2) Add three more examples of important forms of art in your culture.

3) In pairs:

● Discuss and agree on a list of all forms of artistic expression.

● Decide which of the arts you have listed are practised in your country.

● Discuss if there are any differences between art forms practised by young people and traditional art forms.

EXPLORING THE SKILLS

We can all have different views about the same situation. The main **point of view** in a text (both written and spoken) is the standpoint from which an author talks about a topic. It is often:

● for/in favour of/positive about/approving of an idea OR

● against/negative about/disapproving of an idea.

4) In pairs, discuss and make notes on this statement: *Hip hop is art.*

Give reasons for your opinion.

5) Speeches and comments often have a strong viewpoint. Read the comments of two people (opposite) about hip hop, and then copy and complete the table.

	Positive points about hip hop	Negative points about hip hop	Overall point of view
Comment 1			
Comment 2			

Watch the winner of the 2017 dance competition!

Sarahdancer 2 days ago

Wrong winner! The ballet dancer should have won, or the salsa group. Hip hop and street dance might be popular at the local club but they shouldn't be welcomed as an art dance form at a national dance competition. There's far too much of it in competitions nowadays. What happened to tap? And ballet? And salsa and African dance? These forms of dance have a long and creditable history and require hours and hours of practice to achieve high levels of technique and mastery. Hip hop does not require this level of practice and cannot be compared to these other higher dance forms. Dancers like these 'winners' think they can get away with less practice, and this decreases agility and coordination. Hip hop's obsession with tricks like balancing on your head reduces dance to mere show; it is not art. Making hip hop an art form also gives status to something that started as a form of aggression, when dance should be about grace, beauty and culture.

All this focus on hip hop takes attention and money away from the more classical forms of dance. There has been too much encouragement of hip hop, and dance schools and competitions like this one should be encouraging young people to learn the basics of dance through concentrating on classical dance.

 30   59

Chu2003 1 day ago

You obviously don't know what you're talking about! Street dance is just as valid as classical dance and they deserved to win. Two years ago I met a lot of hip hop dancers who all belonged to an underground street culture – all with superhuman strength and abilities. They could fly in the air. They could bend their elbows all the way back. They could spin on their heads 80 times in a row. I'd never seen anything like that. Seeing these dancers changed the meaning of dance for me.

When I was growing up, my dance heroes were old-school dancers like Prince. And it seemed like those dance heroes had disappeared. But after seeing hip hop, the truth is, good dancers have not disappeared at all. They're here, getting better and better every day, and our new dancers come from hip hop and street culture. Dance is changing and evolving and people need to realise that. Online videos and social networking between dancers have created a global laboratory online for dance. I've seen kids in Japan take moves from a YouTube video created in Detroit, copy it, change it within days, and release a new video. And this is happening every day. And from bedrooms and living rooms and garages, with cheap webcams, come the world's great dancers of tomorrow. And because these dancers can now talk across different continents, hip hop can start to transform dance and change the world. I expect we'll see far more competitions being won by street dancers. Maybe you should enter if you think you can do better?

 40   3

DEVELOPING THE SKILLS

You have read Sarahdancer and Chu2003's opinions about hip hop. However, you may have a different point of view.

6) Now answer these questions about the speeches, giving your opinion.

a) What solution does Sarahdancer offer to the 'problem' of hip hop?

b) What is your view of Sarahdancer's solution?

c) Which of Sarahdancer's points do you agree with and which do you disagree with?

d) What is your view of Chu2003's idea that hip hop can *transform dance and change the world*?

e) Do any of Sarahdancer or Chu2003's ideas seem unreasonable? Why do you think that?

f) People can often sound very direct when they are commenting online and they can be more aggressive than they might be if they were speaking face to face. Identify lines in Sarahdancer's and Chu2003's comments that are direct. Do you think they are aggressive? What effect does this have on how persuasive you find each comment?

g) Which comment is the most persuasive? Give reasons for your answer.

h) Which comment is the most inspirational? Give reasons for your answer.

GOING FURTHER

If you have to write a summary, it is usually a good idea to make some notes first. Remember, notes are not written in sentences. They are usually single words or phrases that just give you the basic meaning.

Here are some notes on the last paragraph of Chu2003's comment on hip hop dancing:

- dance is changing
- technology is helping the change
- people all over the world can see one another dancing

7) Look at the photo on the next page. Calligraphy, or the art of writing, is an important part of traditional Chinese culture. Read the transcript above the picture of a dialogue between a Chinese girl and her father living in the United States. Then make some notes ready to write a summary of:

a) the girl's point of view

b) the father's point of view.

> **TOP TIP**
> Notes are not sentences. They are usually single words or short phrases that help you remember an idea.

Girl: Hi Dad. Look at this. We just got the list of subjects we can choose for higher secondary school. And I was thinking about taking Fine Arts.

Dad: Wonderful. I approve, but any reason why?

Girl: Well, I'm really good at drawing and I love painting – all that colour. A lot of people have admired the paintings that I've done.

Dad: Why don't you specialise in calligraphy instead? You're also really good with your brush and ink. You know that universities in China prize calligraphy above other art forms. Calligraphy was **revered** as a fine art long before painting.

Girl: But Dad. You know that I'll never get into a Chinese university. And I want to work in colour. Calligraphy only uses black ink and paper and concentrates on learning characters by heart. I reject the old-fashioned idea that colour is distracting.

Dad: But it's also a way of staying Chinese. That's important.

Girl: But calligraphy isn't creative – it's just copying what ancient scholars wrote years ago.

Dad: Okay, but don't just dismiss the idea. What about studying calligraphy after school and then doing art as your school option?

GLOSSARY **revered** be held in high esteem and respected greatly

8 In pairs, share your notes with each other and make comments. Check that the notes:

- are short
- use your own words
- give information about each point of view.

LANGUAGE BOOSTER Read the list of words below. Sort them into two lists: words that mean 'have a good opinion of' and those that mean 'have a bad opinion of'. Find the words in the dialogue.

| revered | reject | prize | approve | admire | dismiss |

Complete the following phrases about your own culture.

One thing my culture prizes is …

One thing my culture rejects is …

8.2 Celebrations and culture

WRITING SKILLS IN FOCUS

In this section you will learn to:
✓ use examples to support your point of view when writing
✓ use powerful language to make your opinions persuasive
✓ include opposite points of view to develop your own.

GETTING STARTED

1. In pairs, discuss three different celebrations in your own communities using these headings to help you:
   - Name of celebration
   - When it is celebrated
   - Where it is celebrated
   - Why it is celebrated
   - How people celebrate.

2. On your own, choose one celebration and make notes for a short one-minute talk. Don't forget to use the headings above to structure your talk.

3. In groups, give your talk to the rest of the class.

Chinese New Year festival

Whale Temple festival, Vietnam

EXPLORING THE SKILLS

When you write or speak, you can support your opinion and be more convincing and persuasive by giving reasons and examples.

An example can be from your own experience or what you have seen or heard. Examples back up your opinion because:
- they give proof that something exists
- they show how/when/where something takes place.

4. Every year in the south of Vietnam, there is a fishing festival to celebrate the whale, called Cau Ngu. Look at the photo of Cau Ngu above and, in pairs, write five questions you would like to ask about Vietnam and the Whale Temple festival.

5. Now quickly read the extract on the next page from a travel brochure about Vietnam and the Whale Temple festival. Does it answer any of your questions?

Vietnam

With its renowned hospitality and breathtaking landscapes, Vietnam has something for everyone.

The sea

Looking for an active holiday? For example, take a full-day scuba-diving tour with a qualified and experienced Dive Master at Doc Let beach. Nha Trang is the perfect base from which to explore the amazing coral reefs.

The countryside

Looking for attractive scenery? Take pleasure in a **trek** on the slopes of Hon Ba Peak, wandering through the forest and taking a dip in the waterfall. After long, hot days at the beach, come and soak up Hon Ba's pure atmosphere and cool temperatures and discover some of the area's rare flowers and animals.

Food

More of a foodie? Vietnamese food has more to offer than just spring rolls. What about eating freshly caught seafood caught in the morning and dining near the beach?

Activities

Like sightseeing? Take a tour and visit historic monuments such as Long Son Pagoda, a striking Buddhist temple with a 14-metre high statue of the Buddha. Then visit the Po Nagar Cham Towers, an ancient **complex** of eighth-century temples, to discover a little of the hidden culture of Cham through its traditional dance shows.

Cau Ngu, the Whale Festival

Looking for more excitement? It's worth making the seven-hour journey by coastal road to the Nam Hai Whale Temple for the fascinating fisherman's festival, Cau Ngu. The festival to honour the whales and pray for a prosperous life and **bumper hauls** of fish is held twelve days after the Vietnamese Lunar New Year. After prayers and the ceremonial ritual of the **palanquin** procession, there are vibrant traditional games to celebrate the area's rich fishing heritage followed by music.

GLOSSARY		
trek	a long, difficult journey
complex	a group of buildings
bumper hauls	very large quantities
palanquin	a large box on two horizontal poles, carried by four to six people called bearers

6 Read the travel brochure extract again. It gives five reasons and examples for visiting Vietnam. Copy and complete the table about why you should visit the Nha Trang area of Vietnam and the Cau Ngu.

Reason given	Example
If you like active holidays ...	You can take a full-day scuba-diving tour with a qualified and experienced Dive Master.
If you ...	

DEVELOPING THE SKILLS

You can persuade people by describing things in a strong, positive way. For example:

The fireworks were good. ——————————— less persuasive

The fireworks were spectacular. ——————— more persuasive

7 Re-read the passage on Vietnam. Find strong, positive words in the passage that mean the following:

- eat
- enjoy
- walk slowly
- lively
- well-known
- large quantity
- old

8 Now copy and complete the table with all the strong and positive phrases that are used to describe Vietnam.

What	Descriptive phrase
Vietnam	*renowned hospitality and breathtaking landscapes*
the sea	
the countryside	
food	
the monuments	
the Cau Ngu	

9 Write five sentences about your community and region using strong positive descriptive phrases. Use the following prompts to help you:

- the countryside
- the town
- the food
- the history/monuments
- the things to do.

10 You are going to write a letter to a friend, persuading them to come and stay in your home town during a festival or celebration. Use the diagram below to plan your letter.

- Give examples of what you can do together during the festival.
- Make your town and the celebration sound appealing and be persuasive by using lots of positive language.

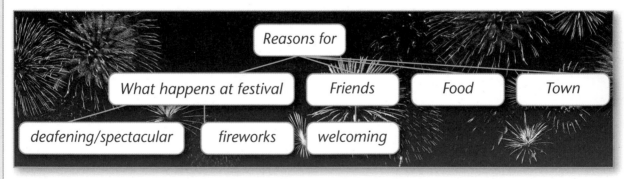

Reasons for

What happens at festival | Friends | Food | Town

deafening/spectacular | fireworks | welcoming

11 Next, write the first draft of your letter.

DID YOU REMEMBER TO ...?

✓ Have I written about the festival?

✓ Have I given good reasons and examples?

✓ Have I used strong, positive words and phrases?

✓ Have I checked my spelling and punctuation?

GOING FURTHER

You can often be more persuasive by **acknowledging** another viewpoint and then trying to overcome this with your own arguments.

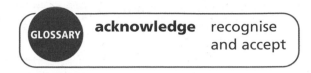

GLOSSARY **acknowledge** recognise and accept

12 The Lord Mayor's Show is a traditional parade in London. Read the following text, which argues that we should cancel the celebrations. What phrases are used to acknowledge another viewpoint?

I think that the amount spent on the Lord Mayor's celebrations is too much, and for this reason we should cancel it or severely reduce the amount spent on the festivities.

While I fully understand that we need to celebrate and, in truth, I take great pride and joy in celebrating how wonderful London can be, I believe there is good evidence to show that we spend too much on the celebrations. I've been told that some celebrations in the city can cost over £50 million on fireworks, displays, pageants and floats. Meanwhile, London's hospitals and schools are in a very bad state. Our hospitals badly need this £50 million to invest in new equipment.

13 Match each viewpoint with its opposing argument.

Acknowledge other point of view	Oppose the argument
a) While it is true that some people suffer injuries during the celebrations,	**1.** however, the number of children that are involved every year in preparing for and celebrating the march-past is enormous.
b) In the eyes of some, Independence Day is just a celebration of the military;	**2.** we could make sure there are extra trained first aid helpers on hand during the festivities.
c) To some extent, it is true that fewer adults take part in the celebrations;	**3.** in fact, the entire nation wakes up on this special day to celebrate life and freedom.

14 Write sentences to overcome or oppose the following arguments with an argument of your own.

- While it is true that the celebrations are expensive, …
- To some extent, it is true that the festival is just entertainment …

15 Write a 200-word blog arguing in favour of holding a traditional or Independence Day celebration in your country.

- Plan your argument: think of three main reasons for holding a traditional or Independence Day celebration in your country or another country in your region.
- Write your blog: don't forget to acknowledge another viewpoint and overcome this with your own arguments.

WRITING SKILLS

8.3 Modern culture

In this section you will learn to:
✓ use examples to support your opinions while speaking
✓ include facts and expert opinions to support your point of view
✓ use rhetorical questions to make your speaking effective.

GETTING STARTED

1 In pairs, discuss the following questions.

- Do you play computer games? If not, why not?
- What types of games do you or others play?
- How much time do you or others spend playing per day/week?
- Who do you think is the 'average' gamer?
- Why do you think people play computer games?

2 Now, in groups of four, feed back to your group what your partner told you.

EXPLORING THE SKILLS

You can be more persuasive when speaking if you use facts or examples to support your opinion. Facts or examples often give reasons or answer the question: 'Why do you think that?'

For example:

> *Gaming is an important part of young people's culture.*

> (Why do you think that? Because …)

Reason/example:

> *Many young people prefer computer games to traditional board games such as chess.*

3 Organise the following examples (a to d) to support Opinion 1 or Opinion 2.

Opinion 1: We should limit the number of hours young people spend on gaming.

Opinion 2: Gaming can solve the problems of the world.

a) Some online games like *World Without Oil* encourage you to adopt real-life habits, like thinking of ways to reduce the amount of oil you use.

b) The majority of fee-paying online users are under the age of 20, and 10% are under the age of 16 in China.

c) 13% of under-18s who use the web are addicted to online gaming, according to a recent report.

d) Games encourage you to persevere and work hard to achieve a mission.

4 In pairs, research and think of two examples to support both points of view for the following opinion.

Computer games are (not) an important part of modern life.

Now each choose one of the opinions. Interview your partner about why they hold their opinion. Start like this:

So, could you explain a bit more why you think computer games are (not) an important part of...

DEVELOPING THE SKILLS

Facts are a powerful means of supporting your opinion. Facts that are 'expert opinions' will make your argument even stronger. Why is this?

Facts and expert opinions:

- show you have done some research

- give your audience a better idea of exactly when, where and how something takes place.

For example:

Many young people play computer games.	weak fact
Five million people under the age of 20 play computer games more than three hours a day in the Middle East.	strong fact
Evidence shows that playing computer games more than three hours a day means you are more likely to become addicted to gaming.	stronger/strongest fact

> **TOP TIP** You need to do research on the internet or in the library to gather powerful facts or evidence.

5) Read this speech about gaming. Copy the phrases highlighted in colour and match them to the labels in the box below.

[ ]

[ ]

[ ]

[ ]

[ ]

Hi. My name is Soo Kyung and I'm an online game designer. I've been making games for about 10 years now. And during that time, as I am sure you are all aware, we are sold the story that online games are violent. Not only that, they also encourage violent behaviour.

[ ]

So I'm going to investigate these ideas and put them to the test. I am going to argue that these ideas are just a myth. I am going to show you that these negative ideas about gaming are, in fact, incorrect.

[ ]

Let us look at the games. Are they actually violent? In fact many games do not feature any violence. For instance hundreds of millions play games like 'Minecraft' where you spend time building entire worlds. A lot of gaming has moved to smartphones and people love puzzles and quizzes like Quiz Up. Then there are the active sports games people are starting to play with Virtual Reality headsets, or Pokemon Go has people running around their city catching Pokemon with their smartphone. None of these games is violent.

[ ]

[ ]

Next let us look at whether games encourage violence. Critics say that video games where you become an active participant in the killing, mean you will resort to violence in the real world too.

[ ]

An easy way to test this is to look at whether violent crimes have increased together with the boom in video game sales. Is this the case? In fact, the evidence shows that violent crime in America, Japan and China, the three biggest video-game markets, has dropped over the past decade at the same time as sales of video games have soared.

- example   • personal introduction   • use of 'you' or 'we' to involve the audience
- repetition   • numbers/facts to support opinion   • use of expert opinion
- speaker's point of view   • acknowledge other point of view

GOING FURTHER
Good presentations often use rhetorical questions. Rhetorical questions are asked only for effect and they do not expect an answer. Instead, they ask the audience to think further.
For example:

Obviously computers are useful to us in many ways that go beyond a book. But is usefulness the best way to measure the value of something?

6 Now insert one or two rhetorical questions into the following introduction to a speech on the benefits of spending your free time away from the screen.

Obviously I use the computer to do my homework. My free time is precious. Free time I save for doing things off screen. Free time is for chatting to friends, playing basketball and reading.

7 You are going to give a presentation on an aspect of computer games. Choose one of the following titles.

- Computer games are addictive

- Computer games are a waste of time

- Reading is better for you than gaming

Example:

Chosen presentation	Computer games are a waste of time
My viewpoint	I disagree that video games are a waste of time
Supporting point 1	Other games, for example chess, are thought to be strategic.
Expert evidence	
Supporting point 2	
Supporting point 3	

Instructions for giving a presentation

- First choose your presentation title.

- Next, decide your point of view. Do you agree with the title?

- Then do your research. Use the internet or the library to find out three pieces of information or examples which support your point of view.

- Make notes for your presentation.

- Now practise giving your presentation. Make sure you know exactly what you are going to say – practise it to yourself several times.

- Use the advice in the 'Did you remember to ... ?' to make your presentation clear and persuasive.

- Give your presentation to your group.

DID YOU REMEMBER TO ... ?

✓ Clearly state the reason for the speech early in the speech.

✓ Use 'we' to include the audience.

✓ Use examples to support the points made.

✓ Include expert opinions to support the points made.

✓ Use repetition, often in groups of three.

✓ Ask rhetorical questions to make listeners think further.

8.4 Disappearing ways of life

In this section you will learn to:
✓ understand and select relevant information in spoken texts
✓ identify and understand opinions in a range of spoken texts
✓ identify and understand conflicting opinions in an informal spoken text.

GETTING STARTED

Many traditional cultures from the countryside are disappearing. It is not just people's lifestyles that are disappearing, it is also the knowledge they hold of their culture that is being lost.

1 Look at these photos. They both show homes in the Middle East.

In pairs, discuss the following questions.

a) Which photo shows a town (urban) life and which a country (rural) life?

b) Where would you prefer to live? Give one reason.

c) Do you think the photos are a good reflection of urban and rural life where you live now?

2 In pairs, brainstorm and then copy and complete the table with things that you associate or link with country life and town life in your country.

Think hard – maybe some activities are associated with both country and town life.

Town life	Country life
Commuting to work	Commuting to work
Going to the cinema	Using mobile phones
Using mobile phones	

EXPLORING THE SKILLS

There are many situations when you might hear a lot of information in a short space of time. You need to be able to find out quickly whether someone is giving you facts or their opinions. If they give you facts, it is often easier to trust them. Luckily you can spot opinions from particular phrases people use to introduce them. For example:

The majority of people live in cities.

Fact – you can prove this fact by finding out how many people live in cities.

It's normal that most people live in cities.

Opinion – you cannot prove 'it is normal'.

CULTURE AND SOCIETY

Phrases and words that introduce opinions:

✓ 'It's normal that, ...'   ✓ 'Obviously ...'

✓ 'It's a shame that ...'   ✓ 'never'

✓ 'It's wonderful that ...'   ✓ 'always'

✓ 'It's terrible that ...'   ✓ 'better/best'

3 In pairs, listen to some statements about living in the country and in the town. Sort the statements into fact and opinion. Be careful, some of them are a mix of fact and opinion. Explain how the statement can be proved if it is a fact.

8.1

Opinion	Fact	How fact can be proved
The overcrowding in our cities is terrible.	The majority of people live in cities.	Find out the numbers and percentage of the national population that lives in the major cities.

4 Two young people from different countries talk about their home life. Listen once and answer the question.

8.2

Who has a rural life and who has an urban life?

5 Listen again. Are the answers the speaker gives to the questions below facts or opinions? For example:

Where does she live?

She says she lives in an enormous and luxurious house. This is opinion because you cannot prove it is luxurious – what is luxurious to one person may not be to another.

Person 1
a) Where does she live?
b) Is there a school in her village?
c) How does she feel about going to school?
d) What does she think about her city?
e) How does she keep in touch with her parents?

Person 2
a) Where does he live?
b) What happened to his parents?
c) How does he feel about where he lives now?
d) What is the house like where he lives?
e) What are his grandparents like?

6 Listen again to the first few sentences from person 2. Find two facts and two opinions.

8.3

DEVELOPING THE SKILLS

In the next exercise you will be asked to listen very carefully to what your fellow students say. The more carefully you listen, the better you will be able to do the writing task.

(7) Write a 200-word article for your school magazine about the advantages you find of living in either an urban or a rural environment. Prepare for the article using the instructions below:

First, listen to others.

- On your own, list or make notes on the advantages of the places where you live or have lived – and whether they were rural or urban.

- In groups, take turns to give a short talk about the advantages and disadvantages of where you live or have lived.

- All other members in the group should listen carefully and make notes.

Next, plan the article.

On your own, use your notes about living in an urban or rural environment to plan your article. You can use a concept map to help you plan.

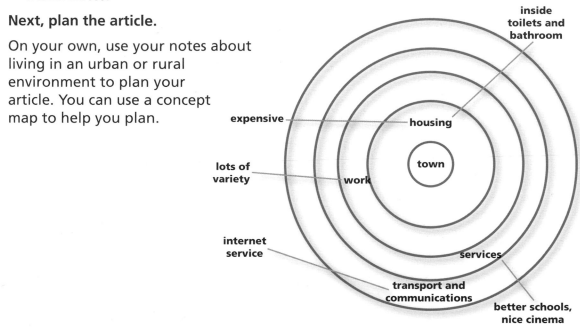

Next, write a first draft of your article.

Read your draft and note any changes that you need to make. Then write it again, checking that you have:

- written about 200 words
- acknowledged other ideas and argued against them with facts and examples
- mixed facts with opinions
- used strong, positive words.

GOING FURTHER

A dialogue, or conversation between two or more people, is often more difficult to understand because different people are likely to hold different opinions about the same thing. When listening, you have to work out who holds which opinion. For example:

Person 1: *It's normal for people to move to towns and cities for work.*

Person 2: *You should encourage people to stay in the villages to protect rural lifestyles and to make sure the languages and knowledge don't die out.*

8 You are going to listen to a short dialogue between a girl and a boy from Indonesia who talk about disappearing cultures.

Before you listen, as a class brainstorm everything you know about Indonesia.

Look at the photos and think about the types of traditional lifestyles the people have.

Now listen to the dialogue and answer the questions. 8.4

a) What special skill and knowledge did the grandmother have?

b) Why doesn't the girl have this knowledge today?

c) What does the girl say has been lost?

d) What is the girl's opinion about the death of a language?

e) What is the boy's opinion about the death of a language?

9 Listen again. Write down the two methods the girl gives for protecting a language.

10 In pairs, discuss what languages you know of in your own culture that are in danger of dying.

Discuss whether you think it is normal for village lifestyles to disappear. (This is an opinion.)

11 Write two sentences about why it is important to protect different languages.

12 Write two sentences about how you can make sure minority languages stay alive.

The big task

Nomadic communities are groups that move from place to place as part of their lifestyle, often to reach new sources of food and water. Did you know that many nomadic communities are disappearing? For example, many people from a European travelling community, the Roma, have abandoned the traditional way of life, including travelling, and now live within mainstream society.

Write a 250-word article for your school magazine about a community whose culture and way of life is disappearing. The last paragraph should give your opinion about whether and how we should preserve the community.

1 First, brainstorm your topic.

- In groups of four, choose a culture that is in danger of disappearing. If you cannot think of one near or in your country, then your teacher can help you.
- Copy and complete the first two columns of the table below.
- Each person in the group researches one of the questions from the 'What I want to know' column.
- Take it in turns to feed back to your group. Your group must listen carefully to what each person has to say.
- On your own, complete the last column of the table.

What I know	What I want to know	What I learned
For example: Many Roma have abandoned travelling as a way of life.	What …? Where …? How …? Why …?	

2 Now plan your article.

- In the first part of the article, write engagingly about what you know about your disappearing culture.
- In the second part of the article, write your opinion. Think of three reasons why and how we should preserve your disappearing culture.

3 Now write your article. Use as many as possible of the following features.

- Use expert opinions (e.g. laws/conventions/evidence/important people).
- Use facts to support the points made.
- Use examples to support the points made.
- Acknowledge other viewpoints.
- Use repetition.
- Ask rhetorical questions.
- Clearly state your opinion in the last paragraph.

Check your progress

Here are the Reading, Writing, Speaking and Listening skills you learned about in Chapter 8.

Use this table to decide how good you are at the different skills, and make a note of what you need to be able to do in order to move up a level.

READING I can …	WRITING I can …
confidently understand and select details from complex texts, and produce concise notes for a summary consistently identify the overall viewpoint and main points, recognising connections between related ideas	consistently and confidently use examples to support a point of view make my arguments persuasive by deliberately choosing powerful language and by utilising opposite points of view to develop my own effectively
understand and select details from texts, and produce adequate notes for a summary sometimes identify the overall viewpoint and main points, recognising some connections between related ideas	sometimes use examples to support a point of view make some of my arguments persuasive by using powerful language and by including opposite points of view to try to develop my own
select a few details from straightforward texts, and produce notes for a summary identify the overall viewpoint and a few more obvious points, recognising a few connections between related ideas	use one or two examples to support a simple point of view try to make my arguments persuasive by using powerful language, and by trying to refer to opposite points of view to develop my own, but find this difficult to do

SPEAKING	LISTENING I can …
consistently make effective use of examples and expert opinions to support my point of view use rhetorical questions effectively to make my speaking persuasive	understand and pick out exactly the details I need when listening confidently distinguish and understand opposite opinions in a range of spoken texts, including more complex, formal ones
sometimes make use of examples and expert opinions to support my point of view use rhetorical questions to try to make my speaking persuasive	understand and pick out many of the details I need when listening often recognise and understand differing opinions in a range of spoken texts
try to include examples, including expert opinions, to support my point of view recognise the effect of rhetorical questions but do not use them	pick out a few of the details I need when listening identify straightforward opinions in simple spoken texts recognise conflicting opinions in simple spoken texts

THE BIG PICTURE

In this chapter you will:

- think about transport – how people all over the world travel from one place to another

- read, write, talk and think about how transport has changed in the last hundred years, and how it continues to change.

THINKING BIG

1 Choose two photos that you find interesting.

- Make notes about the types of transport illustrated in the photos. Note down some ideas covering what you know about them, and why you find them interesting.

- Why are different kinds of transport popular in different places around the world?

2 In pairs:

- Discuss the photos with your partner and share what you know about them. Talk about the countries shown and think about when these different kinds of transport are or were used. Ask your partner questions and look up any information that you don't know.

3 On your own, note down ideas about the following:

- How and why do methods of transport change over time?

- What advantages and disadvantages can you think of for some of our main forms of transport today?

- What is your favourite mode of transport? Explain why.

9
Transport

9.1 Development of transport

In this section you will learn to:
✓ identify and understand opinions in a range of texts
✓ recognise the language used to express opinion
✓ recognise and understand opinions which are implied but not directly stated.

GETTING STARTED

(1) Read the points below and discuss your ideas about them with a partner.

- Think about a journey you have been on recently. What transport did you use and what did you like or dislike about it?

- What are the advantages and disadvantages of cars?

- How do you think transport influences our lives today?

EXPLORING THE SKILLS

When you read a text, it is important to be able to tell the difference between facts and the writer's opinion. Remember:

- A **fact** is something that can be proved, such as a date.

- An **opinion** is what one person or group of people thinks or feels. It cannot be proved beyond doubt.

A writer may use phrases such as *in my opinion* and *I think* to express their point of view. However, if not, a reader still needs to recognise that a comment may just be personal opinion.

Opinions that are presented well are often supported by facts:

> *The development of new forms of transport is the main reason why we have so many opportunities today … we can send items around the world at speeds that were unheard of 100 years ago.*

In this example, *The development of new forms of transport is the main reason* is an opinion, a personal point of view. The fact that follows may be true, but it would be possible for someone to argue that there is another reason of equal or greater importance.

2 Read the text and answer the questions below.

Europe today has many different forms of transport – cars, buses, trains and planes. I think that the development of these forms of transport is the main reason why we have so many opportunities today – we can travel to work, so we can choose from a wider range of jobs. We can send items around the world at speeds that were unheard of 100 years ago. We can go on holiday and visit friends and family.

But this has only been possible in recent years. What did we do before motorways, air travel and the railways? In my opinion, life must have been more difficult and less interesting.

a) Give four types of transport named in the text.

b) Identify four things that transport allows us to do.

c) Identify two sentences where opinions are expressed.

d) Find two phrases the writer uses to say what he or she thinks.

e) Do you agree with the opinions being expressed?

DEVELOPING THE SKILLS

Remember that in order to distinguish between fact and opinion, you need to:

- recognise how facts are presented in a text – look out for dates, numbers and other information that can be proved to be true
- look for phrases that signal the writer's own opinion, such as *in my opinion*, *I think that*
- consider whether something can be proved – if not, it is probably an opinion rather than a fact.

3 Read the text below and on the next page about how transport has developed, and then answer questions 4–6.

With the invention of the steam train in 1803, Britain, the USA and, later, Europe led the modernisation of transport. Today, the world leader, by far, is China. China has 37 900 km of train lines and expects to double that by 2035 to 70 000 km. For comparison, Spain, the world's second largest high-speed train network, has about 3200 km of high-speed tracks.

However, it's not just the size of its network that makes China's achievement appear so incredible. It's the fact that, in 2000, China had only 4% of the world's railway lines and no high-speed tracks at all. In fact, China's rail history got off to a very slow start. While the rest of the world was modernising, in the mid 1800s most of China's transport was either by canal or on foot.

Even when the government began to allow railways in the 1880s and 90s, they were built entirely by foreign companies. But, since 2008, China has rapidly developed its home-grown engineering talent to transform its rail network. China is home to the world's highest train station, Tanggula, (5068 m above sea level) on the Qinghai–Tibet railway and the world's longest railway bridge, the Danyang-Kunshan Grand Bridge (164 800 m). Lives have been transformed as a result of the increase in railways and many people believe that the railways are the most important development of the last 200 years.

4 Read the sentences below. Then read the text again and complete the facts.

Key facts about the railways in China

Length of China's rail network now _____ km
and estimated length in the year_____
with _____ km

The year the Chinese began to invest in modern railways:

_____

The name and length of the longest railway
bridge: _____ with
_____ km

The name and height of the highest railway station:
_____ at _____ km
above sea-level

> **TOP TIP** When you read a text with lots of facts, it can be useful to make short notes to help you remember key information:
>
> *1803 – first steam train invented*
>
> *Spain – world's second largest high-speed rail network*

5 What does the writer think about the following topics?

- China's achievement
- the development of the railways.

6 What is your view of the writer's opinions? Do you agree that the railways are the most important transport development or do you think that other inventions have been more important?

Look at the photos to help give you some ideas, or use any of your own. Research some facts to support your argument.

GOING FURTHER

Adjectives such as 'great' and 'vast' signal an opinion about what someone has seen or experienced. They add more information to a factual account and give you an idea of how the author feels without them having to say it directly.

(7) Read the following extract from an account of a journey.

> Taking thirteen days, passing through nine countries and nine time zones, the main feature of this trip was a journey on the famous Trans-Siberian Railway.

a) In this extract, the writer gives a number of facts: for example, the journey took 13 days. Identify two more facts.

b) The writer also introduces his opinion with the word 'famous'. What do you know about the Trans-Siberian Railway? Find out what might make it 'famous'.

(8) Read the rest of the text. What is the writer's overall impression of the journey?

Coming from a family that has always had strong connections with railways, I had always been interested in trains since I was a small child.

Therefore, I suppose it was only natural that I would always wonder about what it would be like to travel on the world's longest train journey, on the Trans-Siberian Railway.

This 12 300-kilometre journey by train across two continents was a great adventure which went beyond what I had expected and was really exciting. It took me nearly half way round the world, providing the opportunity to see vast contrasts of beauty, culture and climate in a short space of time. The thoughts and memories from the journey will no doubt continue way into the future.

For those who think the Trans-Siberian Railway is just another ride on a train – well, apart from it being the longest train journey in the world, it is much more than that: it's an adventure and one of the very few left on our planet that can be completed by absolutely anyone.

Adapted from a 'A Journey On The Trans-Siberian Railway' by Clive Simpson

(9) Think of more adjectives the writer might have used to describe this journey. Then, in pairs, invent sentences about the journey using these adjectives.

Consider how the writer could express a different opinion about his journey, using negative adjectives. For example:

It was a boring / an unimpressive / an uncomfortable journey.

(10) Read the whole text again and identify:

a) three facts about the journey (think about the distance travelled, where the writer went and why he went)

b) some of the writer's opinions about how he travelled and what he saw on his journey.

9.2 The impact of transport

In this section you will learn to:

✓ use relative pronouns to join sentences and add information

✓ use a variety of structures when writing descriptions

✓ join your ideas and sentences using connectives.

GETTING STARTED

1 Read the questions below and discuss your ideas with a partner.

- In what ways can transport provide people with more opportunities?

- Would you prefer to travel abroad to work, or would you rather go abroad on holiday or for sightseeing?

- Do you think it is good that more people are able to travel wherever they want, or are there disadvantages in this?

EXPLORING THE SKILLS

When you write, you can use a variety of sentence structures to join your ideas together and extend them. In Chapter 3, you learned about ways to combine simple sentences to make compound and complex sentences. Here you will look at other ways to join or extend sentences using relative pronouns.

Relative pronouns

'Where' introduces information about places, for example:

This is the park <u>where</u> we like to play.

'Who' introduces information about people, for example:

Mr Moss was the teacher <u>who</u> encouraged me most at school.

'That' or 'which' introduce information about things, for example:

These are the trainers <u>that</u> everyone wants at the moment.

2 Nisha has moved to a new country to start a job. She is emailing her friends and family at home to tell them about her first few days in a new country. Read the text on the next page. How did Nisha travel to the island, and where did she spend the first night?

3 Read the text again and identify at least four relative pronouns.

Hi Mum and Dad, I've shared all the photos from my trip on Facebook but here's a selection for you non-Facebook users!

This is the boat I arrived on. I flew to the main airport and then took a **ferry** to the island. The ferry, which was quite small, was good fun because I met some friendly people and I also saw dolphins on the journey!

Luckily, there was a helpful lady who showed me where to catch the ferry. It was really busy at the **port**, and my phone didn't have any signal so I couldn't look it up online. I was really glad she helped me because I was lost!

And this photo is of the hotel where I stayed on the first night. The place where I'm working is a long way from the ferry port, so I stayed here for the night and set off again the next morning by coach. The hotel, which was in the town centre, was really noisy but the breakfast was tasty! So, don't worry about me and I'll write again when I get the chance.

GLOSSARY

ferry   a boat that transports passengers and sometimes also vehicles, usually across rivers or short stretches of sea

port   (a town with) a harbour

4) In pairs, read the following sentences and discuss:

- the main idea of the sentence
- what information is given about the main subject.

a) This is our classroom where we study English.

b) This is my friend who lives next door to me.

c) I've got a bike which is quite old.

d) These are the tickets that we need for the plane.

Can you identify why each relative pronoun is used? Look back at the previous page to check your ideas.

5) In pairs, think of different endings for the following sentences. Remember to use the correct relative pronoun.

a) Here's the book …

b) There's the plane …

c) She's the girl …

d) Have you seen the hotel …

e) This is the airport …

DEVELOPING THE SKILLS

When you are describing something, try to use a range of structures to add interest to your writing. Think about using sentences of different lengths, as well as of different types (simple, compound and complex sentences). Also try to use a variety of ways to add description – adjectives, noun phrases (see Chapter 3) or relative pronouns to add further information. For example:

> We reached the hotel early in the evening. It was breathtaking. The hotel, which was a small, white building, was set on the side of a hill overlooking the sea. In front of us we could see blue sea and a clear sky. The beach was spectacular. It had white sand and was surrounded by large palm trees. We could hear the waves gently crashing on the sand. The sky was full of beautiful colours because the sun was starting to go down.

- simple sentence
- relative pronoun
- compound sentence
- noun phrase
- complex sentence

6 Work in pairs. Discuss a holiday you have had or would like to have. You could show each other photos of a place you would like to visit.

- What do you like about the place?
- What can you do when you are there?
- How can you travel there?

7 Imagine you have been on a journey overseas for work, study or sightseeing. You are going to write an email to your friends or family to describe why you chose this place and how you travelled there.

a) First, make notes to help you structure your ideas. Look at the photos and think about what each one shows. You can use these or any of your own ideas.

b) Read through your notes and think of ways you can expand them into simple and longer compound sentences.

8 Now write your email describing your journey.

You could start:

Look at these photos. This is the yellow taxi which I took to the city centre.

> **TOP TIP**
> When writing informal emails, use expressions such as 'Hi', 'Hello', 'Hi there' to start the email and 'Take care', 'Write soon', 'Keep in touch' to end the email.

GOING FURTHER

Sentences can be connected in different ways in order to make complex sentences. Connectives have different uses, as shown below.

> **LANGUAGE BOOSTER**

Connectives	Use
even though	to make a contrast – shows that something happened despite a problem or difficulty
because	to show cause and effect – gives a reason or reasons why something happened
although	to make a contrast – similar to 'even though' – introduces a statement that makes the main statement seem surprising
when	to add further information about an event

9 Read the following sentences. Referring to the table above, decide on the use or function of the underlined connective phrases.

a) <u>Even though</u> I like driving, I take the bus to work.

b) <u>When it is raining</u>, the bus is always busy.

c) <u>Although I got up at 5 a.m.</u>, I missed the train.

d) We walked to the cinema <u>because the underground was closed</u>.

e) The plane, <u>which was very big</u>, had comfy seats.

10 Make notes on the following questions.

a) What opportunities do you have because of transport in your area?

b) What improvements could be made to the local transport system?

c) How could an improved transport system improve young people's lives?

11 Now imagine you have to write an article for a school magazine to explain the importance of a good transport system for young people. Use your notes from above to help you structure your ideas.

> **TOP TIP**
> Try to give reasons for your ideas, using a range of sentence forms (simple, compound and complex) and connectives.

9.3 Problems with transport

In this section you will learn to:
✓ use a variety of grammatical structures accurately and effectively when you speak
✓ vary the tense of verbs you use according to the situation.

GETTING STARTED

❝Restore human legs as a means of travel. Pedestrians rely on food for fuel and need no special parking facilities.❞
Lewis Mumford, American historian and sociologist particularly famous for his study of cities, 1895–1990

1. Read the quote above and discuss in pairs what you think it means. Use a dictionary to look up any words you don't know.

   Then consider the following problems that can be caused by transport:

   - Pollution – what effects do different forms of transport have on the environment?

   - Congestion – what is it like to be on a very busy road?

   - Cost – how expensive are different forms of transport?

EXPLORING THE SKILLS

When you are speaking it is important to be able to express yourself clearly and fluently. This includes using the correct verb tense in the correct situation, depending on whether you want to talk about the past, the present or the future. For example:

> *I ride my bike to college.* (present tense)
>
> *I walked to school when I was younger.* (past tense)
>
> *When I'm older, I will drive to work.* (future tense)

2 Read the speech bubbles below and identify the past, present and future tenses. One of them uses complex verb forms which are not any of these, called 'conditionals'. Can you spot it?

> *When my parents were young, they didn't have a car and they used to travel by bicycle a lot. It was better for the environment, and it was probably fun too.*

past tense

> *Transport causes pollution, and I think cars, which often only have one person in them, are the worst for the environment.*

> *In my opinion, aeroplane travel is the worst in terms of pollution. Each journey releases a lot of dangerous gases. It's also cheaper to fly today than it used to be, which means that people are flying more often and further.*

> *People say that transport is progress, but in my opinion, digging up the countryside to make roads and railways isn't progress – it damages our environment. Soon there will be too many roads and not enough open spaces.*

> *I think that in the future, people won't use cars in city centres at all. There will be new kinds of public transport which will be more environmentally friendly, and cheaper to use.*

> *If we didn't have a good transport system, we wouldn't have all the things we take for granted these days. Businesses wouldn't be as successful, and life wouldn't be as interesting.*

3 Identify which speakers think that transport was better in the past, and which think it was worse. Then read again, and identify the speakers who think transport will be better in the future, and those who think it will be worse.

4 Which of the comments above do you agree with? In pairs, discuss your ideas and give reasons for your opinions.

5 Listen to two people talking about their views on transport. 9.1

   a) Why is Maria asking Luca these questions?

   b) What does Luca think about the bus service?

6 Listen again and match the following incomplete sentences to make sentences you hear. Then decide which full sentence is a simple sentence, which is a compound sentence and which is a complex sentence.

   a) It used to be quite quick,

   b) I usually

   c) Although it might make a difference now,

   A) I don't think it will help in the future.

   B) but now it's really slow.

   C) cycle everywhere.

DEVELOPING THE SKILLS

'Used to …' is one way of talking about what things were like in the past and comparing them with the present. Read this example from the recording:

> *It used to be quite quick, but now it's really slow.*

It compares what the bus service was like in the past (quick) with what it is like now (slow).

> *It used to be quiet in my town, but now it's very busy.*
>
> *We used to walk to school, but now we get the bus.*

(7) In pairs, think up more sentences to describe a situation that you knew in the past and how it is different now, using 'used to'.

(8) Read the following extract. Do you agree or disagree with the point of view? How does it compare with the transport situation where you live?

> I think there are lots of problems with transport today. For example, lots of people in my town drive to work every day. There is a good train service here, which goes straight to the city centre. However, the trains are a lot more expensive than they used to be. They are too expensive for most people to use every day. But petrol is also very expensive – and I think it will get more expensive in the future.
>
> In my opinion, there should be a better bus service. Buses are cheap, practical and they don't cause as much pollution as lots of cars.

(9) In pairs, think of similar sentences about transport that join ideas together in a variety of ways. Try to think of at least one example for each use. Look back at the Language booster in Section 9.2.

(10) Which form of transport do you think causes the biggest problems?

a) Note down ideas about:

- how often it is used
- how many people use it
- how expensive it is to use and to run
- how much pollution it causes
- how it has changed over time, and how it might change in the future.

b) Can you think of any alternatives to this method of transport? In what ways are your alternatives better?

11 In pairs, discuss the notes you made in task 10. If possible, record your conversation. Then listen to it again and see if you can think of ways to improve the way you join your sentences and ideas. Have you used verb tenses correctly?

12 Act out your dialogue again, this time using more ways to join sentences and express your ideas. Make sure that you use the right tenses for your verbs.

GOING FURTHER

You can use **modals** to express your arguments and opinions in a more sophisticated way. These are small words that can be added to a verb to show subtle shades of meaning, such as possibility, intention, obligation or necessity. For example: *I can walk / I ought to walk / I could walk / I should walk*.

Start with simple modals (e.g. *can, must, should*) before changing to the past (e.g. *should have walked*) and using more complex forms.

Read the following conversation.

    A   I should walk to college more often as it's good exercise.

    B   That's a good idea. I could walk with you.

Speaker A feels an obligation to walk to college. Speaker B suggests the possibility of walking with her.

13 Match the following incomplete sentences to make the correct full sentences.

a) I should have set my alarm clock to wake me up early

b) I think the government should have spent a lot of money on railways

c) I could have cycled to school today

A) because the service is awful at the moment.

B) although it was raining a little bit.

C) because I overslept and I missed the bus!

14 You are going to role-play a dialogue between two people who are discussing the transport in their home town. Before you start, note down ideas about:

- what is good about the current system where you live
- what is bad about it.

When you have finished, team up with a partner. One of you will present the positive points and the other will present the negative points. Decide on your roles and spend a few minutes preparing your ideas.

Remember that this is a conversation between friends, so the language can be quite informal. However, try to use a variety of sentences correctly in order to join your ideas more fluently.

Act out your role-play, without looking at your notes.

> **TOP TIP** If possible, record yourself and listen to the conversation afterwards. Can you think of ways to improve it?

9.4 Where will we go and how will we get there?

LISTENING SKILLS IN FOCUS

In this section you will learn to:
✓ understand connections and differences between related ideas
✓ understand what is implied but not directly stated in a formal spoken text.

GETTING STARTED

1 Read the questions below and discuss your ideas with a partner.

- What do you think the most popular form of transport will be in the future? Will it be cars, trains, bikes or something new that hasn't been designed yet?

- What reasons do we have for needing new kinds of transport?

- If we are developing new kinds of transport, what qualities should they have?

2 Because of the problems with many of our current forms of transport, lots of people around the world are trying to design new types of transport. Look at these photos and match each one to its description below.

The future of transport

a) Passengers will board the cloud using ladders and sit on the surface during the journey.

b) Great for short, personal journeys, for people who have always wanted to fly!

c) It's a train made up of pods that travels at high speed through a vacuum tube.

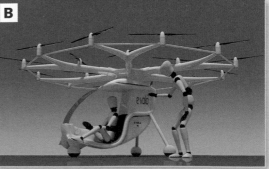

> **TOP TIP**
> Remember to study any images linked to a text as closely as you can. These will give you important information right away, and will help you to understand what you read or hear.

EXPLORING THE SKILLS

When you answer multiple-choice questions, or true/false questions, about listening texts, as with other listening tasks, first read the questions and identify any key words to help you listen out for the answers. You are listening for ideas, opinions and attitudes, and any connection between them. You also need to understand what the speaker is saying even if it is not actually said.

(3) Listen to a radio programme about future forms of transport. Which one of these forms of transport do you think is the most likely to be successful?

🎧 9.2

(4) Listen again and decide whether the statements below are true or false. Remember that the information you need may be implied and not directly stated.

The first one has been done for you as an example.

> False – the speaker thinks we don't have an environmentally friendly way to travel long distances.

a) The speaker thinks that bikes are an environmentally friendly alternative way to travel long distances.

b) The Hyperloop will use expensive fuel.

c) We need to test the Hyperloop on humans before we know how travelling through a tube at such a high speed will affect our bodies.

d) The Volocopter can be used by more than one person.

e) The person controlling the Volocopter has to use a computer.

f) The Volocopter can be used for long journeys.

g) The Passing Cloud idea is useful if you want to get somewhere quickly.

h) The design features small, separate spherical shapes.

i) The Passing Cloud uses an electric engine to move about.

Then listen again and check your answers. What did you hear? How did this help you find the answers?

DEVELOPING THE SKILLS

When you answer multiple-choice questions, or true/false questions, the answer options may not present the information in exactly the same form as you hear it. For this reason, try to think of different ways in which the information could be presented. For example, instead of 'it uses expensive fuel', you might hear 'it isn't cheap to use'.

(5) In task 4, statement **c)** says 'We need to test the Hyperloop on humans before we know how travelling through a tube at such a high speed will affect our bodies.'

Listen and find out how this information is presented on audio track 9.2.

LISTENING SKILLS

183

LANGUAGE BOOSTER

Match the words to the definitions.

a) bamboo
b) sustainable
c) zero emissions
d) heat-resistant
e) synthetic
f) waterway
g) infrastructure

1 not damaged by high temperatures
2 a canal, river or narrow channel of sea that ships or boats can sail along
3 tall treelike tropical grass with hollow stems
4 producing no harmful or polluting gases
5 basic facilities such as transport, communications, power supplies and buildings, which enable a country or organisation to function
6 using natural resources, kept at a steady level that is not likely to damage the environment
7 made artificially

In pairs, look at the photos and think about what you are likely to hear. Then read through the questions. Have your ideas changed on what you think you are likely to hear? Are there words you need to listen out for? Are you listening for synonyms?

6 Listen to the descriptions of each design for new kinds of transport, and then answer the multiple-choice questions below.

9.3

i) Who designed the Bamboo Ajiro bicycle?

   A a student from Austria
   B a student from America
   C a student from Australia

ii) What are the advantages of bamboo?

   A It is strong and needs light to grow quickly.
   B It grows quickly and is light and strong.
   C It grows quickly and does not use much energy.

iii) Which is the best description of 'aramid', the fabric used to make the Adhoc canoe?

   A an artificial material which is waterproof and resistant to heat
   B a material which is naturally waterproof and heat-resistant
   C an artificial material which is waterproof and easily damaged by heat

iv) What is the Adhoc canoe powered by?

   A a fuel with low emissions
   B water
   C human energy

v) What is the Aquatic water taxi made from?

   A metal which is sustainable
   B metal which is not very heavy
   C metal which is soft to the touch

vi) How does it travel?

   A on waterways that are already there
   B on new waterways
   C on a new infrastructure

(7) Listen to a presentation about space travel. What is the main reason for space flight, according to the speaker?

 LANGUAGE BOOSTER Use a dictionary to find definitions for these words and phrases:
propel   *gravity*   *launch pad*

(8) Listen to the text again and answer these multiple-choice questions.

i) Why is it now possible to travel into space?
- **A** We can afford it.
- **B** We have the right vehicles.
- **C** Enough people want to go.

ii) What does the speaker say about sending human beings into space?
- **A** Spacecraft can't go into space without humans.
- **B** Spacecraft must not have human beings on board.
- **C** Spacecraft can go with or without humans.

iii) What example does the speaker give of a spacecraft which does not carry any passengers?
- **A** the Shuttle programme
- **B** communication satellites
- **C** the Space Station

iv) What is needed to make a spacecraft take off?
- **A** a rocket and gravity
- **B** tools and a satellite
- **C** a rocket and a launch pad

v) What is the most important reason why scientists want to explore space right now?
- **A** so they can discover other planets with vital minerals and metals
- **B** so they can find out about other planets and other life forms
- **C** so they can develop space tourism

GOING FURTHER

Just as when you read, sometimes you have to work out what a speaker means by using clues. When we talk to one another, we do not always 'spell out' exactly what we mean. In the same way, when you listen to a speaker, you have to be ready to understand what is implied but not directly stated.

(9) Listen to the text about space travel again. Answer the questions below in sentences.

a) Is the speaker positive or negative about what humans have achieved as regards space travel so far?

b) Explain two ways in which the speaker seems very hopeful for the future possibilities of space exploration.

In pairs, discuss your answers and explain which clues led you to these answers. In other words, what did you hear that helped you understand what was being implied?

The big task

Imagine that there is a competition to design a new transport system for your town or city. You are going to work in a group to design an entry. You have to produce a leaflet which presents your idea, lists its advantages and explains why it is needed.

(1) What factors do you think are important for the new transport system? Here are some ideas:

*cheap   environmentally friendly   made of sustainable materials
convenient   safe   quick   healthy   easy to make   easy to use*

Think about these and other ideas and make some notes.

(2) Working in groups, talk about ideas for a new form of transport. Try to agree on:
- what features are the most important
- what type of material it should be made from (e.g. metals, plastics, carbon-fibre, sustainable materials, recycled materials)
- what form of energy it should use.

You will need to draw up a list of possibilities and discuss which ones are the most suitable.

You can use the internet and other resources to get ideas and conduct research. You could also create an image of your chosen form of transport.

(3) As a group, produce a leaflet for your competition entry. This will need to tell people how good your idea is and why. You will need to:
- say what is wrong with the existing forms
- describe your proposal and say how it works – use diagrams and plans if necessary
- explain why it is a good idea by listing its advantages.

(4) Present your ideas to the class. Be prepared to explain your design and answer questions about it.

Check your progress

Here are the Reading, Writing, Speaking and Listening skills you learned about in Chapter 9.

Use this table to decide how good you are at the different skills, and make a note of what you need to be able to do in order to move up a level.

READING
I can …

consistently understand the opinions expressed in texts, including the more complex ones

securely recognise the language used to express opinions and understand what is implied but not directly stated

understand the opinions expressed in a range of different kinds of texts

recognise the language used to express opinions and understand some of what is implied but not directly stated

understand some basic opinions expressed in straightforward texts

identify the language used to express opinions and understand literal meanings

WRITING
I can …

use a wide variety of structures effectively when writing descriptions

use a variety of connectives, including relative pronouns, securely to good effect when writing

use some different structures when writing descriptions

use some different connectives, including relative pronouns, to link ideas and sentences

use some basic structures when writing descriptions

use some basic connectives and understand how relative pronouns link ideas and sentences

SPEAKING
I can …

confidently use a variety of grammatical structures accurately when speaking

confidently and accurately vary the tenses of verbs I use, according to situations

use a variety of grammatical structures with reasonable accuracy when speaking

use some different tenses when speaking, though I may make errors when I try to be ambitious

use some straightforward grammatical structures when speaking

use some basic tenses well enough to be understood

LISTENING
I can …

understand connections and differences between related ideas in quite complex listening texts when answering multiple-choice questions accurately

usually understand what is implied but not directly stated

understand some connections and differences between related ideas in listening texts when answering multiple-choice questions

understand some of what is implied but not directly stated

understand a few connections and differences between related ideas in straightforward listening texts when answering multiple-choice questions with a little success

answer some straightforward questions about literal meanings

THE BIG PICTURE

Fashion is all around us: from the street to magazines to what everyone around us is wearing. In this chapter you will consider the importance of clothing, what is meant by 'fashion', how it expresses who we are and the rich, beautiful, cultural differences that make fashion what it is.

THINKING BIG

1 Look carefully at the photos and pick the two that interest you most. What questions would you like to ask about each? Make notes on each one, using these questions as prompts.

a) Which time periods are the photos from?

b) Can you identify the people in the photos?

c) Can you identify the country or culture represented in the photos?

d) Why does the picture interest you?

2 Consider the following and then write about:

- an item of clothing, shoes or jewellery that is special or lucky for you

- how your style of dress reflects your culture.

3 Now read the following quotes. Explain to your partner what you find interesting or about them. What do you learn about each speaker from their words?

> *I did not have three thousand pairs of shoes. I had one thousand and sixty.* Imelda Marcos

> *A fashion is merely a form of ugliness so unbearable that we are compelled to alter it every six months.* Oscar Wilde

> *I don't do fashion, I am fashion.* Coco Chanel

> *They think him the best-dressed man, whose dress is so fit for his use that you cannot notice or remember to describe it.* Ralph Waldo Emerson

> *I don't design clothes. I design dreams.* Ralph Lauren

> *Fashion is what you adopt when you don't know who you are* Quentin Crisp

10
Fashion

10.1 Fashion and fabric

In this section you will learn to:

✓ find facts and details from complex texts that present information in different forms

✓ understand and use information presented in different forms.

GETTING STARTED

1 Fashion can be a great way to be creative and artistic, but the desire to be 'in fashion' can also have negative effects. Think about the following points and note down your thoughts:

- The ways people use natural products such as silk and cotton, and where they come from.

- Whether fashion puts pressure on people to spend money and change the way they look.

- What part fashion plays in climate change.

EXPLORING THE SKILLS

The life cycle of a T-shirt

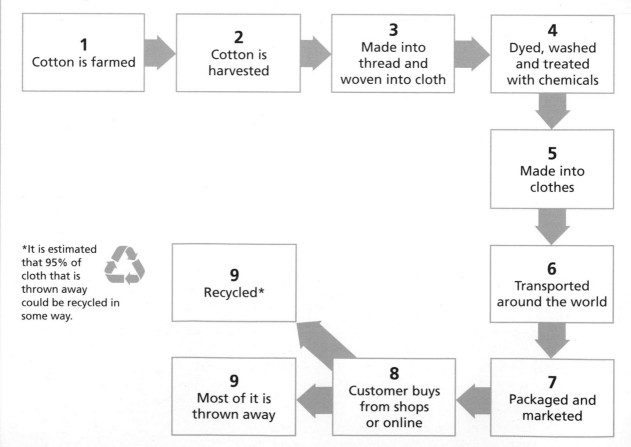

1 Cotton is farmed	**2** Cotton is harvested

3 Made into thread and woven into cloth

4 Dyed, washed and treated with chemicals

5 Made into clothes

6 Transported around the world

7 Packaged and marketed

8 Customer buys from shops or online

9 Most of it is thrown away

9 Recycled*

*It is estimated that 95% of cloth that is thrown away could be recycled in some way.

Information in texts can be presented in different forms, such as diagrams, maps, flow charts or timelines. Being able to read and understand information presented in different ways helps you to understand complex texts.

Look at the flow chart on the previous page which summarises the life cycle of a T-shirt. To find information in the flow chart:

- Look for labels and arrows that explain the different stages of the process.
- Notice the direction of the arrows.
- Notice the shape of the flow chart. Does it go in a full circle or not?

2 Cotton is the most used natural fibre in the world. Look at the flow chart and answer the questions.

a) At which step does cotton move from the farm to the factory?

b) Non-natural things get added to cotton. Which step is this?

c) At which steps in the process can people affect the life cycle of a T-shirt?

3 Silk is another natural material but it is a lot more expensive to produce than cotton. It is one of the most valuable and luxurious fashion fabrics in the world. Read the text and diagram below to answer the questions on the next page.

How Silk is Made

The tiny silkworm is the caterpillar of the silk moth. Its life begins as an egg laid by the adult moth. Larvae (caterpillars) emerge from the eggs and are then known as silkworms. They survive by eating the leaves of the mulberry tree.

To become a moth, the silkworm spins a protective cocoon around itself so it can safely transform into a chrysalis. The chrysalis then breaks through the cocoon and emerges as a moth.

Once the silkworm has spun its cocoon, the chrysalis inside is destroyed by plunging it in hot water before it can break out of the cocoon. This is to ensure that the valuable silk filament remains intact. To make one yard of silk material, approximately 3000 cocoons are used.

The cocoon is soaked in hot water to kill the chrysalis.

The silk is threaded from the cocoon onto a wheel.

Crepe de chine

Crepe

The thread is washed, dried and twisted to make different fabrics.

GLOSSARY

cocoon the silky protective covering of a silkworm

chrysalis the hard protective covering that protects a caterpillar when it is transforming into a moth or butterfly

emerge come out of a closed space

intact not changed or damaged in any way

filament a very thin piece or thread

a) What does the caterpillar eat?

b) What comes out of the eggs laid by the moth?

c) Why does the silkworm weave a cocoon around itself?

d) What would naturally happen to the cocoon of the silkworm?

e) What is different about cocoons raised for silk?

f) Looking at the diagram, explain the purpose of the wheel in silk-making.

g) Why are the cocoons soaked in hot water?

h) Summarise in 50 words the process of silk-making from the diagram. Use your own words as far as possible.

DEVELOPING THE SKILLS

Sometimes writers find it useful to use timelines to clarify what they mean.

4 Read the text below and answer the questions that follow.

Silkworm cocoons

The Story of Silk

According to Chinese legend, Lady Hsi-Ling Shih is the Goddess of Silk. The stories say she was the wife of the Yellow Emperor, who ruled China in about 3000 BC. People believe that she discovered silk when a silkworm in its cocoon fell into her cup of tea. In the hot tea, the cocoon fell apart and she saw that it was made of a single thread. She then introduced silkworm farming and invented the loom.

Traders first sell silk in Rome.

Silkworm farms appear outside China, in Asia.

3000 BC Silk is made in China.

750 BC Rome is founded.

0   100 AD 200 AD 300 AD 400 AD 500 AD 600 AD

Countries in Asia start making silk cloth from Chinese silk thread.

Silkworm farms appear in Europe.

Silk was so important for China that they kept their methods secret for about 2000 years. The Chinese made a fortune from trading silk for precious stones, sandalwood and metals along the Silk Road. It is believed that traders would pay up to 600 grams of gold for a high quality length of silk. Eventually the secret got out, probably because of Chinese travellers to other countries. One story says that a Chinese princess around 300–400 AD hid silkworm cocoons in her hair when she went to India to marry a prince there.

No one knows if these stories are true. But we do know that silk was invented in China and there is evidence that fits the dates in the legends. Scientists have dated silk found wrapped around bodies in Henan province to around 5500 years old.

a) How did the Chinese Empress discover silk?

b) What else do people believe she did to develop silk-making?

c) Why do you think the Chinese wanted to keep silk-making a secret?

d) How did silk-making spread to other countries?

e) How old is the oldest silk we have found?

 GLOSSARY **loom** a machine for weaving cloth

GOING FURTHER

When you are faced with complex texts that include diagrams and dates, it can be useful to simplify them, in your own words, to understand them better. This is a helpful study technique for all your subjects.

5 Look at the information you have collected on cotton and silk. As a class, create a colourful poster for younger students which:

- EITHER explains how silk is made OR describes the life cycle of cotton clothes
- uses a diagram or flowchart with simple illustrations to make the information easy to understand
- answers frequently asked questions (FAQs) about silk or cotton.

Do your own research to add to what you already know about silk or cotton. Present information in a variety of ways, including diagrams, and use your own words.

TOP TIP Note that you will be using the present tense when you are talking about the process of silk-making. However, you will be using the past tense to talk about historical events in the past, such as the silk trade in ancient times.

10.2 Teenage fashion

In this section you will learn to:
✓ use a range of appropriate vocabulary in your writing
✓ use formal and informal vocabulary appropriately.

GETTING STARTED

1 Look at photos of fashion in the past or in different parts of the world. Match the vocabulary below with the relevant photo.

a) bell-bottom trousers   **e)** salwar kameez

b) maxi dress   **f)** sari

c) drain-pipe trousers   **g)** jumpsuit

d) bandana   **h)** cowboy boots

EXPLORING THE SKILLS

Building a wide and varied vocabulary is the key to sounding like an expert on a subject.

When you come across new vocabulary, try the following:
- Guess what the word means from its **context** – the words around it.
- Identify the form of the word – is it a noun, verb, adjective or adverb?
- Look for picture clues that might tell you what the word means.
- See if you can make sense of what the word might mean from its description. For example, *cut-off jeans* and *hipster trousers* both have clues that might help you guess their meaning.
- Look out for **metaphors** or **similes** used to describe fashion.
  For example: *The **cupcake** bridesmaid dress is strictly out of fashion. The skirt tends to stick out **like an upside-down plastic flower**.*

LANGUAGE BOOSTER

A **metaphor** is an imaginative way of describing one thing as another, e.g. *Sheets of rain* poured down the windowpanes. *Armies of dark clouds* gathered menacingly on the horizon, promising more rain.

A **simile** is a comparison in which a person or thing is described as being similar to another. Similes normally use the words 'like' or 'as', e.g. *His teeth are as white as pearls. The dress fits like a glove.*

(2) Quickly write down some useful vocabulary for today's fashion – clothes, hairstyles, shoes. Now let's look at a social media post from a fashion influencer talking about what they're wearing.

As you read, note down specific nouns and verbs related to fashion and style.

Hey, it's Friday, it's not quite winter yet and it's time to rock the animal print for the office! Leopard print is bang on trend. Team it with a block colour to break it up, like I am here with these classic wide-leg trousers in forest green. Add some height with this season's must-have chunky-heeled boots. A neutral polo-neck jumper under the jacket stops the look from being too busy. Tie back hair into a smooth ponytail for low effort but high style. Keep accessories simple – sunglasses, check! earth-tone bag, check! – and let the prints do the talking!
#GetTheLook #Autumn #Fashion #Style #LeopardPrint

GLOSSARY

block colour	all one colour with no pattern
check	another word for a tick mark that says you have already got or done something
earth-tone	a colour that's like one found in nature, such as light brown

LANGUAGE BOOSTER

Note these other aspects of the influencer's style.
- Written in the present tense to express the immediate, 'here and now' feel of the post, which is about this moment in time: *It's Friday, it's not quite winter yet*
- Uses imperative verbs to give advice: *Team it with..., Add some....*
- Has a light, casual tone and uses informal vocabulary: *Sunglasses, check!*
- Uses hashtags with key words at the end: *#Autumn, #Style*

(3) The influencer uses key adjectives, such as *simple*. What do *bang on trend*, *classic* and *busy* mean in the context of fashion? Write a short explanation for each.

DEVELOPING THE SKILLS

Social media posts are examples of writing in an informal friendly style. This is because influencers want their audience to feel like they're 'talking to' a friend.

- Informal writing can start with a casual greeting like *Hi* or *Hey*

- Informal writing may use more exclamation marks. How many can you find in the influencer's post?

LANGUAGE BOOSTER Fashion writing uses specific words and expressions. Match the words from the influencer's post with their meanings. Then try to use them in your own writing.

1	To rock	a	clothing, shoes, hair and accessories together
2	To team with	b	make [something] the main focus
3	To add some height	c	to make yourself look taller
4	A look	d	to put together with
5	Let [something] do the talking	e	to wear proudly

(4) Now write a short social media post of about 120 words describing a look that is in fashion now or that you like.

First, find a photo you can describe. You can use a picture of yourself if you feel comfortable doing that.

Make sure you...

- describe the complete look: clothes, shoes and hair
- use adjectives, present tense and imperatives
- choose hashtags that make sense with your post

Your post should have the same informal, friendly tone as the one on the previous page and use vocabulary appropriate for fashion. You could begin:

'Check out this must-have outfit...'

GLOSSARY **check out** (informal) have a look at

GOING FURTHER

It is important to choose words that give your writing the right tone. This will depend on why you are writing and for whom. A formal piece of writing needs formal vocabulary. So, although you may want to say *white socks are really uncool these days*, in a formal style you would write: *white socks are no longer considered fashionable, except for sport*. Notice how the passive makes the second sentence sound more formal: *'are no longer considered'*.

(5) Below are some examples of informal language used in blogs or in spoken language. Copy the table and fill in the gaps for both formal and informal language.

Informal/spoken/blog language	Formal language for a serious context
Check out...	Look carefully at...
	Dresses will be longer and sleeves are wider.
	Denim jackets are an extremely popular fashion item this year.
Get yourself some chunky heels asap!	
Get the new look!	
	Teaming a plain outfit with accessories is often the cheapest way to make it new again.
Silk shirts to die for!	
A look that works for day and evening – office to restaurant, just like that!	

(6) Read the situation below and then write the letter.

Until now your school/workplace has had a flexible, casual dress code. However, the new principal/boss has decided that neither staff nor students are allowed to wear denim in any form, at any time. You think that this is unfair as well as inconvenient.

Write a polite letter to the principal/boss in which you:

- explain the benefits of wearing denim, for example: *Jeans match with everything, wash easily and last a long time.*

- give evidence of how denim is popular worldwide, for example: *Surely you have noticed that denim is now accepted as a sensible and smart option around the world. Even Barack Obama, when he was the President of the United States, was photographed wearing denim.*

- make clear that more extreme denim fashions wouldn't be acceptable, for example: *Ripped jeans will not be worn.*

TOP TIP
You are writing a formal letter to the management of your organisation. Keep your language formal and accurate.

10.3 Clothes and culture

In this section you will learn to:

✓ use the right words when speaking about culture and clothing

✓ use more specialised vocabulary appropriately.

GETTING STARTED

1 Culture can be defined as the combination of language, art, food, literature, clothing, music and ideas that are special to a particular part of the world. Fashion is therefore one part of culture.

In pairs, think about the following questions about what people wear and note down ideas or information that is new to you.

● What styles of hair or clothing is fashionable at the moment amongst your friends?

● What clothes do people typically wear to formal occasions where you live?

● Is there a traditional or national dress where you live? If so, what is it?

● What colours of clothing are significant to particular occasions? For example, black is worn to funerals in some parts of the world while white is worn in others. Some brides wear white to their wedding while others wear red or vibrant colours.

EXPLORING THE SKILLS

To talk about clothes and culture, it's important to learn specific vocabulary as well as more general vocabulary about clothes.

2 In pairs, consider the following culture- or country-specific words to do with clothing and match them with the relevant photo:

a) sarong

b) jodhpurs

c) kimono

d) beret

e) kilt

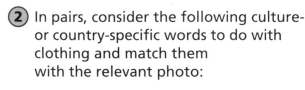

(3) Vocabulary can also be categorised into groups of similar words. Look at the lists of words below related to culture and clothing.

Headwear: turbans, crowns, tiaras, feathered hats, bowler hats, peaked hats, helmets, fur-lined hood, berets, bonnets, headscarves, veils.

Styles of clothing: flared, tapered, gathered, baggy, fitted, high-waisted, low-slung, hipster, full-skirted, tight-fitting, loose-fitting.

In groups of three, take turns to quickly draw one of the clothing items from the list above while the others guess what it is. Give a time limit of 30 seconds for each drawing. If you are unsure of meanings, check them in a dictionary.

(4) Add your own words to the categories above and explain them to each other. Are some of these special to your own or another culture?

DEVELOPING THE SKILLS

(5) Read the text below, which explains some reasons for wearing different types of clothing. Discuss it with your partner.

Clothing is so much more than just a covering for our bodies or protection from the environment. Clothing can represent who we are, what we believe and even how we worship. Some cultures and civilisations define themselves through their clothing.

Of course, choices of clothing are also based on factors like gender, climate and geographical location. As we know from old paintings and photographs, clothing is constantly changing over time to reflect the needs of our lifestyles. Clothing is also worn for more complex reasons, for example, to show membership of a group like a basketball team. Some types of clothing are worn only at special ceremonies, like a graduation cap and gown or a wedding dress. Some clothing is worn to indicate emotions, such as joy or sorrow. Different cultures believe different colours are appropriate for mourning.

Some cultures have distinctive clothing that is associated with them. Silk kimonos are Japanese, saris are Indian and kilts are associated with the Scots. Fashion and traditional clothing can help us understand the people who wear them, as well as their cultural beliefs and values.

(6) Work in groups to prepare notes for a short talk for your class on describing a specific type of clothing in your region or culture.

- Name and describe the item.

- How does this particular type of clothing differ by gender?

- Explain the origin of this form of clothing: religious, cultural, climate, environment, group membership or ceremonial.

(7) Now identify any gaps in this information and agree together on how you will gain information to fill these. For example, each of you could take responsibility for one type of clothing. Remember first-hand sources around you might be more reliable than internet searches. Think about teachers, parents, support staff, grandparents and family members that you could ask.

(8) As a group, prepare to give the talk to the rest of your class, making sure you divide up the speaking equally. You could bring in items of clothing or pictures to illustrate your presentation.

(9) Choose a piece of clothing to show to the class which you think represents a particular culture, for example a robe, a piece of headwear, jewellery or a scarf. Either bring it in to the next lesson or find a picture to present. Think about the best vocabulary to describe the item and be prepared to answer questions about it. Remember to cover each of these questions when you describe the item:

- What?
- When?
- Who?
- Where?
- Why?
- How?

GOING FURTHER

Intonation is the rise and fall of your voice when you speak. Using intonation correctly when you ask and answer questions is a key skill. The better your intonation, the better you will be able to express what you want to say and the easier it will be for the listener to understand you.

The 'Wh-' words (*What, When, Who, Where, Why*) and '*How*' are useful when asking questions.

(10) Listen to the following questions and decide if the **intonation** is falling or rising:

- When did you get your new trainers?
- Your school football team wears red and white, doesn't it?
- What's the first belt colour in karate?
- I hate wearing tights in our dance classes.
- Do you have to wear a swimming cap in competitions?

Asking open ('wh' or 'how' questions), which require information: usually falling intonation.

- *Where did you buy your new sports kit?*

Asking closed ('do/'does' or 'tag' questions), which require a 'Yes/No' response: rising intonation.

- *Do you like your school team's colours?*
- *The national cricket team in your country wears blue, doesn't it?*

Answering questions with simple statements: falling intonation.

- *No, I don't like wearing a skirt to play tennis.*

Answering questions with complex statements: rising intonation then falling at the end.

- *I think my new cycling shorts are comfortable, practical and stylish.*

(11) You are going to hear part of a presentation by a sportswear designer.

10.2

- Why do you think the presenter asks questions during his talk
- What intonation does he use for each one?

(12) Listen again and prepare four questions that you would like to ask the presenter at the end of his talk. Use these words or phrases to construct your question:

Where...?　　When...?　　How...?　　Why...?
What...?　　...isn't it?　　...doesn't it?

Now work in pairs to practise asking the questions and inventing answers. Remember to use the correct intonation.

(13) Work in groups to prepare notes for a short talk for your class on fashion and brands in sportswear.

Group A: in favour of people wearing branded sportswear.

Group B: against people wearing branded sportswear.

As you listen to each group's talk, prepare questions to ask them at the end of their presentation.

10.4 The price of fashion: who pays?

In this section you will learn to:
✓ listen effectively to fellow students
✓ understand and select detailed information supplied by fellow students
✓ understand what is implied but not directly stated in a conversation.

GETTING STARTED

1 Although fashion is a popular and rich aspect of our culture, the modern fashion industry can sometimes exploit both people and the environment in its search for luxury and low-cost products.

In pairs or threes, discuss what you know and what you think about one of the following issues related to the fashion industry:

● the impact that making, buying and throwing away clothes has on the environment

● workers being paid an unfair wage relative to the profits made by big fashion companies.

Now make a note of some questions for a group to answer on the other topic. They will do the same for you. Try to answer their questions and highlight any points that you will need to research as a group.

EXPLORING THE SKILLS

In the last task you had to listen carefully to what your fellow students were saying. You used this information to help you learn more and see where there were gaps in your knowledge. Together, you had to write some notes. To do this, you needed to:

- listen attentively

- ask questions – to make them explain things in more detail when you were unsure – and listen carefully to the questions they asked you

- make use of as wide a vocabulary as possible.

Did you have to use any other skills?

2 Now you will work together on a listening task. You are going to hear a news story about an environmental-rights group, Earth Friends, speaking out against fast fashion. 10.3

Answer these multiple-choice questions. Choose the option that you think best answers each question.

a) Earth Friends believes that the major fashion brands only care about:
   A the cost of producing clothes
   B the quality of their clothes
   C the health of the workers

b) Why does the representative from the fashion industry think that it's not fair to make life difficult for customers?
   A because the environment is less important than having freedom to buy clothes
   B because not everyone can afford to buy high quality clothes
   C because so many people want to buy clothes made out of fur

c) What is her biggest positive point about the fashion industry?
   A there is a lot of demand for clothes
   B people can choose which shops they want to buy from
   C it gives jobs to people

d) Which word best sums up the environmental activist's attitude to fast fashion:
   A uncaring
   B realistic
   C angry

3 Listen to the news story again and answer the questions below.

a) What did the protestors do to attract attention?

b) What was the first protester shocked by when they investigated clothes factories? Give two details.

c) Do the Earth Friends protestor and the representative from the fashion industry agree on anything? If so, what?

4 In pairs, discuss your answers to question 3. Now listen again to check your answers.

DEVELOPING THE SKILLS

'Sweatshop' is a slang (very informal) word that is used to describe factories where people (often women and children) work under difficult working conditions. They get paid very low wages and have no medical care. They often do not have unions or ways of complaining. A lot of fashionable clothes are made in sweatshops around the world.

5 You are now going to work together again. Divide into two groups. Group A reads points 1 to 4 of the Facts About Fast Fashion. Group B reads points 5 to 8. Discuss the meaning of the words in bold and be ready to summarise your information in your own words.

Fast Facts About Fashion

1. Sweatshops are found all over the world, including in countries like the UK and USA.
2. 85–90% of sweatshop workers are women. Children are also forced to work in sweatshops and there are as many as 168 million child **labourers**, in different industries, aged 5–14.
3. Fast fashion relies on selling very high numbers of very cheap clothes in styles that change from week to week. Huge, online **budget** clothes brands could not exist without sweatshops keeping **production costs** low.
4. Fast fashion is also cheap because it uses chemicals to grow cotton and destroys clothes it can't sell because it costs less than **storing** or recycling them.

> Group A

5. Research showed that if sweatshop workers were paid twice as much, it would only add 1.8% to the price of the clothes.
6. **Surveys** of shoppers suggest they would happily pay up to 15% more to be sure clothes came from factories that were not sweatshops.
7. The Fashionchecker, a research organisation, looked at 250 fashion brands and found that 93% of them are not paying their workers enough to live on. The brands include famous high street shops and **luxury designers**, as well as online brands.
8. A survey showed that 1 in 3 young people feel like a piece of clothing is old if they've worn it once or twice.

> Group B

6 Now work in pairs, one person from Group A and one person from Group B, and give a summary of your Fast Fashion Facts.

GOING FURTHER

Good listeners understand what other people may imply but not say directly. This is probably most important when you are listening to people who have different points of view.

You need to pay attention to the tone they use, their body language and, above all, to their language and their choice of words.

7 You are going to listen to two students talking about sweatshops and what they can do to prevent companies taking advantage of people who desperately need a job.

Take a look at the questions before listening to the recording.

First read questions a) to d).

a) Why is Celine glad to put her phone down and have a coffee?

b) Name two things that Celine has bought.

c) How does Celine feel about her shopping?

d) How does Celine feel about the amount of money she has spent?

Now listen to the first part of their conversation.

 10.4

Discuss your answers in pairs.

Listen to the recording again. Which phrases made you use clues to understand what is implied (meant but not stated directly)?

8 Read the next questions before listening to the rest of their conversation.

a) What is Barry annoyed by first of all?

b) What really shocks him even more?

c) How much might some sweatshop workers get paid per day?

d) What is the key phrase used to describe a certain group of customers, for example, a particular age group?

e) Why does Celine think they should be careful when contacting companies?

f) What is Celine's idea to get more public support against sweatshops?

g) How does Celine feel about the campaign that she and Barry will start?

Now listen to the whole conversation and answer the questions. 10.5

Check your answers. Put a star by the ones where you had to understand what was implied but not directly stated. Listen to the whole conversation a second time.

Check your answers.

The big task

You are going to organise a unique fashion show. You will present clothes that represent your very own style and your opinions on fashion.

1 First, read this flyer and summarise the main points quickly for your classmates.

Welcome to:

'Be Yourself' – a fashion show with a difference!

'Be Yourself' is organised by a group of teenagers interested in culture, art and design. We are aspiring designers, graphic artists and fashion enthusiasts who would like to see a forum for their work and that of their peer group. We want to give young people the chance to show just who they are, how they feel and the things that express their creative talent in a marvellous fusion of fashion, culture and teen couture.

Being a 'fashion show with a difference', we would like you to be careful to steer away from the following negative fashion issues – fashions that:

◆ promote the 'cult of skinniness' either through choice of models or styles: we are looking for healthy teenagers of all shapes and sizes and the aim is to look and feel good

◆ use animal fur or fur trim in any form

◆ promote the products or use of sweatshop brands.

(N.B. Any entries that have or promote these will not make it to the final competition.)

So, what is likely to impress judges? Here are some examples that have impressed our judges in the past:

◆ colours and textures that are thrown together in new and exciting ways

◆ designs and styles for people with all body types aged between 14 and 21 (feel free to enter different designs for different age groups)

◆ designs that promote fair employment and fair trade for all producers

◆ sustainable green designs that use natural and biodegradable fabrics and materials

◆ designs that reuse old garments to promote sustainable fashion.

2 Now that the formalities are over, here's what you need to do to get cracking on your own fashion show.

● Get your design team together – four designers are ideal for four to six design ideas. Sign up as above.

● Draw or sketch your fashions or put them together for real.

● Write your own commentary/voiceover for the show, describing and explaining your design/fashion item. Each entry must include the following:
  – a descriptive statement about the outfit
  – an explanation of what inspired it
  – why it is innovative/versatile/practical.

Check your progress

Here are the Reading, Writing, Speaking and Listening skills you learned about in Chapter 10.

Use this table to decide how good you are at the different skills, and make a note of what you need to be able to do in order to move up a level.

READING

I can …

consistently and accurately locate facts and details in complex texts containing graphics

sometimes find facts and details in a range of texts containing graphics

find a few facts and details in straightforward texts containing basic graphics

WRITING

I can …

make effective use of a good range of vocabulary, including comparatives and superlatives, in my writing

consistently use formal or informal vocabulary appropriately according to reader and purpose

use a fair range of vocabulary, including comparatives and superlatives, in my writing

distinguish formal and informal vocabulary and attempt to choose the right word according to reader and situation

use a limited vocabulary, including basic comparatives and superlatives, in my writing

use informed vocabulary, but do not adapt my choice of words according to reader and purpose

SPEAKING

I can …

use a good range of specialist vocabulary accurately and confidently when speaking

use some specialist vocabulary correctly when speaking

use a basic range of vocabulary when speaking

LISTENING

I can …

consistently listen thoughtfully to other students and can understand and select information accurately from what they say

usually understand what is implied but not directly stated in a conversation

listen to other students attentively, so that I can understand and select information from what they say

understand some of what is implied but not directly stated in a conversation

listen to other students politely, so that I understand and pick out a few details correctly from what they say

understand what is said during straightforward conversations

THE BIG PICTURE

In this chapter you will:

- think about what you do to amuse yourself
- hear about, read about and write about some favourite forms of entertainment
- consider other people's favourite forms of entertainment.

THINKING BIG

1 In pairs, look at the photos and discuss them.

- What forms of entertainment do they show?
- Create a list of all the forms of entertainment you can think of.
- Which forms of entertainment are the most expensive?
- Which forms of entertainment are the most popular in your country?

2 In pairs, explain your usual forms of entertainment. Give details of:

- what you like to do
- when you do it
- why you like it.

3 Draw a pie chart to show the balance between the time you spend studying and relaxing or playing. It should look something like this. Do you spend most of your relaxing/playing time looking at a screen? How much screen time do you have?

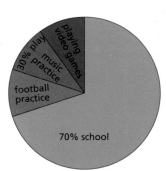

4 In groups, discuss whether you agree with this quote when you think about your study/play balance.

❝Anyone who tries to make a distinction between education and entertainment doesn't know the first thing about either.❞
Marshal McLuhan, Educator, Writer and Social Reformer, 1911–1980

11 Entertainment

11.1 Music

READING SKILLS IN FOCUS

In this section you will learn to:

✓ understand and select relevant information

✓ identify points for and against a point of view in a text

✓ recognise a point of view when it is implied and not directly stated.

GETTING STARTED

In pairs, discuss what types of music you enjoy listening to. Do you play an instrument?

EXPLORING THE SKILLS

Articles for magazines and newspapers often try to build a balanced argument by giving both reasons for and against an issue. When you are reading it is useful to be able to:

- identify the reasons given

- decide if they are for or against an issue

- decide yourself whether the reasons given are valid.

(1) Although it means not owning music, lots of people are happy to stream it instead. In pairs, discuss the following questions. Find out where you agree and disagree with each other.

- How do you usually get your music?

- How much is a CD in your country? How much does it cost to stream music? Are either of the prices 'too expensive'?

(2) You are going to read a newspaper article about streaming music. Before you read, with your partner, brainstorm and then copy and complete the table below with all the reasons you can think of:

- for streaming music

- against streaming music.

For	Against
People can listen to anything they want	Many artists don't earn much from their music

3 Read the article and answer the questions.

- Which paragraph introduces the discussion, which argues for and which against?

- Write down the main idea (the main reason for or against) in each paragraph.

- Add the reasons for and against to the table you created in task 2.

TO STREAM OR NOT TO STREAM?

Streaming music from the internet is fast replacing owning music. As long as you have an internet connection, you can listen to music for free (with adverts interrupting the songs) or pay a monthly fee that's less than a CD. That's great for music fans, and for musicians. Even new artists without a record deal can reach global audiences. This 'democracy' has almost certainly helped music like K-pop travel beyond a local audience in Korea to win major music awards in America and Europe.

Moreover, streaming solves one of the music industry's biggest problems: piracy. Before streaming, artists were losing millions as people illegally downloaded their music for free. Now fans can listen to any music they want, without breaking the law, and artists earn royalties each time their song is played.

However, musicians are forced to accept tiny royalty payments. It has been estimated that artists earn about $3 per 1000 streams while the music industry makes as much as $1.8 billion in profit. If musicians can't survive by creating music, then their future looks as uncertain as it did when piracy was their biggest problem.

DEVELOPING THE SKILLS

There are some signals that a writer is giving you a reason to support or oppose an argument. Often they will use phrases that structure the reasons. For example:

Reasons supporting	Reasons opposing/against
On the one hand	In contrast
Moreover	However
Furthermore	On the other hand
Firstly, Secondly	
Since	
In view of the fact that	

4 You are going to read a newspaper article which discusses whether classical music is still relevant to young people today. Before reading, in pairs:

- Discuss and choose the best two synonyms for 'relevant'.

  - meaningful
  - useful
  - significant
  - important
  - practical
  - popular

- Discuss your experience of classical music. Talk about opportunities to:

  - take part in an orchestra or choir at school
  - listen to classical music.

5 Read the article below. Identify the paragraphs (labelled A to G) that give reasons for and against. Complete the diagram with the reasons.

A Many people believe that classical music is not relevant to young people today. However, this issue frequently generates heated debate.

B On the one hand, many people say that classical music is associated only with small numbers of people from privileged backgrounds and older people. For instance, if you look at the audience at a classical concert, the majority is over the age of fifty.

C In contrast, others say it is more popular than we first imagine. Many young people listen to classical music without realising. It is often used in films and advertisements. For example, a famous piece of classical music was used as the theme music for the 1990 Fifa World Cup. Not many people could have given its name – 'Nessun Dorma' – but millions recognised it and, more importantly, enjoyed it.

D Also, some people point out that young people reinvent classical ideas to produce new music: for instance, some people claim that rap developed from the music of a classical composer, Arnold Schoenberg (1874–1951).

E However, young people point to the fact that classical music has been outstripped by technology. To play a classical instrument, such as a violin or cello, you need to study hard and practise for hours. Nowadays, you do not need to get aching arms and blisters on your fingers from practising. A teenager can write and produce a professional-sounding track using a computer program in the comfort of their own bedroom.

F A final point to bear in mind is that the term 'classical music' can be used to refer to a dazzling variety of music, from jazz to pieces for large orchestras. This makes it even more difficult to say whether classical music is relevant to young people.

Reasons against

G So, it may be only a minority of young people who play classical instruments, but when it comes to enjoying classical music – well, it depends on the piece of music. It may be more relevant to young people in the modern world than they realise!

Associated with privileged backgrounds and old people, classical music is still relevant to young people today

Reasons for

More popular than realise

IS CLASSICAL MUSIC RELEVANT TO YOUNG PEOPLE?

6 In pairs, copy three reasons from task 5 – it doesn't matter whether they are for or against – into the table and complete with the supporting evidence.

Reason	Supporting evidence
More popular than people imagine, many young people listen to classical music without realising	Classical music is often used in films and advertisements – used as the theme music to the World Cup in 1990

7 In pairs, discuss these questions.
- if you think the article gives a 'balanced' view
- which of the reasons given were the most persuasive for you and why.

GOING FURTHER

We often need to be able to work out someone's opinion even when they do not state it directly. For example:

> *The band strutted on stage but only managed to sing three songs.*

Poor opinion: the word *only* implies that three songs is not enough.

Here is another example:

> *The band strutted on stage and wowed the audience from the first minute with the stunning power of their guitar playing.*

Good opinion: the words *wowed* and *stunning* are strong positive words.

8 Read this series of texts between two friends about a karaoke evening.

What is the opinion of each friend about the following?
- the singing
- the food
- the venue
- overall

Hi. Last night's karaoke evening. What did you think?

> *Had such a laugh. Nearly died laughing trying to sing Fantasy.*

But I didn't get a go!

> *How come?*

Not sure. None of my favourites on playlist. But still enjoyed it!

> *What did you think of the venue?*

Too many people chatting. It put me off performing.

> *Yes, but then everyone was dancing.*

Yes. I could have danced till dawn.

> *And food?*

Yum! Verdict?

> *Ten out of ten! When can we go again?*

11.2 Books, books, books

In this section you will learn to:
- ✓ communicate information clearly and accurately
- ✓ punctuate speech correctly
- ✓ use a wide range of punctuation correctly and effectively.

GETTING STARTED

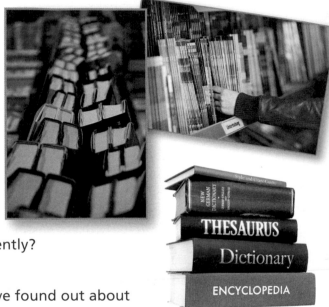

1 On your own, look at the photographs on this page. As a class, brainstorm and create a list of all the different types of reading texts you know.

2 In pairs, discuss the following questions. Listen carefully to what your partner says and make notes.

- When do you read?
- Where do you read?
- What do you read the most frequently?
- What do you like reading?

3 In groups of four, share what you have found out about your partner's reading habits.

EXPLORING THE SKILLS

Punctuation used correctly makes your writing clearer and easier to understand. Quotation marks are used to show the exact words that people say.

> *I prefer graphic novels.*

- You put the quotation marks around the words that someone says. For example: *"I prefer graphic novels,"* *said Lara.*
- When the spoken words come first, put a comma or question mark **inside** the speech marks after the last word spoken. For example:

  "What happened?" she asked.

- When the spoken words come last, put a comma before the first quotation mark. For example:

  The teacher said, "Everyone stand up."

- The speaker's first word uses a capital letter. For example:

  The sorcerer proclaimed, "Let the magic begin!"

- When a new person starts speaking, start a new line.

4 Write out these sentences, inserting quotation marks where necessary.

a) This book really inspires me said Hassan.

b) My best friend asked why don't you read this book?

c) Amina maintained books are better than television any day.

d) I cried at the ending because I found it so sad admitted my brother.

e) Bao Zhi added the suspense nearly killed me I couldn't put the book down!

5 You are going to write a short story about the world's most successful spy. Imagine the spy goes into the underground car park of an abandoned office block to meet the leader of a criminal gang. Describe what happens, writing two sentences about each of the following:

- what the gang members look like
- what the gang leader says to the spy (using direct speech)
- what the gang members say to each other (using reported speech)
- what the gang members decide to do with the spy (using direct speech)
- how the spy feels
- what the spy does next.

 LANGUAGE BOOSTER What people actually say is called **direct speech**. You put what people say inside the quotation marks.

When you tell what people said (for example, *Lara said that she prefers graphic novels*) this is called **reported speech**.

DEVELOPING THE SKILLS

Apostrophes are used to show that letters have been missed out (apostrophe for omission). For example:

We are reading a book.　　　　*We're reading a book.*

The apostrophe is also used to show that something belongs to someone (apostrophe for possession).

Use *'s* for a singular owner. For example:

The girl's writing is neat. (To show that the writing of one girl is neat.)

Use *s'* for plural owners. For example:

The girls' writing is neat. (To show that the writing of all the girls is neat.)

6 Put the apostrophe in the correct places in the following sentences.

a) Well write up our science experiment.

b) Borrow Yousefs textbook to read all the punctuation rules.

c) Mum says she cant take the book back to the library. Shes at work.

d) The girls writing is very similar to her brothers.

e) The boys bedrooms are very tidy. Theyve put all their clothes away.

(7) Alex Rider is a boy who is the world's most successful international spy. Copy the passage below, which comes from the Alex Rider series, where Alex discovers a dead man but is then kidnapped by a criminal gang. Insert quotation marks and apostrophes where necessary.

> And then there was a man standing in front of him. Alex looked up.
> Come with me the man said.
> What?
> The man opened his jacket, revealing a gun in a holster under his arm. You heard what I said.
> A second man had crept up behind him and dragged him to his feet. Both of them were in their thirties, clean-shaven with sunglasses. The man with the gun had spoken with an American accent.
> We have a car. Were going to walk you there. If you try anything, well shoot.
> Alex didnt doubt them. There was a seriousness about them, a sense that they knew exactly what they were doing. For a brief moment he considered a countermove. Right now, before it was too late, jabbing with an elbow then swinging round to kick out.
> But the first man had been expecting it. Suddenly Alexs arm was seized and twisted behind his back. Dont even think about it! the man warned.
> Alex was bundled into the waiting car.
>
> Extract from *Scorpia Rising*, by Anthony Horowitz

GOING FURTHER

Mistakes in punctuation and spelling make your writing difficult to read. You need to be able to use a wide range of punctuation marks, from full stops and capital letters to colons, brackets and pairs of commas. You need to use punctuation to help you express your ideas clearly.

The **semicolon** is used to contrast two sentences or ideas that are closely related. For example:

I like going to the cinema; I don't like watching TV.

The **colon** is used to introduce a list of items. For example:

I like the following types of entertainment: TV, film, music and board games.

Colons are also used to introduce people's words in a dialogue or interview. For example:

Reporter: What kind of things do you write?

Author: I usually write adventure or mystery stories.

Pairs of commas can be used to add more information to a sentence. The information between the commas is not essential, but adds more detail. For example:

Her father, who is retired, spends hours every day reading the newspapers.

Brackets (or **parentheses**) are also used to give extra information in a sentence. They set the information apart more strongly than commas do. For example:

The journalist wrote articles (often more than four a day) at an astonishing rate.

In this sentence the basic information is that the journalist wrote quickly. The fact that he wrote more than four articles a day is the extra information and is put in parentheses.

8 Rewrite the sentences below using colons, commas and full stops.

a) The following authors have won the Nobel Prize for literature Naguib Mahfouz, Doris Lessing and Orhan Pamuk

b) Literature covers a wide range of genres poetry drama novels and non-fiction

c) After writing the following need checking punctuation spelling and number of words

d) There are many types of fiction romance thriller science fiction horror historical fiction and the graphic novel

9 Write your own lists, introducing each list with a colon. Use full sentences.

a) Four recent books I have read

b) Four recent films I have seen

c) Games I play

10 Insert pairs of commas or parentheses around the extra information in the following sentences.

a) What is the value if any of studying literature?

b) The teacher told me in an excited voice that *The Theory of Code* was an excellent book.

c) The number of books available in schools, in libraries, on the internet is beyond counting.

11 As a class, create a list of recent reading. Then:

● Write a 100-word review of something you have read recently in class. It can be long (e.g. a novel) or short (e.g. a football report).

● Add a comment at the bottom of your review. For example:
The Hunger Games *by Suzanne Collins: "I was obsessed with this book," says Bassem.*

● Make a class display of all your recent reading.

12 Write a 250-word imaginary interview with your favourite writer.

● First, think about the type of books/texts your author writes.

● Decide what questions you want to ask. Use the key question words:
What   When   How   Why   Where

● Imagine the answers your author gives.

● Write up the interview, using colons to show each speaker. For example:
Reporter: What inspired you to start writing?

● Finally, check your work for:
punctuation   spelling   number of words used

 11.3 Television

In this section you will learn to:
✓ disagree politely in a conversation
✓ keep a conversation going by rephrasing what the previous speaker has said.

GETTING STARTED

(1) Nowadays lots of people use streaming services to watch TV. What types of programmes do you like to watch? Do you like comedies, documentaries, dramas, true crime shows or sport? As a class, find out the most watched TV programmes in the class.

- First, make a list of the kinds of programmes you watch. Then choose the top five most popular types of TV programmes.

- Each person in the class should tick the programme they watch the most.

- Make a class bar chart showing the most popular TV programmes in the class, like the example below.

- Give a brief talk using your bar chart.

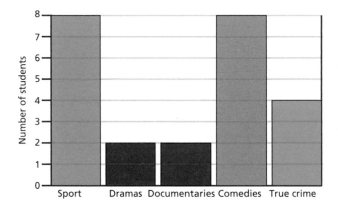

EXPLORING THE SKILLS

When disagreeing, try not to say 'no'. People will think you are impolite. Try instead to use one of the many polite ways of disagreeing.

(2) Read the list of phrases below, which express disagreement. In pairs, sort them into 'polite' and 'impolite'.

- I take your point, but that's not the way I see it.

- Perhaps, but I can't help thinking that …

- You must be joking!

- No thank you. I'd rather not.

- I see what you mean, but I'm not convinced that …

- That's rubbish.

- I'm not sure about that; however, what about …?

(3) Listen to the following short conversations. For each one: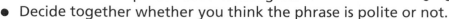
- Write down the phrase used to disagree.
- Decide together whether you think the phrase is polite or not.
- Add any new phrases to your list from task 2.

(4) Listen again and listen to the intonation of the speakers.

(5) Look at the phrases used for disagreeing politely in tasks 2 and 3 again and categorise these into the formal phrases, less formal phrases and informal phrases. When you use the phrases for disagreeing, think about who you are talking to and the situation.

Formal	Less formal	Informal
I take your point but that's not the way I see it.	Although what about…?	Maybe later.

DEVELOPING THE SKILLS

Remember that when you want to disagree or introduce your own (different) idea, there are many phrases you can use to disagree politely. Refer to the list you created for tasks 2 and 3.

(6) Imagine four young people who are flatmates and have all agreed to spend the evening together watching something together.
- In groups of four, take on the role of person A, B, C or D.
- Hold a polite conversation where you try to watch your chosen programme.

Person A

Wants to watch: live sport (a tennis match) tonight at 7pm.

Person B

Wants to watch: to **binge-watch** the latest **costume drama**.

Person C

Wants to watch: a **documentary** on **veganism**.

Person D

Wants to watch: the live broadcast of Glastonbury Festival that starts at 8pm.

GLOSSARY		
live television	when an event or performance is broadcast at exactly the same time as it happens
binge-watch	watch several episodes of a programme one after another in a short time
costume drama	a drama in which the actors wear costumes from a particular time in history
documentary	a TV or radio programme or film which shows real events or provides information about a particular subject
veganism	someone who practises veganism does not use any animal product for food, clothing, etc.
screen time	time spent using a device with a screen, such as a phone, tablet or television

(7) In groups of four, repeat task 6 but as yourselves. What would you like to watch when you come in from school?

(8) In pairs, role-play a scene between a mother and young person disagreeing politely about the amount of **screen time** in the evenings. Arrive at a solution which works for both of you. You could use these prompts or develop your own ideas for the role-play.

Mother

Thinks child spends too much time on their phone.

Would prefer child to play football/do homework/practise their instrument.

Child

Has homework to do.

Has Grade 5 piano exam next week.

Wants to message friends. Must watch one online video for homework.

GOING FURTHER

Remember, you can keep a conversation going by:

● Listening carefully and then asking questions to find out more. For example:

English was my best class today.

Oh really. What did you do?

● Agreeing and then giving your opinion. For example:

I read a lot more non-fiction than fiction.

Oh yes, we read a lot of non-fiction in school, for instance …

● Rephrasing (saying what the other person has said in similar words) to show you have understood. For example:

I can't afford to get a new TV.

Mmm, yes, the new flat-screen TVs are very expensive.

(9) Listen to two people discussing what they saw on TV last night and answer these questions:

● What do their mothers want them to watch?
● What alternative phrases or synonyms are used to describe *The Big Bang Theory*?

(10) Listen again and answer the questions.

● What phrase does the boy use to mean the same as 'educational'?
● In the end, what programme does the girl want to watch and why?

11 Read this section from the listening passage. Identify any techniques used to maintain the conversation that are listed in 'Going further'.

> **Girl**: Do you watch *The Big Bang Theory*? I do. It's so funny.
>
> **Boy**: Yes. I agree, it makes me laugh a lot, but it gets boring in the end because they are all repeats.
>
> **Girl**: True, the repeats are tedious. But I like to watch something light at the end of the day. So what do you watch?
>
> **Boy**: I tend to watch the sports highlights because I can watch it on the computer in my room – I just watch it when I want.
>
> **Girl**: Good point, although …

12 You are going to discuss TV-watching habits. First, read the article about how watching TV is changing.

> According to a recent report, Americans aged 18 and older spend on average more than four hours a day watching TV. When comparing this to the amount of time the average American spends on their smartphone, surprisingly, the time spent watching TV is slightly more. This report shows that television is still relevant in the digital age. However, looking more closely the results reveal that there is a large generation gap in TV viewing. While adults aged 50–64 spend nearly six hours a day in front of the TV and adults aged 65+ spend more than seven hours a day, young adults watch significantly less TV. Some of the difference could be explained by the fact that many people over the age of 65 are retired and therefore have more time to watch TV. However, the fact that younger people are more likely to use streaming services on their devices instead of watching traditional television channels plays a large role in this.
>
> Adapted from 'The Generation Gap in TV Consumption', Statista

13 Discuss TV-watching habits with a partner. If they don't watch television, then they can invent when, where and what they would like to watch.

Prepare for your conversation.

- Write down at least five questions you would like to ask.

- Write down two prompt phrases you can use to agree with your partner.

- Write down two prompt phrases you can use to disagree politely with your partner.

- Plan what you will say about your TV-watching habits.

Hold the conversation.

Maintain the conversation for at least five minutes. Both of you should try to use different techniques to keep the conversation going.

11.4 Film

In this section you will learn to:

✓ understand and select facts in both formal and informal spoken texts

✓ recognise and understand opinions and attitudes in a more formal dialogue.

GETTING STARTED

1 On your own, think of a film. Take turns asking and answering other students in your class if they have also seen the film. If they have, ask them what they thought about it.

EXPLORING THE SKILLS

Most texts mix both fact and opinion. It is important to be able to tell facts from opinions so that you can decide for yourself whether you believe something or someone.

As you have learned in earlier chapters:

- a fact is something you can prove to be true, whereas

- an opinion is what someone thinks or feels about a subject and cannot be proved.

> **GLOSSARY** **epic** a long book, poem or film whose story extends over a long period of time and tells of great events

2 Shahnaz and Swayam are deciding which film to see and where to eat afterwards. Listen to what they say. Identify the facts and opinions to complete the table below. **11.3**

Fact	Opinion
At 7 o'clock there's the spaghetti Western *The Good, the Bad and the Ugly*.	It's an epic.

DEVELOPING THE SKILLS

You have just listened to a conversation between two friends and identified some facts and opinions. Now you are going to hear a more formal text. It is a talk about a serious subject – film-making in Nigeria. Here, you will have to listen a little more closely to identify some facts and opinions.

LANGUAGE BOOSTER | Match the words to their definitions.

Word	Definition
a) on location	**A:** record/make a film
b) prolific	**B:** a room where a film company makes films
c) at an astonishing rate	**C:** very fast
d) shoot a film	**D:** very productive
e) studio	**E:** at the site of a film production away from the studio

3 Listen to the talk about Nollywood, Nigeria's Hollywood. Write down any facts you hear and how you could prove each one. Remember – you should not write down opinions. 11.4

Nollywood fact bank	How can I prove this?
Second largest film industry in the world	Find out how many films made in Nollywood, Hollywood and Bollywood and compare

4 Now listen again. How does the speaker describe Nollywood?

Listen carefully. Copy the sentences and fill in the gaps with the correct information (the gaps are often more than one word). Which of the sentences are facts and which are opinions?

- Nollywood is _____ – so that it is now the second largest film industry in the world.

- Nollywood usually makes about _____ films annually.

- Movies are not produced in film studios but _____.

5 Now listen to a radio interview in which a film critic is discussing whether an Indian Bollywood film, *Bombay*, should be included in a top 100 all-time best movies list. Listen once and make notes on the questions the radio presenter asks.

11.5

6 Listen again. Complete the sentences (the gaps can be filled with up to four words) and then decide whether the sentence is a fact or an opinion.

Bombay

a) *Bombay* was made in _____.

b) It was _____ Mani Ratnam.

c) It is about a Hindu man who _____ a Muslim woman.

d) The film _____ Mumbai during a time of rioting and violence.

e) The best thing is the _____.

f) The film was a bit too _____ for me.

g) The director and editors _____ some of the romance scenes _____.

h) Manisha Koirala, _____, was the best for me.

i) The film won _____.

j) It was one of the biggest grossing films _____.

k) The _____ sold 15 million copies.

l) It is a must-see from one of the most _____.

m) If you want to go and see a great _____ movie, then you should go and see *Bombay*.

n) Five stars _____ five.

7 Listen again and answer these questions in writing.

a) Give **two** facts that the guest knows about the film.

b) Give **three** opinions that the guest holds about the film.

c) Give **two** reasons the guest gives for including *Bombay* in the top 100 films.

d) Do you think these are good reasons?

8 In groups, discuss if you would you like to go and see *Bombay*. Make sure you give a reason for your answer.

GOING FURTHER

Sometimes one word can change a fact into an opinion, for instance, an adjective can change a fact into an opinion. For example:

fight scenes **(fact)**

thrilling fight scenes **(opinion)**

Films are often described using extreme adjectives, which may be hyphenated.

Example: Bombay *is a must-see, award-winning movie.*

Read the following adjectives and then discuss the questions below in pairs.

star-studded	*action-packed*	*nerve-wracking*
slow-moving	*jaw-dropping*	*laugh-out-loud*

Think of:

- a film with a star-studded cast. Who played in it?
- an action-packed movie. What happened?
- a nerve-wracking movie. Why was it frightening?
- a slow-moving film. Why was it slow?
- a jaw-dropping moment in a film. What happened?
- a film that was laugh-out-loud funny. Why was it funny?

9 In pairs, talk about your favourite film or your imaginary favourite film.

- Make notes and then copy and complete the table below with one fact and two opinions on your favourite film.

- Listen carefully to what your partner says. Add details to the table about their favourite film.

- Compare your notes with your partner's. Are they the same?

Item	What	Fact	Opinion	Opinion
My favourite film	The Monkey King	The budget was $82 million.	Chow Yun Fat makes an awesome Jade Emperor.	It's got gripping fighting scenes.
My partner's favourite film				

10 In groups, discuss the last film or TV programme you saw. Take turns to speak, giving your film a rating in stars as shown on the right.

> ★ = Deadly dull and boring
> ★ ★ = Okay
> ★ ★ ★ = Good
> ★ ★ ★ ★ = Great
> ★ ★ ★ ★ ★ = Fantastic – an all-time great

11 Make a film or audio recording of your discussions (using your phone). Play back the recording, listening carefully to what each person said about their film. Was it mostly fact or opinion?

The big task

In groups of four, hold a debate about whether lots of screen time is good for you or not.

Group 1: argue *for* lots of screen time.

Group 2: argue *against* lots of screen time.

1 First prepare for the discussion:

- Choose roles.
- In your group, sort these facts and arguments into *for* and *against* lots of screen time. Throw out any arguments that are irrelevant.

> ○ Good quality apps, TV show, movies, etc. can help teenagers understand real-world issues.
> ○ Too much screen time can result in bad posture, eye strain or neck pain.
> ○ Learning strategies to manage screen time is an essential skill.
> ○ I don't own a smartphone.
> ○ A lot of screen time can affect your sleep.
> ○ Too much screen time takes time away from sports which keep you active and healthy.
> ○ The ability to spot adverts and know how adverts works is an important life skill for teenagers.
> ○ There's lots of educational stuff online. You can do research for your studies online.
> ○ Can keep in touch with and chat to friends.
> ○ When disasters happen and there is lots of distressing news, this can upset teenagers.
> ○ Young people need to learn to be smart consumers and choose good quality content.

- Add any further arguments of your own.
- Allocate arguments to each person and decide the order in which people will speak. Usually the strongest arguments are presented first and last.

2 Now write up each argument, adding an example, a statistic or an expert opinion to support your argument.

3 Now hold your debate in front of the class. Take turns so that a person from Group 1 speaks first, followed by a person from Group 2, then the next person from Group 1 followed by the next person from Group 2, and so on.

> **TOP TIP** Introduce your opinions using one of the phrases for disagreeing politely.

4 Now take a vote in class. Which side won? Do you think that screen time is good or bad for you?

Check your progress

Here are the Reading, Writing, Speaking and Listening skills you learnt about in Chapter 11.

Use this table to decide how good you are at the different skills, and make a note of what you need to be able to do in order to move up a level.

READING I can ...	WRITING I can ...
consistently and accurately locate facts and details in complex texts identify most of the points for or against a point of view, even when they are implied and not directly stated	use a wide range of punctuation in my writing, accurately and to good effect
find some facts and details in a range of texts identify some points for or against a point of view, including some implied but not directly stated	use a fair range of punctuation in my writing and with a reasonable degree of accuracy
find a few facts and details in straightforward texts identify a few obvious points for or against a point of view	use a basic range of punctuation in my writing

SPEAKING I can ...	LISTENING I can ...
disagree politely and confidently in a conversation sustain a conversation for some time and can use rephrasing effectively	consistently understand and pick out details accurately from a range of spoken texts, including the more complex usually understand opinions and attitudes in a formal spoken dialogue
disagree politely and clearly in a conversation take part in a two-way conversation and sometimes make use of rephrasing	confidently understand and pick out details correctly from a range of spoken texts understand some opinions and attitudes in a formal spoken dialogue
disagree in a conversation take part in a conversation, but will need support from the other speaker to keep it going	understand and pick out a few details correctly from some straightforward spoken texts understand a few simple opinions and attitudes in a formal spoken dialogue

THE BIG PICTURE

In this chapter you will:

- think about what it means to be young, and what it means to be old

- research, think, talk and write about what young people and old people do, what they want and how people change as they get older.

THINKING BIG

1 Look at the photos and make notes on what they show about different stages in life.

- What do you think are the advantages and disadvantages of each stage of life?

- How does age change your attitude to learning new things?

2 In pairs, look at the photos and then discuss these questions:

- In what ways do different cultures differ in their attitudes to children and very old people?

- What do you think about each of the activities shown? Talk about the differences between people's abilities when they are young, and when they are old.

3 On your own, note down ideas about the following points. You will come back to these later in the unit.

- What do you think are the best things about being young?

- Are there any problems or difficulties with being young?

- Think about how much your life has changed since you were a young child. What can you do now that you couldn't do before? Are there things you can't do now that you used to enjoy?

- In what ways do you think that getting older will make your life easier? In what ways could it make life more difficult?

- Consider your own culture's attitude to childhood. What childhood experiences do you share with other cultures? In what ways might they be different?

12
Young
and old

READING SKILLS IN FOCUS

In this section you will learn to:

✓ recognise both facts and opinions in different types and lengths of text

✓ understand how the use of language may suggest a viewpoint.

GETTING STARTED

(1) Read the questions below and discuss your ideas about them with a partner.

- Do you help to make decisions about things that affect you at home and at school? Think of examples.

- In what ways can young people play a part in the decisions which affect their lives?

- Do you think that young people should be involved in political decisions?

EXPLORING THE SKILLS

When you read a formal text, such as a newspaper report, you need to be able to tell the difference between facts and opinions, and also to identify the author's **viewpoint**. Articles that you read in newspapers, magazines and websites often express the viewpoint of the author. This is the main belief that the author wants to convey, and he or she will use facts and opinions to present his or her viewpoint.

(2) Read the introduction to an article about voting rights for young people. What is the main idea in this piece of text? Choose one of the answers below.

A More people should vote.

B More young people should be allowed to vote.

C Young people are not interested in voting.

One of the issues that is often discussed in politics is at what age people should be allowed to vote. In some countries, campaigners want to lower the voting age to 16. This would increase opportunities for young people to help shape their own future.

In fact, people under 18 are already shaping the future. In 2014, Malala Yousafzai won a Nobel Peace Prize at the age of 17 for her work fighting for children's rights. Greta Thunberg, the environmental activist, spoke in front of the United Nations Climate Action Summit when she was 16. Many young people work in responsible positions. For example, lifeguarding is a popular teenage job where kids as young as 15 are responsible for the lives of hundreds of people and regularly save adults from drowning.

Yet in most countries, none of these young people would have the chance to vote.

When you read an article like this, it is important to realise that the writer has researched the topic and formed a viewpoint based on what they have discovered.

Consider the viewpoint of the author, given in the first paragraph.

Then notice the facts the author uses to support their viewpoint:

Malala Yousafzai won a Nobel Peace Prize at the age of 17.

Greta Thunberg, the environmental activist, spoke in front of the United Nations Climate Action Summit when she was 16.

Lifeguards as young as 15 are responsible for the lives of hundreds of people and regularly save adults from drowning.

3 In pairs, read the rest of the article and discuss the questions on the next page. Explain your ideas in your own words.

A Most countries have set the minimum voting age at 18. This is because of tradition more than social, economic and political realities. It is also often linked to the age people were allowed to join the army. But, nowadays, many under 18-year-olds not only fight for their country, they work and pay taxes and they may be treated the same as adults if they break the law.

B After World War II most European countries lowered the voting age from 21 to 18. But there are still many countries in the world where it remains high. For example, the minimum voting age is 21 in Gabon, and 20 in Cameroon. Singapore also has a minimum voting age of 21, and so does Malaysia although this is due to be lowered to 18.

C Lowering the voting age to 16 for all countries would be a better reflection of the general age of the population and improve political participation of millions of people. This is especially true in growing countries with young populations. Some of the handful of countries which have lowered the voting age to 16 are Austria, Brazil, Cuba, Scotland and Nicaragua. In Bosnia and Herzegovina, 16-year-olds can vote if they are employed. The voting age in Indonesia, North Korea and Timor-Leste is 17.

D In many countries, there continues to be a lot of discussion about the pros and cons of lowering the voting age. One of the main arguments against it is that young people of 16 are too immature to make an informed decision. However, many young people already have responsibility for caring for older parents or younger siblings, may have jobs, and are often contributing to the household income.

E Young people are expected to follow the laws of their country so it is only right that they should have a say in electing representatives who make the laws. Just because they're younger doesn't mean that they're less interested or knowledgeable about political, social and economic issues. In fact, many teenagers are politically active. Government policies affect the future of the next generation so young people need to have their interests represented.

(4) Re-read paragraph A.

    a) Why has the voting age been set at 18 in most countries?

    b) Why does the writer think that this reason doesn't make sense?

(5) Re-read paragraph B.

    a) What was the minimum voting age in Gabon and Cameroon when this article was written?

    b) Is the writer stating a fact or an opinion here?

(6) In paragraph C, how does the writer support their opinion that the voting age should be lowered?

(7) In paragraph D, the writer says, 'young people of 16 are too immature to make an informed decision'. Is this the opinion of the writer, or of somebody else?

(8) Re-read paragraph E. Does the writer think that older people always know more about political issues than younger people?

(9) In groups, discuss the following questions.

- At the moment, in your country, are you able to vote?

- Do you think it is important to vote, or do you think it does not make much difference?

- What is the minimum voting age in your country? Do you think it should it be higher, lower, or stay as it is?

DEVELOPING THE SKILLS

Online newspapers often let readers express their points of view about material published on the site. This means readers can respond to and engage with topics they read about.

(10) Read these comments about the voting age article.

> 'I disagree with the idea that the voting age should be lowered. I think that people of 16 are too young to vote.'
>
> 'People can get married, have babies and fight in the army before the age of 18, so why shouldn't they be able to vote?'
>
> 'Young people have great responsibilities – they often work and earn money, and pay taxes, all before they are able to vote. This doesn't make sense to me.'
>
> 'Surely voting isn't important – there are more important things to think about, such as healthcare and ending poverty and disease. We should be worrying about this instead.'

(11) In pairs, discuss what you think about each of the comments.

(12) Working individually, write a short comment like those above, expressing your opinion about the age at which people should be allowed to vote.

GOING FURTHER

Just as **adjectives** can give you a strong impression of the writer's opinion (for instance, 'The *spectacular* scenery...' tells us the writer loves the scenery), so **nouns** and **verbs** can also tell us about the writer's attitude. Each word can have an emotional connection. For example:

Nouns: a *crowd* of people, might be a *mob* or an *audience* or a *congregation*.

Verbs: the man *walked*, might mean he *swaggered boastfully* or *marched smartly*.

13 Discuss the words in the examples above with a partner and look them up if necessary. Which is positive, negative, neutral?

14 Read the texts below. What problem do they highlight?

> In my town I see a lot of young people hanging around aimlessly on street corners, wasting their time idly chatting to friends, kicking balls around and talking rudely to other, more respectable members of society. And then they complain that there is nothing for them to do. My response to this is that they should find something to do – find some more useful way to pass the time.

> I was disgusted to read the letter and felt I had to reply. I am a young person and I feel insulted by the way this reader dismisses all young people. I believe that the vast majority of young people in this town are hardworking, conscientious and courteous. The school has an excellent record, and we try hard to be responsible members of the community.

15 What type of texts are these – factual accounts or expressions of opinion?

Identify the words and phrases which express the emotions in each text. Copy and complete the table.

	Positive	**Negative**	**Neutral**
Letter 1		hanging around	
Letter 2			

16 Sum up the viewpoint of each writer.

12.2 Setting the tone

In this section you will learn to:

✓ choose the correct tone and style for different readers and different situations.

GETTING STARTED

1 Read the points below and discuss them with a partner.

- Describe any interesting websites or blogs you have visited or read recently.

- Do you ever write material such as reviews or news stories for websites?

- What is the difference between formal newspaper articles and informal blogs?

- What different reasons can you think of for writing websites, blogs or social media posts?

EXPLORING THE SKILLS

When writing an informal text, it is important to use the correct tone and style to suit your reader. Think about who your text is for. If you are writing in a formal situation, for example to your employer, you need to use the formal writing techniques covered in Chapter 6. If you are writing in an informal situation, to your friend perhaps, you will use a very different style. You might use different vocabulary, as well as different sentence structures.

2 Read this blog post about someone who taught their great-grandmother to blog, and then do the Language booster task on the next page.

Last month I posted here about <u>my successful attempt to explain the internet</u> and how to use a tablet to my 95-year-old great-grandmother, Patrizia. Lots of you have messaged me to ask what happened next. To be honest, I didn't think she'd do much more than video call family but she's surprised us all and … started a blog!! She's always been really into baking and swapping recipes with her friends but they mostly copied the recipes out by hand. Now she's sharing them online with millennials sixty years younger than her. It just goes to show, you're never too old to learn something new!

I showed her a few basics, like buying a domain name and choosing a design, and she was completely hooked. She even worked out how to make videos of herself baking and posted those! The only problem she's had is with fake comments and bots because she doesn't realise they're not real. So, my next internet lesson for her is going to be online safety. I'd feel terrible if she got scammed just because I introduced her to the internet.

LANGUAGE BOOSTER

Look at some of the words from the blog. Are they formal or informal? What do you think these words mean? Match them to their meanings.

a) hooked

b) a millennial

c) a bot

d) get scammed

A a computer program that can do things online like a person

B be tricked, often for money

C a person who became an adult around the year 2000

D enjoying something and wanting to do it again

Language develops to fit new experiences in the world. New words and phrases, such as *bot* and *millennial* develop to describe new situations.

3 Read this article about internet use in Spain.

Internet use

In Spain, just like the rest of Europe, far fewer people over the age of 65 are online compared with their millennial children or their Generation Z grandchildren. This shows that older citizens are missing out on the digital revolution. This is despite the fact that they make up a growing percentage of the population.

'Age is more important in determining internet use than income, gender ... or level of education,' said an official in Spain's Ministry of Industry.

After the age of 65, the proportion of internet users decreases even more steeply. However, technology is a useful method for breaking down the isolation often experienced in old age. 'Although nothing can make up for affection, the internet can help communication, with mail, chat or messaging, and it's fun and always available,' he said.

4 The writer of the article works in the Spanish government. How does his tone and style differ from the tone and style the blogger used on the previous page?

5 With her baking blog, Patrizia started communicating with people much younger than her and in a completely different way than she had before. Discuss these questions in pairs.

- How have computers or the internet affected the lives of some older people you know?

- Can older people where you live feel isolated, or are they part of the community?

- What can older people gain from using the internet?

DEVELOPING THE SKILLS

Remember to think about your reader and use the appropriate style of writing.

6 Imagine that you are going to start a blog. Consider the points below and make notes.

- Who are you writing your blog for?

- Will your blog have a serious topic, such as your views on politics, education or global issues? Or will it be informal and deal with more personal issues?

- How will your choice of topic affect the tone you use in your blog?

7 When you write letters or emails, you need to decide how to create the tone you want to use. For example, in Chapter 6 we looked at formal writing conventions, such as using full forms rather than contractions. Match the features across the two sides of the table.

Formal writing (e.g. a letter to/from a teacher)	Informal writing (e.g. an email to a best friend)
1. Full forms: 'I have written a letter to your father'	A Friendly language to end: 'Best wishes from'
2. Formal language to start: 'Dear Sir, Thank you for '	B Contracted forms: 'I've written a letter to your dad '
3. Formal language to end: 'Yours faithfully'	C Use idioms: 'It was blazing hot today'
4. Avoid using idioms: 'It was extremely hot weather '	D Friendly, conversational start: 'Hi, Thanks a million for …'

8 Now write two letters, one to your teacher and one to your school friend, explaining why you were away from school yesterday. Try to use the different techniques shown in the table.

GOING FURTHER

Just as you need to adjust your tone for different readers, you need to think about the purpose of what you are writing. Here we will look at how to write instructions.

The internet is a very useful learning tool but, at any age, people need to know how to go online safely. Imagine that you have to write a set of instructions for someone who doesn't know much about online safety. The instructions must give advice about the safest way to proceed, what to do and what not to do.

Read the extracts below and decide which is the most suitable introduction to those instructions:

> *Internet safety is the knowledge and practices for making sure users are as safe as possible online. This includes protecting yourself against cyber crime and guarding privacy and passwords.*

> *The internet is a bit like a giant library inside your computer. You wouldn't want to leave the doors open for anyone to walk in and mess up the books, take whatever they want and steal your personal possessions.*

The second extract is a better introduction for someone who is new to internet safety. The writer:

- uses a friendly, direct tone
- uses less sophisticated vocabulary
- writes about the experience in an accessible way, making comparisons with familiar settings (a library) rather than using unfamiliar technical language.

When you write instructions, it is important to present the information in the correct sequence, using clear language.

9 Choose your reader. Will you write instructions for a young child, or an elderly person? Your tone and style will be different depending on your reader. In pairs, read the phrases in the box and put them into the correct columns in the table. Some phrases will fit in both.

> - clear, simple words
> - more sophisticated language
> - short sentences
> - variety of sentence types
> - not too much technical language
> - fun and interesting

Young reader	Older reader

10 Now work individually to write your instructions about keeping safe on the internet. Remember to adjust your language according to your reader. You should write about 150 words.

12.3 Growing up

In this section you will learn to:

✓ speak clearly and use the correct stress when speaking

✓ vary your tone to interest your listener.

GETTING STARTED

1 Discuss the questions in pairs.

- At what age do you think people become adults? Is this because of what you are allowed to do, or because of how mature you are?

- Is there a clear moment at which you become an adult in your society, or is it a gradual process?

- In your country, are there any traditions which you associate with the change from being a child to being an adult?

- Do you think the step from being a child to being an adult is exciting, or is it something that makes young people nervous?

EXPLORING THE SKILLS

In situations where you want to tell a story or talk in a way which will interest your listener, there are different techniques you can use to make your speech more exciting, or to convey your emotions more clearly. For instance, you might:

- emphasise particular words and use a wider range of expression

- pause before some words to build up greater dramatic expression

- repeat certain words, or vary the volume of your voice.

Remember – it is not just *what* you say, but *how* you say it, that conveys your ideas.

2 Listen to Carmen, Adil and Keiko describing how children become adults in their country. How do you think they feel?

3 Listen to the extract. What techniques from 'Exploring the skills' are being used here?

🎧 **12.2**

Listen to the whole thing again. How does each speaker show their emotions? Consider *what* they are talking about and *how* they present their stories.

🎧 **12.1**

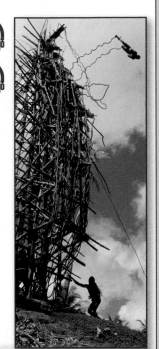

4 Think about a time when you first felt that you were being treated like an adult. What happened, and how did it make you feel? Practise describing this situation in pairs, using the three techniques on the previous page to make your story sound interesting. Then present your ideas to the class.

5 Look at the photographs on this page and read about more ceremonies from around the world. Note down ideas about how you might feel in each situation. Use the words below to help you.

| excited | proud | nervous | happy | scared |

Land diving – South Pacific

On Pentecost Island in Vanuatu in the South Pacific, there is a ceremony that started a world-famous sport. When young boys are ready to become men, they take part in a land-diving **ritual** called Naghol. A 20–30-metre-high tower is made from wood. Then local men and boys jump off the tower, with only a **vine** attached to their legs. The vine takes them all the way down to the ground – to complete the ritual, they have to brush the ground with their head! The vine doesn't stretch, so if the length isn't right, the diver could be seriously injured, or killed.

This ritual influenced bungee jumping, but the festival has a strong spiritual significance for the islanders, as it is thought to make the land **fertile**.

Initiation by bullet ants – the Amazon rainforest

The bite of the bullet ant of the Amazon rainforest is said to be the most painful bite of any insect in the world. Its name shows that the bite from this ant is like being shot. But young men from the Satere Mawé tribe of the Amazon have to experience bites from the bullet ant as part of their **initiation** into adulthood. The pain can make them unable to move their arms for a while, and they may **shake uncontrollably**. If they can cope with the pain, they are seen as men.

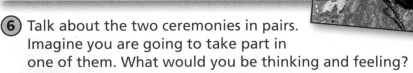

6 Talk about the two ceremonies in pairs. Imagine you are going to take part in one of them. What would you be thinking and feeling?

GLOSSARY

ritual	a series of actions performed in a fixed order, often as part of a religious ceremony
vine	the long stem of a climbing plant
fertile	(for land) able to grow crops
initiation	the process by which someone officially becomes a member of a particular group, often involving special ceremonies
shake uncontrollably	be unable to stop moving your body

DEVELOPING THE SKILLS

7 In 'Thinking big' you made notes about being young: what was good about it; what you can do now that you couldn't do as a child; how your life changes as you get older. Did any of these topics come up in your notes?

LANGUAGE BOOSTER When talking about the future, you can use phrases such as 'I hope', 'I can't wait', and 'I'm looking forward to' to describe your hopes and plans.

- learning to drive
- leaving home
- marriage

In pairs, discuss what each of these things means to you, and your hopes and plans for the future.

8 Read these comments from young people about their experiences. Are they similar to or different from your ideas?

> I'm so excited about learning to drive – I've been saving up money for lessons, and my parents have helped me too. I'm starting lessons on my seventeenth birthday, and hopefully I'll pass my test soon! I'm looking forward to having more freedom. I won't have to ask my parents to take me to places any more!

> I can't wait to leave home. My parents are great, but I'm 19 now and I think I'm ready to have my own space. I'd like to live with friends, I think that would be really, really good. I'm looking for a job at the moment, and when I find one, I'll think about moving out.

> My parents want me to get married and maybe start a family. But I think I'm too young for that! I'd rather go travelling, see the world, just ... do what I want for a bit! Then I want to find a really interesting job.

9 Are these people excited about the topics they are discussing or are they nervous about the future? How can you tell what emotions they are feeling? What spoken techniques for adding interest have they used? Discuss your ideas in pairs.

10 Listen to a conversation between two friends. Why is one of them very excited?

11 Listen to the conversation again. How can you tell Eliza is excited?

GOING FURTHER

Telling a story to one person or a group of friends is one thing, but what about talking to a large group of people? Giving a presentation is an important and useful skill, and you can use many of the same techniques to interest your listeners.

12 Read the question and note down your ideas.

How do you feel about the changes in life you will experience as you grow older?

13 a) On your own, read the topics below. Think of any other important life stages or events.

> work   leaving home   university   travelling
>
> having a family   learning to drive   responsibilities

b) In pairs, describe what you hope to do in the future. Using the ideas above, decide what you will do first. How do you feel about the life stage you have chosen to discuss? For example, are you looking forward to having more responsibility, or not? What expectations do people around you have?

c) Carry out your conversation. Take time to listen to each other's points of view, and be prepared to offer advice, if appropriate. For example:

A *I really want to learn to drive, but it's so expensive.*

B *Well, you could get a part-time job. Then you could save money for lessons.*

TOP TIP Record yourselves preparing your ideas and having your conversation, and then listen to it. Does your speech sound interesting, and have you used techniques for expressing emotion? Can you think of ways to improve it?

14 Prepare a presentation about coming-of-age ceremonies in your country, or about a ceremony in another country that interests you.

Research information about it, and then give your presentation to the class. Remember to use your tone of voice to help you express your ideas and emotions. You may have a mixture of factual information and your own opinions and emotions, so think about how your tone of voice should change.

12.4 Achievements of youth and old age

In this section you will learn to:
✓ recognise and understand ideas, opinions and attitudes
✓ recognise connections between ideas

GETTING STARTED

1 In pairs:

- Tell one another about a young person who has achieved something amazing.

- Do you think young people should be encouraged to try dangerous activities? Why or why not?

- If a young person has a talent for a particular sport or activity, how far should they go with this? Should it be more or less important than their education and social life?

EXPLORING THE SKILLS

Sometimes when you are listening, you have to pick out specific information in order to answer questions or follow instructions. Check that you understand what you need to know. If you have to choose between two or more options, there are steps you can take to help you answer the questions correctly.

- First, make sure you read and understand all of the options.

- Then, reject any which are obviously wrong.

- Think about key words you should listen for. Think of synonyms for these words – words with the same meaning – as the text may not be identical.

2 Read the question and the answer options.

- Why is this person famous?

A He is the youngest person to pass his A levels.

B He is an Olympic swimming champion.

C He is a record-breaking English diving champion.

Once you have read and understood the question and options, listen to the text. We can reject option A, because we hear that he was working towards his A levels.

The key words we need to listen for are 'swimming' or 'diving' and 'champion'. We hear 'diving', so we can reject option B, and when we hear the word 'star' – a **synonym** for champion – we know option C is correct.

(3) Look at the photos. Listen to the passage and match the photos to the descriptions.

Round-the-world sailor
Olympic medallist
Climber of the Seven Peaks

(4) Listen to the recording again and answer the questions.

i) What did Jordan Romero achieve to win a new world record?

   A He climbed seven high mountains.

   B He was the youngest person to climb Mount Everest.

   C He was the youngest person to climb the highest mountain on each of the seven continents.

ii) When did Jessica start her journey?

   A October 2009

   B May 2010

   C October 2010

iii) How did Inge prepare for her competitions?

   A She spent many hours each day training in the swimming pool.

   B She travelled all over the world to be coached by experts.

   C She mainly practised in the sea near where she lived.

DEVELOPING THE SKILLS

When you have to answer questions about longer listening pieces, it can be more difficult to follow the main ideas. But the technique is the same as for shorter pieces: read the questions and options, and listen for key words. These will help you focus on what you hear and enable you to answer the questions successfully.

5 Discuss the questions in pairs.

- What achievements are important to you? If you live to be 100, what would you like to do before then?

- Do you think people are more able to fulfil their ambitions when they are old, or when they are young?

Try using some of this vocabulary. Check that you know what these words mean:

achievement   marathon   finish line   exhausted

dehydrated   energy   blood sugar levels

concentration   record breaker   personal best

6 Read this introduction to an article about a marathon runner. What is unusual about him?

World's oldest marathon runner completes Toronto race at age 100

Fauja Singh from east London finishes in 8 hours, 25 minutes and 18 seconds – ahead of five other competitors.

7 Answer the questions.

a) Which marathon did Fauja Singh run in this article?

b) How long did it take him to finish?

8 Listen to the rest of the article. Remember to read all the options before you listen, and use the pauses and replaying to check your answers.   12.6

i)   Where does Fauja Singh live?   iii) When did he run his first marathon?

     A India   **A** when he was a farmer

     B East London   **B** when he was 89

     C Toronto   **C** in 1911

ii)   When was he born?   iv) What does Singh say makes him successful?

     A 11 April 1901   **A** ginger tea and being happy

     B 1 April 1910   **B** curry and cups of coffee

     C 1 April 1911   **C** ginger curry, cups of tea and being happy

GOING FURTHER

Sometimes you might have to answer questions about quite a complex text. In this situation, do not worry about understanding every word. Remember that sometimes the answers have to be 'worked out' from the text.

9 In this chapter you have looked at the different achievements and difficulties of young and old people. Now, in pairs, draw a timeline of life from birth to death, and mark on it what you think are the significant stages and developments which people experience. For example:

10 Listen to an interview with Jago Philips. What has he done? 12.7

> **LANGUAGE BOOSTER** Write definitions for these words. Use a dictionary.
>
> adolescence   infancy   adulthood   responsibility   inadequacy   regret

11 Listen again and answer the questions.

i) What is the subject of Jago's book?

- **A** How his children have developed
- **B** His own theory of how life changes
- **C** An explanation of someone else's theory about how life changes

ii) What is important about the first stage, called Infancy?

- **A** We learn about love.
- **B** We become independent.
- **C** We are very confident.

iii) What can happen in Early Childhood?

- **A** Everyone starts saying 'No' to the child.
- **B** Children can do more for themselves.
- **C** Parents start to do everything for the child.

iv) What is the different between Play Age and School Age?

- **A** We play with different toys.
- **B** We don't learn anything in the Play Age.
- **C** We start to develop relationships outside the family in School Age.

v) What do we try to discover in Adolescence?

- **A** Our own identity
- **B** Who is in charge of the world
- **C** How the world works

vi) Why is Young Adulthood difficult?

- **A** We don't have as many friends.
- **B** We have a lot of new responsibilities.
- **C** It is difficult to find work.

12 Listen to the recording again and answer these questions in your own words:

a) Why did Jago decide to write this book?

b) What kind of a person is Jago? Choose one word to describe him and explain why you think this describes him well, by giving an example from the interview.

The big task

In this unit you have looked at the different rights and responsibilities of young and old people. Now you are going to prepare a presentation about the subject, choosing from the topics in the speech bubbles below.

1 In groups, read the following statements and discuss them. Note down some ideas about your opinions. Then choose one of the statements for your presentation.

> *The age of 18 is too young to vote. Young people need to learn much more about how the world works before they can be trusted to vote.*

> *The internet can be dangerous. Young people shouldn't be allowed to use it because they won't find out anything useful.*

> *Older people aren't capable of achieving success in the same way as younger, healthier people.*

> *It is dangerous for young people to attempt difficult activities such as mountain climbing or sailing, and parents shouldn't encourage it.*

> *There aren't any different stages to life – we just start young, then grow up gradually. We don't 'become' an adult at any particular age.*

2 Prepare a presentation about your chosen statement, giving your viewpoint on the subject. Remember to use facts and other people's opinions to back up your viewpoint and express it convincingly.

3 Once you have agreed on a topic, divide it up into different areas for each person in the group to work on individually. For example:

- one person can research famous people whose work is linked to the topic
- two others can find articles and other sources of information which support your point of view.

4 Once your research is completed, bring your work together and look at what you have found. Think about the best way to present your work – for example, a poster with images and text, or a slide presentation of images, key phrases and lists of arguments. You should try to produce a combination of oral presentation and written work with images.

5 Prepare your presentation. Think carefully about your audience, and use an appropriate style and tone. Remember to express your views clearly.

Check your progress

Here are the Reading, Writing, Speaking and Listening skills you learned about in Chapter 12.

Use this table to decide how good you are at the different skills, and make a note of what you need to be able to do in order to move up a level.

READING

I can …

- consistently and accurately recognise and understand facts and opinions in a range of texts including complex ones
- understand how the choice of language may suggest viewpoint

- recognise and understand some facts and opinions in a range of texts
- sometimes understand how language may suggest viewpoint

- sometimes recognise and understand more obvious facts and opinions in straightforward texts

WRITING

I can …

- consistently and effectively adapt the tone and style to the reader and purpose of my writing

- sometimes choose the right tone and style according to the reader and purpose of my writing

- write for different readers and purposes but use the same tone and style

SPEAKING

I can …

- consistently speak confidently and clearly, using the correct stresses in my pronunciation and varying the tone of my voice for effect

- speak clearly, using appropriate stresses in my pronunciation and varying the tone of my voice so that I can be understood quite easily

- express some simple ideas but do not always use the correct stresses; I tend to use the same tone all the time

LISTENING

I can …

- consistently understand ideas, attitudes and opinions in quite complex spoken texts and then answer multiple-choice questions accurately
- usually understand what is implied but not directly stated in a formal interview

- understand ideas, attitudes and opinions in spoken texts and then answer some multiple-choice questions correctly
- sometimes understand what is implied but not directly stated in a formal interview

- understand ideas, attitudes and opinions in straightforward spoken texts and then answer a few multiple-choice questions correctly
- understand straightforward ideas stated in a formal interview

13 Answering reading questions

SYLLABUS INFORMATION:

Paper 1
2 hours
Reading and Writing
60 marks

The Reading and Writing paper of Cambridge IGCSE English as a Second Language includes four reading and two writing exercises. The reading exercises are based on four different types of reading texts. Examples of texts that may be used are articles, blogs or websites.

The first reading exercise involves giving brief open response questions on a short text of 400-450 words long. The second exercise involves answering multiple-matching reading questions on a longer text of 600-650 words.

The information in these syllabus information sections is based on the syllabus for examination from 2024. You should always refer to the appropriate syllabus document for the year of your examination to confirm the details and for more information. The syllabus document is available on the Cambridge International website at www.cambridgeinternational.org.

This chapter gives you practice in answering both short answer reading questions and longer reading questions. It provides step-by-step advice on how to approach these questions, and this is followed by some example exam-style questions for you to practise and develop your reading skills.

Open-response reading questions

In this type of question, you are given a short text to read and need to select details to answer a question. The answer may be a single word or a phrase.

Skills required for this type of question include:

1 skim and scan to find details

2 identify key words in questions.

APPROACHING OPEN-RESPONSE QUESTIONS: STEP BY STEP

STEP 1 **Skim read the text**

This will give you a quick idea of how the information is organised. Do not worry too much if there are words you do not understand – you may not need them for the answers anyway!

● You learned and practised the skill of skim reading in Chapter 1 Section 1.1.

STEP 2 **Read through all the questions**

This will give you a quick idea of the information you will need to find.

STEP 3 **Find the detail**

Answer the questions one at a time, and find just the information you need. Use the scanning skills you practised in Chapter 1. In Chapter 3 you also learned about using the question words (who, what, why, where, when, how) to help you decide what kind of information is needed. Remember that the answers are to be found in the text in the same order as the questions.

> **REMEMBER TO...**
> ✓ Skim read the text and read the questions before you start writing.
> ✓ Underline key words in the questions to help you focus on the information you are looking for.
> ✓ Scan the text to find the details you need.
> ✓ Keep your answers brief and concise.

Now that you understand what to do, and the order in which to do it, you are ready to read a text and answer questions which require short answers.

PRACTISE OPEN-RESPONSE QUESTIONS

Read the following newspaper article about the problems faced by American beekeepers, and then answer the questions below.

Where have all the bees gone?

Richard Ford, first started beekeeping ten years ago when he bought a large field of nut trees in California. He began with just two bee boxes, each containing 10 000 bees. As time went on, he bought more boxes and eventually had about 100 000 000 bees. He was proud of his achievement, so imagine his shock when he went to examine his boxes one day, to find that half of all his bees had just disappeared. Standing on his precious land, Richard said, 'I have never experienced anything like this.'

Other beekeepers across the USA had also had similar shocks. Bees have been disappearing rapidly and for no apparent reason over the past decade. This is obviously a problem for the beekeepers, as it is leads to a loss of personal income. There is, however, a more concerning issue on a wider scale, which is the threat to the production of certain crops, including the most profitable, Californian almonds.

The mysterious disappearance of so many bees highlights the importance of honeybees in the successful production of the fruit and vegetables that feed people across the USA. Although there had been regional bee crises before, this was the first time there had been a national crisis. Bees are flying off in search of food and simply not returning to their old homes, once they have found new plants and flowers to feed off.

Worried beekeepers met with researchers in Florida this month to try to find out the cause of the problem and how to cope with it. They discussed a range of possible causes, including diseases which affect the bees and in some cases their poor diet.

Another problem is that queen bees are producing fewer worker bees and only living half as long as they did a few years ago. This is thought to be because on non-organic farms there are still many chemicals being used to protect the crops. Some of these, like herbicides, do not necessarily affect the bee population. Others, however, like insecticides, are often responsible for harming the queen bees.

Producing honey is not, in fact, the main way beekeepers earn money. They make much more from renting their bees to other people, who then use them to help produce more of their own crops. Over the past ten years, the costs of fuel and equipment have doubled and then trebled, as has the cost of controlling bugs. In addition, the price of queen bees has gone up from $10 each to $15 each.

1. Approximately how many of Richard Ford's bees were missing? [1]
2. What is the most worrying problem about the sudden disappearance of so many bees? [1]
3. What are the bees looking for when they fly off? [1]
4. What do some farmers use which can cause harm to bees? [1]
5. How do beekeepers earn money from their bees, apart from selling honey? [1]
6. What is more expensive for beekeepers today, than ten years ago?
   Give three details.
   ....
   ....
   .... [3]

[Total: 8 marks]

Remember that a phrase is a group of two or more words that form a unit of meaning, such as *colourful parrots*, *first national lockdown* or *gains money by working*.

Multiple-matching reading questions

This type of question provides a longer, more demanding text from which you find details and match them to the questions. It can be a continuous text divided into several sections, or a collection of related texts. The texts may include extra details that require you to understand what is implied but is not directly stated.

Skills required for this type of question include:

The reading skills you need: the ability to:

1 reading closely for details

2 understanding what is implied but not directly stated.

APPROACHING MULTIPLE-MATCHING READING QUESTIONS: STEP BY STEP

STEP 1 Skim read the text

Find out quickly what the text is about. Focus on the first sentence of each paragraph to give you an idea of how the information is organised and the differences and similarities between the texts.

STEP 2 Read all the questions through

This will give you a quick idea of the information you will need to find.

STEP 3 Find the detail

Answer the questions one at a time. Identify key words in the questions and use your skim-reading skills to find the information you need. The answers in this question <u>are not in the order of the text</u>. Therefore, to start with, you will need to skim read each paragraph to find the answer.

STEP 4 Avoid distractors

There may be something in one section or paragraph that seems to relate to a question, whereas in fact, the answer is in another section or paragraph. Check the detail.

Your brain is like a movie camera – sweep over the whole text to get the full picture, then focus in a bit closer to get a sharper image, then zoom in for the close-up shot – click! You've got the information you need.

Check your answers

Check that the information you have found is exactly what is asked for. Remember, you may use **A**, **B**, **C** and **D** more than once in your answers.

STEP 6 **Read 'in between the lines'**

You need to understand what is implied but not directly stated. You learned this skill and practised it in Chapters 1 and 7.

Now you understand what to do, you are ready to answer a multiple-matching reading question.

REMEMBER TO...

✓ Skim the text and read through the questions. Underline key words in the questions to help you focus on what you need to find.

✓ Read for detail, and underline the information you need for your answer.

✓ Check that you have understood what was implied in the text.

✓ Check all your answers.

PRACTISE A MULTIPLE-MATCHING READING QUESTION

Read the text below about four young people (A–D) who shop online. Then answer questions (a)–(i).

Shopping online

A *Joe admits to spending too much time playing computer games and contacting friends through social media, so his favourite method of shopping is online. 'I can shop without leaving the house and there's more choice online than in local shops,' he says. I can't remember the last time I went into a shop to buy anything! I only use my corner shop for collecting and returning things I've bought online. Of course, this is very convenient for me – I actually work there for two hours every morning before college, but I never spend any of the money I've earned in the shop! I have had a few problems with online shopping – I once bought a football shirt that was the wrong size and there was a long delay getting my money back. I still think there are lots of advantages, though, in particular because I don't want to waste money on petrol and parking when I'm shopping.'*

B *Alex, like most young people, spends quite a lot of time online, both chatting with friends and doing school work. However, she says she no longer shops online. 'I had some bad experiences,' she explains. 'Once, I ordered some trousers, and when they arrived, they looked nothing like the picture and didn't even fit my little sister! Now I prefer shopping in real shops. I also realised that going shopping with my friends is a good way for us to actually meet up in person, particularly at the weekends. We meet in the local shopping mall at our favourite café, and we chat about what we're going to buy. I've got a part-time job, so I'm quite independent – I don't have to ask my parents for money for clothes, although they do pay for my school uniform! I've also just passed my driving test and my parents bought me a small car, but I have to pay for petrol and other expenses.'*

C Danni spends a lot of time playing sport at the weekends and going out with his friends in the evening. He also volunteers as a part-time coach for his local football club. So he doesn't have much time for shopping and his friends aren't keen on it. '*I am very interested in fashion and I enjoy buying new clothes online. My favourite way of shopping and one that I would recommend to everyone, is actually to order online and then go to the shop to collect what I've bought. This 'click and collect' method is great. It takes a little more time than having goods delivered to the house, but I prefer to shop this way. I can try on the clothes and if I'm not happy, I can buy something different or leave the items at the shop and get a refund. I still have to drive to the shop and pay for petrol and parking, but I'd rather do that than have to send things back through the post,*' he adds.

D Mariko likes shopping online because she thinks it's cheaper. '*I love it!*' she says. '*I often go to a shop and spend a long time trying on clothes. Then I walk out without buying anything, which embarrasses my friends. I just make notes about the clothes I like, and then go home to search for the best price on the net.*' Some businesses are not happy with 'showrooming', as this practice is called, but Mariko feels that as a student, she should look for the lowest possible price. '*I've had a few problems buying things online,*' she admits. '*A leather handbag I ordered turned out to be just plastic but the company wouldn't return my money. Generally speaking, though, I'm happy with my online buying experience.*' Ironically, Mariko has a Saturday job in a shop and she gets very cross when customers waste her time looking at things that she knows they will go home and buy online!

For each statement, write the correct letter A, B, C or D on the line.

Which person gives the following information?

a) a time when they were sent clothing that was too small .... [1]

b) the fact that they are not paid for their part-time job .... [1]

c) the suggestion that going shopping is a good way to meet up
with friends face-to-face .... [1]

d) an example of how sometimes shopping online can lead to
losing money? .... [1]

e) an explanation of why they go to a shop every day but don't
buy anything .... [1]

f) the idea that they have not had any problems with
shopping online .... [1]

g) the wish to be able to not spend any money on petrol and
parking when shopping .... [1]

h) a recommendation for how to combine buying things online
and in shops .... [1]

i) the idea that they mainly socialise online .... [1]

[Total: 9 marks]

14 Answering note-taking questions

> SYLLABUS INFORMATION:
>
> **Paper 1**
> 2 hours
> Reading and Writing
> 60 marks
>
> The Reading and Writing paper includes four reading and two writing exercises. Exercise 3 requires students to read a text of 400-500 words long and to answer questions by completing some brief notes.

This chapter gives you practice in answering reading questions that require you to take notes. It provides step-by-step advice on how to select details from a short text in order to make notes and to organise them under given headings. It also provides some example exam-style questions for you to practise and develop your reading and note-taking skills.

Skills required for this type of question include:

1 selecting relevant details

2 recognising the difference between facts, ideas and opinions

3 finding and organising related details.

APPROACHING A NOTE-TAKING QUESTION STEP BY STEP

STEP 1 Make sure you understand the task

First, use your skim-reading skills to get an idea of the text's content, what it is about and how it is organised. If the text has no subheadings to help you do this, read the first sentence of each paragraph. Then, carefully read the headings that you are asked to use in the question before going back to the text to start selecting the details you need.

STEP 2 Find the related details

It is a good idea to use different colours to underline the information you think you are going to need. If there are two headings, use two different colours to underline each of the two different kinds of information. Sometimes the information you need will be all together in the text and you may have to sort out the points. Other times the information will be spread through the whole text. Make sure you put the detail under the right heading!

Here is an example exam-style exercise to practise these steps. It develops the note-taking skills you will need for a question that asks you to read text and make notes. Remember, you are not to write anything yet – you are just going to read and underline the points you need. (You will need to have a copy of it so you can write on it.)

Read this speech which was read out at a school assembly and then follow the instructions carefully.

JOIN OUR GREEN CLUB

We are a group of four students in Grade 12 here at Stocklea High School and we have been doing a lot of work recently on how to make our planet a better place to live, for ourselves and for future generations. We have decided, with the help of our Form Tutor, Mr Hussein, to make sure that our school plays a bigger part in helping to improve the environment – not just in our school itself, but in the area around it.

It all started because we were really shocked to hear from Mr Hussein, that the cost for the council – the wages, the transport costs, etc. – of collecting all household rubbish, has doubled in the last two years. This is despite a 5% improvement in recycling used cardboard boxes, newspapers and unwanted office papers. They said that people are still throwing away plastic bottles, yoghurt pots, takeaway food containers and other similar things, instead of recycling them. This all adds to the landfill problem, because we are running out of places to bury it all and we really think that the situation is getting seriously out of control! It's like a monster on the loose!

It's not just how people deal with their household waste that causes the problem. We have all noticed how the town is being spoiled as well, by all the litter lying around. People don't seem to care about the consequences and it makes us really angry – why can't we all just look after our town properly? After a typical Saturday afternoon shopping, the town is disgusting – food wrappers, drink cans, cardboard cups, newspapers – all sorts of things. It's so unhygienic. Our lovely River Mim, which flows through the middle of town, always has empty glass bottles and rusty old cans floating in it and sometimes even broken shopping trolleys. There is also the park, which should be an attractive place to go with friends and family for picnics and to play games but now it's quite ugly and dangerous too. Most parents won't even take their little children there anymore.

So now, we are asking all of you in Grade 11 to come and help. We intend to have a collection through town, this weekend, when we will be going round with black bin bags to collect empty sweet papers, chip packets, cans, etc. and take them to be recycled. Some of our parents have already offered to help, by driving us to the recycling centre. In the afternoon, we will work on cleaning up the river and the park so that they are both attractive and safe once again. It would be great if you could bring some bags or thick gloves or gardening tools with you and you'll need to wear old clothes and boots too, if you have some. We aim to tidy up the footpaths completely by picking up all the newspapers and cans, etc. We are also going to cut back any bushes which have grown too large and get rid of some of the weeds, both of which make the paths difficult to walk down in places. Please come and help. The bigger our group, the faster the results. Meet us in the town square at 10am. Oh and bring a coat in case it rains!

LANGUAGE TIP Always check the spelling of words transferred from a text. If the word is misspelled, you may make a new word which changes the meaning or make the meaning unclear.

Imagine you are going to give a talk about the Green Club to your classmates. Use words from the article to help you write some notes.

Make short notes under each of these headings:
The problems the Green Club has seen in the town

....
....
.... [3]

Actions the Green Club will carry out this weekend

....
....
....
.... [4]

[Total: 7 marks]

TOP TIP Remember, you can always neatly cross out an answer and write in the correct one if you need to.

STEP 3 Make your notes

Read the headings again carefully as you make your notes. Double-check that each detail is one you *really* need. Remember, notes do not need to be full or proper sentences – save time and keep them brief. The number of dotted lines show how many points you need to make; the lengths of the lines give you an idea of how long each point should be. Make sure you have not written the same point twice.

LANGUAGE TIP Remember, it may help you to identify each bullet point for your notes if you find the **topic sentence** that gives the main point of each paragraph in the text.

STEP 4 Keep the notes brief

Imagine you had to use paragraph 2 of the speech to produce a poster to inform people about the facts of the situation in the town.

Here are some sample notes on household waste problems:

i)	the cost of collecting all the rubbish from households – the wages, the transport costs, etc. – has doubled in the last two years; we thought this was a shocking statistic
ii)	despite a 5% improvement in recycling used cardboard boxes, newspapers and unwanted office papers
iii)	people are still throwing away plastic bottles, yoghurt pots, takeaway food containers and other things like these, instead of recycling them
iv)	adds to the landfill problem because we are running out of places to bury it all; the situation is getting out of control – it's like a monster on the loose!

There is not enough room for all of this text. How can you cut it down?

Some advice

You can:

- delete all the examples
- miss out any unnecessary detail
- omit any irrelevant opinions, emotions or comparisons
- use one word which sums up a longer phrase.

And so **i)** becomes:

cost of household rubbish collections has doubled in two years

Look back and see what has been left out and why. Now reduce notes **ii) iii)** and **iv)** in the same way.

Then, with a partner, compare your reduced notes and see if you can make them even briefer. Each one should be between seven and ten words.

Finally, use steps 3 and 4 to complete your notes on other problems in town and on the Green Club's planned actions.

> **TOP TIP**
> You do not have to use your own words for these notes, but sometimes it can save you space and time.

> **LANGUAGE TIP**
> Finding **synonyms** (words with similar or the same meaning) can help you put other people's ideas into your own words when note-taking.

REMEMBER TO...

✓ Skim through the text first; then read the headings carefully before you start to select the details you need.

✓ Read the headings carefully again as you make your notes. Double-check that each detail is one you really need.

✓ You do not need examples, details and comments – unless you are asked for them!

✓ Remember, notes do not need to be in sentences – save time and keep them brief.

✓ In the practice question below, the number of lines tell you how many points to make; the lengths of the lines tell you how long each point should be.

✓ Check that you have not written the same detail twice.

✓ You do not always need to use your own words for these notes.

PRACTISE A NOTE-TAKING QUESTION

You are ready to do an exam-style note-taking question.

Read the following magazine article about the Inuits. Then follow the instructions to make notes.

An Inuit Way of Life

The Inuits are a fascinating group of people, living in the Arctic region. They used to be called 'Eskimos' but are now known as 'Inuits', the name they call themselves, meaning 'the people'. It is remarkable how they have spread from a small region across a huge geographical area, from Greenland to Russia. Today, for example, there are more than 40 000 Inuits living in Canada and over 55 000 in Greenland. It is clear, however, that they have managed to maintain their own values, traditions and beliefs.

Two things that are very important for the Inuits are hunting and art. Hunting has always been necessary as they eat sea creatures like whales and fish, and also birds such as ducks. Their main food source is still the sea, and this will certainly continue to be the case in the future. Now, though, they can use guns rather than the traditional pointed weapons and fishing lines. Art, on the other hand had a more spiritual value for them. They used to make small figures out of stone or bone, that they believed had magical powers, as well as useful items such as pots and weapons. Nowadays, art is important for a different reason. They still use bone or stone, but produce beautiful items like rings and necklaces, which they sell around the world to generate income.

In the frozen north where the Inuits live, there are few building materials. No trees grow there, so houses cannot be constructed from wood and the ground is frozen, so no bricks can be made from mud or stone. However, the Inuits discovered a skilful way of building, involving cutting out large blocks of ice and cleverly making them into shapes, to build circular 'igloos'. These completely enclosed the Inuits and formed protection from snow storms. In summer, after the ice melted, the Inuits lived in tents made from animal skins. To travel across the snow, the Inuits used whatever material was available to make something to sit on, before then being pulled along by teams of dogs. Nowadays, the Inuits still build igloos and use dogs to help them travel, but they live in more solid buildings, designed as more permanent homes. They can also use petrol-driven vehicles.

What does the future hold for the Inuits? Many traditions show no sign of changing. The older generations will still be completely comfortable living in the frozen, Arctic regions of Canada, Greenland and Alaska. Radio and TV programmes using the Inuit language will ensure it continues into the future. Inuit film makers will produce films reflecting Inuit values and ways of life. The Arctic Winter Games, held every two years, will continue and these will also help to keep the Inuit sense of identity strong in the future. Perhaps, however, a more negative aspect is that younger Inuits may find themselves divided between their cultural background and modern society. Some will have to leave the traditional way of life behind as they look to earn a living in cities, either within Canada or other industrialised countries.

Imagine you are going to give a talk about the Inuits, past and present, to your classmates.
Use words from the article to help you write some notes.

Make short notes under each of these headings:
How the present way of life for the Inuits is different from the past

....

....

.... [3]

What will not change for many Inuits in the future

....

....

....

.... [4]

[Total: 7 marks]

15 Answering multiple-choice reading questions

SYLLABUS INFORMATION:

Paper 1
2 hours
Reading and Writing
60 marks

The Reading and Writing paper includes four reading and two writing exercises.

Exercise 4 involves reading a text of 550-600 words long and answering six multiple-choice questions. Questions may focus on the main ideas or details in the text, or on the attitudes or opinions expressed. There are six questions, each with three options to choose between for the answer.

This chapter gives you practice in answering reading questions that require you to pick out details from a text in order to answer multiple-choice comprehension questions. It provides step-by-step advice on how to approach these types of question, using an exam-style question as an example for guidance. It then provides some more exam-style questions for you to practise and develop your comprehension skills.

Skills required for this type of question include:

1 finding relevant details

2 recognising facts and ideas

3 understanding implied meaning

4 understanding the purpose of a text.

APPROACHING MULTIPLE-CHOICE READING QUESTIONS

Here is an exam-style multiple-choice exercise, which is followed by five steps to help you understand how to approach questions like these. Read the step-by-step guidance first before completing the answers.

Read the blog post written by 16-year-old Natalia, who has just started a new hobby, scuba diving, and then answer the questions.

Hello all you fans of online gossip. First of all I'm sorry for being so quiet, but I did say that I would be busy for a while. Anyway, I'm back and I've so much to write! Anyone discovering my blog for the first time, you won't have a clue what I'm talking about, but my lovely regular readers will, of course, know exactly what I have been doing. I sincerely hope that both sets of readers, particularly all you in the latter group, will be as excited as me by my latest adventure! Maybe after reading, you too will all feel brave enough to try something you've never done before!

When I told everyone that my dream was to learn to scuba-dive, I wasn't prepared for such mixed reactions. My new blogging friends were really excited and I think some were quite jealous. Those from my village, who are a lot closer to me – we've known each other since we were four – just thought I was having a laugh and even my six-year-old twin sisters thought I was mad. I remember one of them saying, 'but you don't really like getting wet – you won't even take us to the park if it's raining!'

But – I did it! After getting my medical certificate of fitness, I booked myself into a hostel in London and onto two courses for beginner divers. My swimming was a bit rusty but good enough, so I didn't need extra lessons, which was one less expense. The courses, in the pool and then in open water, were not cheap, although thankfully the cost included the exams. Actually, what should have been the most expensive course – in open water – ended up being the cheapest, because of the voucher that my parents gave me for my birthday – you may remember that was why I decided to take up the hobby in the first place. I must say they have been behind me all the way, from first planting the idea in my mind with that voucher, to looking over the details of the course that I had chosen. They even gave me money towards the equipment, that I had to buy before the open-water dive, which would have been the highest cost of all.

I thought I'd find the open-water diving the most challenging training, but I have to say that it was actually the first pool dives that proved to be the trickiest. I just wasn't used to having my head under water but my instructor reassured me that most beginners feel the same, and once I'd got over that, I was already in love with diving. It was when I got into the open water though, that I realised I was entering a whole world of new experiences. So far, it has been all that I expected and more and I'd really recommend it. I've learned new skills, made new friends and never felt so fit and full of energy in my life.

I can't wait for later this year, when I'm going to Wales for my first sea dive. Just imagine – I'll be diving amongst dolphins and seals, amazing plants, colourful fish and things that I have only ever seen in books. I even have the secret hope of catching sight of the remains of old boats that have been lying there in the sea, undisturbed – except by those who are not too scared to dive 18 metres below sea level – like me for example! Not bad for someone who used to be unwilling even to step outside when it was raining!

1. Who does 'you' specifically refer to in line 5?
    A people who love reading online gossip
    B people who have read the girl's blog before
    C people who are reading the girl's blog for the first time

2. How did people who have known Natalia the longest react when she told them about her new hobby?
    A they thought she was joking
    B they thought she was crazy
    C they were jealous

3. What was the most expensive part of the course?
    A paying for the pool training
    B buying the equipment
    C paying for the open-water training

4. In paragraph 3, Natalia mentions her parents to show how
    A they supported her with her new hobby
    B they paid for all her training
    C they helped her to choose the right course

5. Natalia suggests that most beginners will find the pool training the most difficult because

    A they are not fit enough

    B they are not confident swimmers

    C they are not used to being underwater

6. What does she hope the readers will gain overall from reading her latest post?

    A an understanding of the challenges of starting a new hobby

    B the courage to try something new

    C the inspiration to go and try scuba-diving

[Total: 6 marks]

STEP 1   Understanding the task

In a multiple-choice reading task, you do not need to write any words or phrases. Instead, you need to demonstrate your understanding of a text by choosing the correct answer from a choice of a few different options.

Multiple-choice questions test some of the language skills that you have practised in other sections, such as understanding synonyms and paraphrasing. They also test reading skills that you are already familiar with from other types of reading comprehension tasks, such as the ability to:
- skim and scan a text to find specific factual information
- identify and select details for a specific purpose
- demonstrate an understanding of implied meaning
- understand the purpose of a text.

Remember, when preparing to answer a multiple-choice question:
- In the exam-style question on the previous pages the order of the answers are in the same order as the questions. You can also see that question 6 is a question about the purpose of the text overall.
- Skim read the text to get a general idea of the overall topic and the content of each paragraph.
- Read the questions carefully to understand what is required, underlining any key words.
- Go through the choices of answers carefully. You may be able to use your common sense to eliminate an option that does not seem possible.
- Remember that all of the possible choices may be found somewhere in the text but only one of them will be the correct answer to each question.
- Read the text again more carefully to find the correct choice for each question.

STEP 2   Answering 'what' and 'how' multiple-choice questions

Remember that **What** questions require you to read the text to find specific details about an event, a situation or something that happened.

How questions require details about the way something happened, or the way someone feels about an event or situation.

It is a good idea to first find the paragraph in which you think the correct answer is contained. Then underline appropriate sentences in that paragraph, before going back to the choices to eliminate the two which are incorrect.

2.1 Look at question 2 from the previous example exercise. The answer can be found in paragraph 2. The key words in the question are, 'who have known Natalia the longest'. Look at the highlighted sentences in the following paragraph to eliminate the incorrect answers.

● *How did people who have known Natalia the longest react when she told them about her new hobby?*

When I told everyone that my dream was to learn to scuba-dive, I wasn't prepared for such mixed reactions. My new blogging friends were really excited and I think some were quite jealous. Those from my village, who are a lot closer to me – we've known each other since we were four – just thought I was having a laugh and even my six-year-old twin sisters thought I was mad. I remember one of them saying, 'but you don't really like getting wet – you won't even take us to the park if it's raining!'

There are three different groups of people mentioned, however, we know that:
● her blogging friends are new
● the girl is 16 and her sisters are six so they have known her for six years.
● her friends from the village have known her since they were four, so for 12 years.

The people that have known her the longest, therefore, are her friends from the village, who 'thought she was having a laugh'. Which choice of answer, A, B or C would be correct?

The above example also shows you an example of **inferring** an answer, which we will explore again in Step 4.

2.2 Now look at the following question. The answer can be found in paragraph 3. The key words in the question are 'the most expensive'. Look at the highlighted sentences in the paragraph below to eliminate the incorrect answers.

● *What was the most expensive part of the course?*

But – I did it! After getting my medical certificate of fitness, I booked myself into a hostel in London and onto two courses for beginner divers. My swimming was a bit rusty but good enough, so I didn't need extra lessons, which was one less expense. The courses, in the pool and then in open water, were not cheap, although thankfully the cost included the exams. Actually, what should have been the most expensive course – in open water – ended up being the cheapest, because of the voucher that my parents gave me for my birthday – you may remember that was why I decided to take up the hobby in the first place. I must say they have been behind me all the way, from first planting the idea in my mind with that voucher, to looking over the details of the course that I had chosen. They even gave me money towards the equipment, that I had to buy before the open-water dive, which would have been the highest cost of all.

There are actually five references to cost, however we know that:
● extra swimming lessons were not necessary i.e. no cost
● the exams were included in the price i.e. no additional cost
● she had a voucher for the pool course, so that was cheaper than the open-water course
● the equipment 'would have been the highest cost of all'

Which choice of answer, A, B or C would be correct?

STEP 3 Answering questions about the meaning or purpose of an individual word or words

One of the questions you may be asked in an exercise like this is about what a particular word or words mean or refer to in a particular line of the text. To find the best answer, you will need to read the whole paragraph. Look at question 1 in the exercise for an example.

● *Who does 'you' specifically refer to in line 5?*

Anyone discovering my blog for the first time, *you won't have a clue what I'm talking about, but* *my lovely regular readers will, of course, know exactly what I have been doing. I sincerely hope that both sets of readers, particularly all you in the latter group, will be as excited as me by my latest adventure!*

All three possible answers have been mentioned somewhere in the paragraph but here you need to understand what 'the latter group' means to be able to identify the correct option.

Which choice of answer, A, B or C would be correct?

3.1 Another of the questions you may be asked may be about why a particular word or words are used in a paragraph or what the overall meaning of the paragraph is. To find the best answer for these purpose questions you have to read the whole paragraph. Look at question 4 in the task for an example.

● **In paragraph 3, Natalia mentions her parents to show how…**

Having read the whole paragraph again, which choice of answer, A, B or C would be correct?

STEP 4 Answering multiple-choice questions about implied or inferred meaning

We saw one example in Step 1 of how the best choice of answer may be inferred or implied rather than stated directly and other examples in Step 2. Another common question of this type may be one which asks 'what is suggested by' something.

Look at question 5 from the task. The answer can be found in paragraph 4.

● **Natalia suggests that most beginners will find the pool training the most difficult because**

The key words in the question are 'pool training' and 'the most difficult'. Look at the highlighted sentences in the paragraph below to eliminate the incorrect answers.

I thought I'd find the open water diving the most challenging training, but I have to say that it was actually the first pool dives that proved to be the trickiest. I just wasn't used to having my head under water but my instructor reassured me that most beginners feel the same, and once I'd got over that, I was already in love with diving.

You can eliminate choices A and B as they are not mentioned in connection to difficulty for other people. The writer states that having her head under water was the trickiest and her tutor reassured her that most beginners feel the same.

Which choice of answer, A, B or C would be correct?

STEP 5 Answering multiple-choice questions about the overall purpose of a text

Remember that a writer always has a different reason or purpose for writing their text. There are different words to describe this text purpose and you need to look at the text overall to see what the writer is trying to achieve and communicate to their readers.

> **TOP TIP**
> The basic purposes of non-fiction texts can be divided into four groups:
> Descriptive
> Informative
> Persuasive
> Instructive
> Remember DIPI.

- **What does she hope the readers will gain overall from reading her latest post?**

In the previous task the purpose of the text is identified in the first paragraph:

Maybe after reading, you too will all feel brave enough to try something you've never done before!

It is also reiterated in the tone of the final paragraph.

Which choice of answer, A, B or C would be correct?

Now that you understand what to do and the order in which to do it, look again at the example multiple-choice exercise and complete the answers.

REMEMBER TO…

✓ Skim read the text to get a general idea of the overall subject.

✓ As you are skim reading for the overall subject, take note of the content/topic of each paragraph.

✓ Read the questions carefully to understand what is required.

✓ Underline any key words in each question.

✓ Read the text again more carefully to find the paragraph which contains the correct answer.

✓ Go through the answer choices carefully, eliminating those that are incorrect to leave the best one.

PRACTISE A MULTIPLE-CHOICE READING QUESTION

You are now ready to do an exam-style multiple-choice exercise.

Read the blog written by Jenni about the role of non-verbal signs in communication and then answer the questions that follow.

My cat speaks sign language with her tail
(A quote by Robert A. M. Stern; architect and author)

I'm 17 years old and about to go to university to study Kinesics. If that means nothing to you, it is the study of body language, eye contact and facial expression – in other 'words', non-verbal communication.

Let me just start by telling you a sad story with a happy ending! I've always had a close bond with my cousin, so was horrified when my aunt phoned to say that Justin had been in an accident and was in hospital. Imagine my next shock, when I visited him and whilst perfectly conscious, he was completely deaf. The thing is that despite his deafness, we could still communicate perfectly, just by using our hands, face and eyes. Justin's condition was temporary, thankfully; still, it got me thinking and I realised that I wanted to learn more about non-verbal communication.

My parents had never tried to influence my decisions but they were thrilled when I first told them my intention to follow in my dad's footsteps and study veterinary science, particularly Mum. She is a great believer in doing something at university, which leads to a worthwhile future career. So, when I announced that I was studying Kinesics instead, she commented, 'Well Jenni, it's not something I've heard of and I really don't know what job it will lead to.' Being a veterinarian, my dad understood about animals communicating without words – but his reaction was similar. After a long chat with them, though, they felt reassured. We talked about the degree and possible future careers – in health or social care for example. I expressed an interest in working with people who lose their hearing later in life, or have problems communicating verbally because of mental health issues or Alzheimer's.

I was reading a book on Kinesics, when I remembered Dad telling me how Beethoven had lost his hearing, yet continued to perform and compose incredible music, which some believe was better than his earlier work. If anything, it seemed to make him even more of a genius. Dad also talked about other incredible people with little or no hearing – the inventor Thomas Edison, the activist Helen Keller, actress Marlee Matlin, YouTuber Rikki Poynter and lifestyle bloggers Hermon and Heroda Berhane. Then I had to laugh because my cat, Sushi, came in with her tail upright and jumped up, purring and rubbing my book with her nose. Like Dad I had always understood animals, without acknowledging that it was their non-verbal communication I was connecting with.

Nowadays, we have more channels of communication than ever, yet sometimes it seems like we are actually talking to and understanding each other less. All I see, is people everywhere, with their heads down, looking at a screen; people doing anything to avoid accidental eye or body contact. If we continue like this, talking will become less of a feature of our lives, but at the same time we still need to be able to understand each other. It would be great if you all now rush out for a DVD on sign language, but I realise that's unlikely. I do suggest, however, that we take more time to observe body language, look people in the eye during conversations and be aware of the expression on our face. Just this morning I gave my neighbour a big smile and a wave. It felt good to see how his shoulders lifted immediately and he got a spring in his step. So, what are you waiting for – go and non-verbally communicate with someone! Just don't, I beg you, start staring complete strangers in the eye, whilst smiling madly, because you run the risk of being reported!

1. In paragraph 2, Jenni talks about her cousin, to explain:

   A how she helped him to recover from his accident.

   B how she first became interested in Kinesics

   C how she learned the importance of communicating with family

2. How did Jenni's mum react when she first told them about her change in degree?

   A she was surprised that it was possible to do such a degree at university.

   B she was thrilled by her daughter's choice

   C she wasn't certain what job it would lead to in the future

3. What does 'it' refer to in line 3 of paragraph 4?

   A Beethoven's incredible music

   B Beethoven's loss of hearing

   C Beethoven's earlier work

4. What understanding of non-verbal communication does Jenni share with her father?

   A how it is used to communicate with people who have dementia or mental health issues

   B how it is used by famous people who have lost their hearing

   C how it is used by animals

5. Jenni suggests that:

   A people understand each other better now, thanks to having more channels of communication

   B people will talk to each other less in the future

   C people should stop using technology so much

6. Jenni hopes that by reading her blog, people will:

   A become inspired to learn sign language

   B become more confident about making changes to their academic and career choices

   C become more aware of the importance of communicating with each other non-verbally.

[Total: 6 marks]

16 Answering informal writing questions

SYLLABUS INFORMATION:

Paper 1
2 hours
Reading and Writing
60 marks

The Reading and Writing paper includes four reading and two writing exercises.

The first writing exercise involves writing 120-160 words in the style of an informal email in response to prompts giving information about the purpose of the piece of writing and its audience. Marks are awarded for both content and language.

This chapter gives you practice in completing a writing task which informs, explains or describes. Using an example exam-style question, it provides step-by-step guidance on how to approach informal writing questions. This type of question requires you to adapt language and style according to the reader and the purpose, to use informal vocabulary and structures, to use accurate grammar and punctuation, to organise your ideas into coherent text, and to use a range of informal linking phrases appropriately. At the end of the chapter an exam-style question is provided for you to practise and develop your writing skills.

Skills required for this type of question include:

1 writing to describe, inform or explain

2 adapting your style according to the form, reader and purpose of the writing

3 using a range of grammatical structures accurately

4 using a range of appropriate vocabulary and spelling accurately

5 using linking phrases and connectives correctly

6 using punctuation correctly.

APPROACHING AN INFORMAL WRITING QUESTION

Informal writing questions require you to produce a piece of writing to explain or describe something, or to give an account of something. You are asked to imagine you are in a particular situation and you are given some guidance about what to include in the writing. There may be a picture guide and a short explanation of the context of the situation as well as some prompts of points you need to include in your writing. In this type of writing you have to be clear and write something which the reader will enjoy.

Here is an example exam-style question to practise this style of writing. Read the steps that follow for guidance before attempting to answer it.

You recently bought a present for someone. There was a problem with it.

Write an email to a friend about the problem.

In your email you should:

- explain why you thought the person would like the present
- explain that there is problem with the present and describe the problem
- tell your friend what you are going to do about it.

Write about 120 to 160 words.

You will receive up to six marks for the content of your email, and up to nine marks for the language used.

[15 marks]

STEP 1 Decide on the form, reader and purpose

Read the details of the task very carefully. The first things to check are:

- What **form** of writing are you being asked for? Is it an email or a blog?
- What is the **purpose** of the writing? Is it to inform, explain or describe something?
- Who is the **reader** – the person you are writing for? Is it a good friend? Is it someone you have seen recently or someone that you have not seen for a while?
- How will you keep the style informal? Are there informal ways to address the reader and engage with them? Are there informal opening and closing phrases that you could use? Are there discourse markers, such as 'well', 'so', 'anyway', 'you know', 'right', 'okay', that you could include?
- How will you keep the language informal? Are there opportunities to introduce contractions, colloquial words or phrases, idioms, phrasal verbs, personal pronouns and less formal vocabulary?

LANGUAGE TIP

Colloquial language is the language we use in everyday conversation. One way of indicating this in writing is to use **phrasal verbs** such as *call off* meaning to cancel or *bring up* to raise a topic. They are formed by combining a preposition with a common verb to create a verb with a different meaning. They can add informality to writing.

All these things will affect the way you write. You need to write in an appropriately informal style.

You learned about style and degree of formality in your writing in Chapters 6 and 12.

Before you write anything, in the question underline who the reader is. Discuss this with a partner and decide together on informal opening and closing phrases/sentences. Then discuss how you could personally engage the reader throughout the email or blog, for example with the use of discourse markers.

STEP 2 Look at the picture and the explanation of the context of the question

In this example question there is a picture guide. The picture is of a girl who seems to be disappointed as she looks at something in a box. The picture is just a visual guide to the context but it does not mean that you have to describe that particular situation or write as if you are the girl opening the box.

In this question there is an explanation of the context. In this case, 'You recently bought a present for someone. There was a problem with it.'

Underline the key words and then in pairs, discuss these questions:
- Why do people buy presents and for whom?
- What present or presents have you bought and why?
- What present or presents have you received from someone and why?
- What type of problems could there be with something that you bought?
- What can people do if they buy something online that has a problem?
- What can people do if they buy something from a shop and there is a problem with it?

STEP 3 Address the bullet point prompts

You must address all bullet point prompts in your content. So it will help if you make a basic plan of your answer. You could do this as a 'concept map', like the example below:

Imagine you decided to buy a radio-controlled car for your brother.

Now look at the three bullet points.
- explain why you thought the person would like the present
- explain that there is problem with the present and describe the problem
- tell your friend what you are going to do about it.

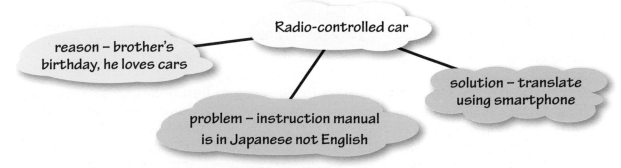

Do not spend more than five minutes on your plan.

If you follow this plan when writing your answer, you can be sure that you have included all the necessary content.

Remember that to address the content appropriately, you need to think about language.

In pairs:

Look at the question again:
- what tense or tenses will you use in your opening and closing sentences?
- are the bullet point prompts requiring you to write in the past, present or future tenses?

STEP 4 Develop your ideas

When writing your final answer, it is important to develop the content so that it is not just three short sentences addressing each bullet point. Remember that your answer should ideally not be too short or too long.

To help develop your ideas:
- Try to imagine a situation clearly in your mind.
- Try to think of something similar that you have experienced or could experience.
- Give small details to develop the points, for example the model of car, how old your brother is, when and where you bought the present.

Here are some ideas on how you could develop each point for this question:

1 **Why you thought the person would like the present:** it was your brother's birthday and you know he loves cars.
   Development: he already has a collection of radio-controlled vehicles / you have been saving up your pocket money to buy him something a little more expensive / it was a very special birthday / your mum and dad gave you some money as well, to buy it.

2 **Explain there is a problem and describe the problem with the present:** the instruction manual is in Japanese not English.
   Development: You had this problem with something you bought before / you wish you could speak Japanese / Your brother doesn't need instructions so it's not a real problem.

3 **Tell your friend what you are going to do about it:** use your smartphone to translate.
   Development: You have no time to return the present before his birthday; you will never buy another radio-controlled car / you will never shop online again / you will buy a book next time / you will also write to the seller to complain / you will write a review on their website.

Think carefully about your choice of verb tenses:

1 – 'why you thought the person would like the present' = mainly past tense

2 – 'what the problem is' = mainly present tense

3 – 'what are you going to do' = future actions so future tense.

The notes in point 1 above explain why you thought the person would like the present. These notes could be used to write:

I bought it for my brother's tenth birthday and thought he would like it because he collects anything radio-controlled. As he is bit obsessed, it was obvious what to get. I ordered a model car, although I don't like cars, so it was really boring!

Looking at the above example:
- What did the writer buy?
- Who did she buy it for?
- Why did she buy it – reason 1?
- Why did she buy it – reason 2?
- How did she feel about buying it?

You can see how a lot of ideas can be included in a small number of words.

In pairs:
- Look at the above ideas for developing the points and discuss which you prefer and why.
- Decide whether there are any other ways that you could add details to develop the points.

 TOP TIP When writing to a word limit you may not be able to include all the points. In which case, choose just one or two of the main points to develop the argument.

STEP 5 Organise your informal writing appropriately

Use paragraphs effectively

Although you are producing an informal piece of writing, such as an email of blog, it is still important to organise your work into clear paragraphs. This will help your reader to understand and follow your ideas easily and coherently.

Here are some ways that you could start your first paragraph in an informal email:

> *I hope you're well   Thanks for your email*
> *It was great to hear from you*

Here are some ways that you could start your last paragraph in and informal email:

> *Say hello to your sister   Hope to hear from you soon*
> *Write soon*

With a partner, think of other ways to start your first and last paragraphs in an informal email.

Then, together, think of ways that you could start and finish an informal blog.

Use informal linking words and connectives

Here are some linking words and phrases you could use to connect ideas between or within paragraphs when writing an informal email or blog to explain, describe or inform:

and	*because*	*although*	*anyway*
also	*so*	*as*	*for example*

Look at the example paragraph again and identify the words that the student uses to connect their ideas together.

Then look at how the writer also uses the pronoun 'he' to avoid repetition of the words 'my brother'.

 LANGUAGE TIP Using **pronouns**, for instance, *he, it, they* after you have used the noun once, help to make sure that the paragraph runs smoothly. For example, *Anyway <u>my brother</u> hardly ever reads the instructions because <u>he</u> knows so much about how radio control works.*

Some of the other methods for organising your email are:
- punctuation such as a colon (:) or a dash (–), to show the link between the ideas at the start of the sentence and the ideas in the rest of it
- relative pronouns, for example, *which, that*
- connectives to show movement through time, for instance, *for a start, then, after that*

Now write the complete email and then compare your answer with a partner or in a group.

REMEMBER TO…

✓ Open and close your email in an appropriately informal and friendly way.

✓ Think about whether you need to use the past, present or future verb tense.

✓ Address each bullet point, adding at least one brief extra detail to fully develop the point.

✓ Write in clear paragraphs.

✓ Keep to the word limit.

✓ Link your ideas between and within the paragraphs with connectives and linking phrases so that your writing flows smoothly.

✓ Use informal language throughout.

PRACTISE AN INFORMAL WRITING QUESTION TO EXPLAIN OR DESCRIBE

Now you are ready to do an exam-style informal writing question.

You were recently going somewhere by train and something unexpected happened during the journey.

Write an email to a friend explaining what happened.

In your email, you should:

● explain where you were going and why

● describe what happened

● say how you felt about what happened.

Write about 120 to 160 words.

You will receive up to six marks for the content of your email, and up to nine marks for the language used.

[15 marks]

> **TOP TIP**
> Don't forget the basics. Remember, sentences always start with a capital letter and end with a full-stop, exclamation mark or question mark. Sentences should also include a subject and a verb.

(17) Answering formal writing questions

This chapter gives you practice in completing a formal writing task. This type of task involves writing to discuss, explain, argue, inform, report, review or make suggestions. A piece of formal writing may involve:
- discussing something or arguing for and against it
- convincing or persuading the reader
- giving your personal opinion
- explaining, describing or informing about something such as a situation, happening or event
- making suggestions, for example, to improve the situation or event.

Formal writing questions include prompts to get you started, for example in the form of speech bubbles which offer different points of view on the subject, but you should also use your own ideas.

Just like informal writing tasks, these questions require you to adapt your language and style to the reader and purpose. But this time you need to use a formal structure and style, including linking words and connective devices, formal vocabulary and accurate grammar and punctuation. They have a set word limit.

Skills required for this type of question include:

1 writing to formally discuss, explain, inform, report or review

2 adapting your style according to the form, reader and purpose of the writing

3 using a range of grammatical structures accurately

4 using a range of appropriate vocabulary and spelling accurately

5 using linking phrases and connectives correctly

6 using punctuation correctly.

APPROACHING A FORMAL WRITING QUESTION INCLUDING OPINION OR ARGUMENT

Let's look at an example exam-style writing task for an article including opinion or argument.

A recent survey of road use reveals that there is too much traffic in your town. So the council is considering setting up a 'congestion charge'. This means that anyone who wants to drive their car into the town centre will have to pay to do so.

Your teacher wants students' opinions and has asked you to write a formal article on the topic for your school magazine.

In your article, discuss the advantages and disadvantages of introducing a 'congestion charge' and give your personal opinion on the subject.

Here are some comments from students in your class:

> *This will hit the poorest and weakest people the hardest; it's not fair.*

> *My parents own a shop in the town centre and this change will mean fewer customers for them.*

> *This is a great idea because it will make our town a safer place.*

> *This is a good idea to help cut down on pollution and noise in the town centre and could raise money for town improvements.*

Now write a formal article for the school magazine.

The comments above may give you some ideas, and you should also use some ideas of your own.

Write about 120 to 160 words.

You will receive up to six marks for the content of your article and up to nine marks for the language used.

[15 marks]

STEP 1 Decide on the form, reader and purpose

As in the informal writing question, the initial things to check are:

- What **form** of writing are you being asked for?
- Who is the **reader** – the person you are writing for?
- What is the **purpose** of the writing? Is it to explain or describe something? Is it to persuade someone to do something? Is it to convince someone of your opinion? Is it to discuss two sides of an argument before concluding with your personal opinion? Sometimes it may be a mixture of several of these.

Before you write anything, underline the words and phrases in the question that tell you the form, reader and purpose of the task. Then discuss these with a partner. Remember that this is a formal writing task so you should aim to show you can adapt your style appropriately.

> You learned about style and degree of formality in your writing in Chapters 6 and 12.

STEP 2 Understand the prompts – the speech bubbles

The prompts for a formal writing task for opinion or argument may be in the form of speech bubbles. These will give different points of view about a topic which you can explore and develop in your writing.

The prompts in this example give different viewpoints on the issue of whether or not the town council should introduce a congestion charge. Unlike an informal writing task, there is no picture guide or bullet points to address or to tell you the content of each paragraph – this is left entirely up to you. Instead, formal writing questions like these just say you have to write an article giving your views. So you need to do some more planning for this task and decide what points to make in each paragraph.

In pairs, answer the following questions:
- Look at the four speech bubbles – which ones are in favour of the congestion charge; which ones are against?
- Who do you think would agree with these points of view – any particular groups/types of people?
- Which point of view do you agree with on balance, and why?
- Try to imagine what other people in the town might think, for example, parents with young children, people in wheelchairs, elderly people, shop owners. How could these ideas help you write your article?

> **TOP TIP** Try to come up with your own ideas, but always make sure they are relevant to the question. Using a concept map or outline plan before you start writing should keep you on the right track.

STEP 3 Use the prompts – the speech bubbles

There are two possible approaches to using the speech bubbles to write a formal article depending on whether:
- the purpose of your article is to **convince or persuade** the reader that your point of view is the correct one so the overall tone of your article is persuasive

or

- the purpose of your article is to **balance both sides of the argument** by looking at the advantages and disadvantages of each one. With this type of article you should still remember to give your personal opinion.

3.1 Let us imagine you decide to argue strongly <u>against</u> the plan to introduce a congestion charge. First, identify which two of the speech bubbles argue <u>against</u> the congestion charge. You are probably going to use one or both of these points to argue your viewpoint.

Next, use the comments as part of a concept map, just as you have in earlier chapters. Draw lines out from the first speech bubble and add the ideas which could develop this point of view. Here is an example:

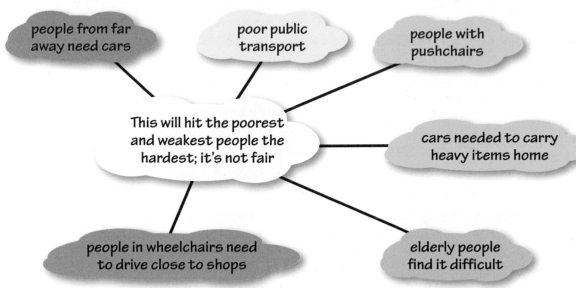

Now do the same for the other speech bubble which argues against the congestion charge.

3.2 What about the points which support the charge? Do you think they are true to any extent? You can use these ideas in order to support your point of view by arguing against them. Here is an example:

Now do the same for the other comment in the speech bubble which supports the congestion charge.

In pairs, compare your notes and see if you can add any more ideas.

Can you think of any reasons why you personally might be against the congestion charge? How would it affect you?

3.3 Now imagine you are strongly <u>in favour of</u> introducing a congestion charge.

With your partner follow the previous steps once more, but this time with the intention of persuading the reader that the congestion charge is a good idea.

Can you think of any other reasons why you personally might be in favour of the congestion charge?

3.4 Now consider how you would write this as a more discursive article, which outlines the advantages and disadvantages of congestion charge before finishing <u>by expressing</u> your own opinion. Decide with a partner what to include or omit from your article.

> **TOP TIP**
> Remember to check how many words you need to write for any formal writing task and to keep this in mind while you are planning your ideas.

STEP 4 Develop your ideas

When you write sentences giving your point of view, avoid just stating your viewpoints in a list.

To help develop your point of view:
- try to imagine the situation clearly
- view it from different angles so you can refer to other viewpoints – either to support your case, or to help you argue against them
- offer details to support your points
- give brief reasons for your opinions.

> **TOP TIP**
> Remember that you do not need to include all the points made in the speech bubbles and that you can also include ideas of your own.

So, for example, these notes:

> People from far away need cars / cars needed to carry heavy
> items home / poor public transport / people in wheelchairs need
> to drive close to shops / elderly people find it difficult / people
> with pushchairs

could become:

> The congestion charge will be bad for people who cannot afford the charges. It will be very hard for people who live far away in country areas without buses or trains to get into town. They need to use their cars. Shopping can be very heavy. It would be difficult for them to carry things like televisions to the car parks on the outskirts of town. Elderly people and people who are sick would be badly affected. They are not able to walk all the way into town. It is the same problem for parents with pushchairs and energetic young children, who need their cars to get into the centre as easily and quickly as possible.

Underline in this example paragraph the reasons given for the viewpoint and the examples.

TOP TIP Never simply copy out the words in the speech bubbles. If you want to include the idea, you must try to use your own words as far as you can.

Now write two more paragraphs: one using the notes you made around the other speech bubble against the congestion charge and one using the notes you made in favour of the congestion charge to support your viewpoint.

STEP 5 Use paragraphs correctly

Here are some connective phrases you could use to link ideas within or between paragraphs when writing to give an opinion and offer a clear line of argument:

> *on one hand... on the other hand   another reason why...*
> *alternatively,   some people think that...*
> *first of all, ... secondly, ...   as well as this...*
> *in addition, I think that ... therefore...*

You can introduce your final paragraph with a phrase such as:

> *To sum up, I think that...   On the whole, my view is...*
> *In brief, I strongly believe that...*

Think of three more connecting words or phrases. Compare your suggestions with a partner or in a group, and see how many words and phrases you can find together.

Read the example article of 160 words below. Try to identify these five linking devices:
- a topic sentence introducing the main idea of paragraph 1
- the word 'them' used to refer back to the previous sentence
- three separate words/phrases linking ideas
- the word 'also' to make a link within a paragraph
- one phrase to introduce the final summary and opinion.

In my opinion, a congestion charge is not a good idea, for several reasons. For a start, many people will not be able to afford it.

Secondly, it will be will be hard for people who live far away in areas without public transport to get into town. In addition, there are people who need to use their cars because shopping, for example, can be very heavy. It would especially be a problem for them to carry things such as televisions to the car parks on the outskirts of town.

A further group of people who will be affected are the elderly and sick, as they cannot walk very far. A similar situation applies to parents with young children in pushchairs, who also need cars to get into town as easily and quickly as possible.

To sum up, I strongly believe the congestion charge would be very unfair and as a consequence I don't think the council should introduce it.

APPROACHING A FORMAL WRITING QUESTION TO REPORT AND MAKE SUGGESTIONS

The piece of formal writing may instead be to inform, report and make suggestions. Much of the information in the previous steps will also apply to this type of writing.

Let us look at an example exam-style writing task for a formal report.

Your class recently took part in a one-day course on 'Improving your computer skills' at the local library. The head of your school wants students' opinions about the course, and you have been asked to write a report.

In your report, say what was good about the course, and suggest how it could be improved.

Here are some comments from students in your class:

> I already knew most of it so I didn't learn very much.

> The computers were more modern than the ones we have at school.

> We did too much reading and not enough practice.

> The instructor was very good.

Now write a formal report for the head of your school.

The comments above may give you some ideas, and you should also use some ideas of your own.

Write about 120 to 160 words.

You will receive up to six marks for the content of your report and up to nine marks for the language used.

[15 marks]

STEP 1 Decide on the form, reader and purpose

You should think about the form, reader and purpose in the same way as you did in STEP 1 of writing a formal article. The main difference will be that the purpose of writing is now to report on a situation, event or happening and make some suggestions, often for ideas on how to make improvements.

STEP 2 Understand the prompts – the speech bubbles

You should think about the comments in the speech bubbles in the same way as you did in STEP 2 of writing a formal article.

The prompts in this example report question give different viewpoints on what students thought was good or bad about the one-day computer course.

In pairs, discuss the speech bubbles in the same way as you did before, but this time in the context of the report question.

STEP 3 Use the speech bubbles

The purpose of your report is to identify what was good about the course and what could be improved, so this time you should look at all the student comments in the speech bubbles.

Use the comments as part of a concept map, to note down your ideas.

STEP 4 Develop your ideas

You should approach the development of your ideas in the same way as you did previously.

In pairs, try to imagine the situation clearly and think about how you could develop the student comments adding some details of your own and offering reasons. What else could be good about the one-day course? What else could be bad about the course? What suggestions could you make to improve the course?

STEP 5 Use paragraphs correctly

You will be using paragraphs and connective words and phrases in a similar way to the formal article. The main difference in a report is that it can be helpful to use sub-headings for each paragraph. These do not have to be complicated but they allow the reader to see at a glance what is contained within each paragraph. The following is an example of how you could organise your report with appropriate sub-headings and linking phrases:

Our one-day computer course at the library

Introduction

The aims of this report are to discuss what students enjoyed about their one-day computer course and make suggestions for improvements.

Good things about the course

Some students thought that .... *Others felt that* ....

Bad things about the course

On the other hand, some people commented that .... *In addition others said* ....

Recommendations

In my opinion, it was a good course and I enjoyed it, but *I would like to make a few suggestions* on how it could be improved.

1 *It would be a good idea to* ....

2 *I would also recommend that* ....

3 *A final suggestion would be to* ....

If these suggestions are taken into consideration, I have no doubt that future courses will be a success and I would have no hesitation in recommending them for other students of our school.

 LANGUAGE TIP Using an **impersonal form** brings formality and authority to your writing. For example *It is clear...*, *It would be wise* or *It will be a challenge...* It is also an effective form to use when giving recommendations.

Now write your report and compare it with a partner's report.

REMEMBER TO...

✓ Read the question through carefully.

✓ Read it a second time and underline key words or phrases which tell you the form, reader and purpose.

✓ Look at any speech bubbles supplied. Remember, these are just ideas you can use if you wish. If you can think of your own ideas, so much the better. If you can't think of your own ideas, it doesn't matter – you can still produce an excellent piece of writing using one or more of the ideas you are given.

✓ Make some very brief notes by each prompt – or a quick concept map – so that you have an idea about what to include.

✓ You may be able to think of each prompt as one paragraph. If you are writing a report, remember that you can include a title and appropriate sub-headings.

✓ Use your own words as far as possible even if you are using the prompts provided.

✓ Leave a few minutes at the end to check your work.

PRACTISE A FORMAL WRITING QUESTION INCLUDING OPINION OR ARGUMENT

Now you are ready to do an exam-style formal writing question including opinion or argument.

In the school magazine, a teacher has written an article about how parents should not allow children under the age of 16 to play computer games. Your class teacher wants students' opinions on the subject and you have been asked to write an article for the next magazine.

In your article you should say whether you agree or disagree and why.

Here are some comments you have heard from different people on the subject:

We can learn a lot from playing computer games.

Computer games are a good way to relax.

Young people should study in the evenings, not play computer games.

Children will start talking to their parents more if they are not playing games.

Now write an article for your teacher.

The comments above may give you some ideas, and you should also use some ideas of your own.

Write about 120 to 160 words.

You will receive up to six marks for the content of your report and up to nine marks for the language used.

[15 marks]

18 Responding to listening questions

SYLLABUS INFORMATION:

Paper 2
Approximately 50 minutes (includes 6 minutes transfer time)
Listening
40 marks

The Listening paper of Cambridge IGCSE English as a Second Language consists of five exercises with a total of 40 multiple-choice questions. Students listen to both short and longer recorded texts and answer questions from three or four possible options. Examples of text types are monologues, interviews or conversations. Each recorded text is played twice. At the end of the test, students have six minutes to transfer their answers onto a separate answer sheet.

The number of multiple-choice questions for each exercise are:
Exercise 1 – 8 questions
Exercise 2 – 10 questions
Exercise 3 – 8 questions
Exercise 4 – 6 questions
Exercise 5 – 8 questions

This chapter gives you practice in answering listening questions. It gives you guidance on how to approach multiple-choice listening questions, and includes some exam-style questions for you to practise and develop your listening skills.

In listening questions, you have to listen carefully to one or more people speaking, find the relevant details from what they say and then use them to select the answer. Types of listening question include:
- a multiple-choice question, with either visual or written prompts
- a gap-fill question, with multiple-choice options.
- a matching question

In the following pages we will be looking at different sorts of listening questions, one at a time.

Skills required for listening questions include:

1 listening carefully for details

2 understanding key words and phrases

3 understanding a speaker's ideas or opinions

4 understanding which information you need to choose for the correct answer

5 understanding what is implied although not directly stated.

APPROACHING MULTIPLE CHOICE LISTENING QUESTIONS WITH VISUAL PROMPTS

This type of question involves listening to a recording of a person speaking, or a short conversation and selecting the relevant details to complete the answer. In the example exam-style questions on the next page, you are given four different visual options and you need to choose the one which shows the correct answer.

Skills required for this type of listening question include:

1 listening carefully for details

2 understanding key words and phrases

3 understanding a speaker's ideas

4 understanding which information you need to choose for the correct answer

REMEMBER TO…

✓ Look at all the visual prompts carefully to understand what each one shows, for example what or where the place is, or who the people are likely to be and where the conversation could be taking place.

✓ Underline key words in the questions to help you focus.

✓ Identify what kind of detail you should be listening for. For example, is it a weight? A time? A day or date?

✓ If the visual prompts or questions relate to numbers, for example weights, times or dates, say them to yourself to think about the way they sound before you listen.

✓ Use your common sense to identify any visual prompts which seem unlikely.

✓ Make good use of every pause in the recordings as you listen.

✓ Use the second playing of the question to check that you have selected the right details and the correct visual prompt.

✓ Avoid choosing the first option that you hear which sounds correct, as there may be two possible answers that are quite similar.

Practise listening: multiple-choice questions with visual prompts

You will hear six short recordings. For each question, choose the correct answer, A, B, C or D.

1. What birthday present is the girl going to give to her mother? [1]

 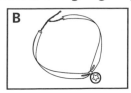 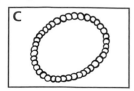 

2. Which museum do the boy and girl decide to visit first? [1]

3. Where does the family decide to go camping? [1]

4. Where did the girl leave her library book? [1]

5. Why can't Alan and Paula go out together in the afternoon? [1]

6. What will the second performance of the evening be? [1]

The key question words – *What, Which, Who, Where, When, How* and *Why* – will help signpost the information you need to find: *what* and *which* = a thing; *who* = a person or group; *where* = a location or setting; *when* = a time; *how* = a process or way; *why* = a reason or cause.

APPROACHING SHORTER MULTIPLE-CHOICE LISTENING QUESTIONS

This type of question involves listening to a recording of a formal or informal monologue or discussion between two speakers, then choosing the correct answer from a number of multiple-choice options. The kinds of texts you may hear include short informal or formal talks, answerphone messages, dialogues, announcements or explanations.

To practise this type of question, complete the exam-style questions below.

Skills required for this type of listening question include:

1 listening carefully for details

2 understanding key words and phrases

3 understanding a speaker's ideas or opinions

4 understanding which information you need to choose for the correct answer

5 understanding what is implied although not directly stated.

REMEMBER TO…

✓ Remember to make good use of every pause in the recordings.

✓ Underline any key words which might help you focus on the detail you need.

✓ While the recording is being played, write in as many of the answers as you can.

✓ Use the second playing to check that you have selected the right details.

Practise listening: shorter multiple-choice questions

You will hear five short recordings. For each question, choose the correct answer, A, B or C. You will hear each recording twice.

You will hear two classmates talking about a school trip they are going on.

1. Where are the students going on their school trip?   [1]

   A to a museum   **B** to a film festival   **C** to an art gallery

2. At what time will the school bus leave to take the students on the trip?   [1]

   A 5.50 am   **B** 7.00 am   **C** 6.00 am

You will hear a teacher giving some information about a demonstration he is going to give.

3. What is the class about to make in their cookery class?   [1]

   A food for a picnic   **B** some biscuits   **C** a chocolate cake

4. How much dried fruit should the students use? [1]

    A 50g   **B** 100g   **C** 150g

You will hear a woman leaving a phone message to explain why she will be late to work.

5. Why is Bernice unable to get to work on time today? [1]

    A she has missed the bus

    B there is a problem with her car

    C she has to wait for an engineer to come and fix her landline phone

6. If her employers want to speak to her, how should they contact her? [1]

    A call her on her mobile phone

    B call her on her landline phone

    C leave a message on her answer phone

You will hear a dialogue between a man and a waiter.

7. What does the waiter give Ali? [1]

    A a smoothie leaflet

    B a food menu

    C a drinks menu

8. Which drink does Ali decide to order in the end? [1]

    A an orange and mango smoothie

    B an orange and banana smoothie

    C an orange juice and lemonade

You will hear two classmates discussing a talk on the environment that they have just attended.

9. How did the girl feel about the talk? [1]

    A She thought it was boring.

    B It made her want to travel more.

    C She thought it was too long.

10. What has the talk inspired the boy to do first? [1]

    A learn more about wild animals

    B learn more about climate change

    C get involved with charity work

[Total: 10 marks]

LANGUAGE TIP Be aware of key question phrases that can alert you to when a question requires information from the recording about either number or quantity: *How many...?, How much...?; At what time...?, On what day...?*, for example.

APPROACHING GAP-FILL LISTENING QUESTIONS

This type of question involves listening to a recording of a longer text and selecting details to complete sentences which have gaps in them. There will be a few different options to choose from. The kinds of texts you may hear include speeches, radio talks, lectures and classroom presentations.

The exam-style questions below help you practise this type of question.

Skills required for gap-fill listening questions include:

1 listening carefully for details

2 understanding key words and phrases

3 understanding a speaker's ideas, opinions and attitudes

4 understanding exactly what detail you need to complete the gaps in the sentences

5 understanding what is implied although not directly stated.

REMEMBER TO…

✓ Use the pauses in exactly the same way to prepare yourself as you did for the earlier listening questions.

✓ Use your pre-reading skills, just as you did before. Look at the questions and their three possible answers very carefully. Make sure you really understand them to prepare yourself for the sort of information or clues you need to listen for.

✓ Underline any key words in the questions which might help you focus and identify the clues you need to answer the question.

Practise listening: gap-fill questions

You will hear a radio talk about Josh Waitzkin, a young man who became one of the world's leading chess players while still a school student. For each question choose the correct answer, A, B or C. You will hear the talk twice.

Now look at questions 1–8.

Chess Master

1. Josh has been a National Champion ☐ times.   [1]

   A 3

   B 21

   C 30

2. Josh first became interested in chess when he was ☐.   [1]

   A in a park

   B in a playground

   C at school

3. Josh became an International Master at the age of ☐ . [1]
   A 16
   B 11
   C 13

4. *How to Win at Chess* was Josh's ☐ book. [1]
   A least successful
   B latest
   C first

5. The speaker recommends that ☐ read *I am a Player not a Piece*. [1]
   A child chess stars
   B chess fanatics
   C people in general

6. Josh was attracted to Tai Chi Chuan because of his interest in ☐ philosophy. [1]
   A western
   B eastern
   C ancient

7. Josh travels the world ☐ methods of learning, mental attitude and the psychology of competition. [1]
   A teaching
   B giving lectures on
   C introducing people to his books on

8. Josh believes that people have to be prepared to ☐ in order to be successful. [1]
   A face new challenges
   B avoid taking risks
   C learn more about the psychology of winning

[Total: 8 marks]

APPROACHING MATCHING LISTENING QUESTIONS

This type of question involves listening to short monologues spoken by different speakers about the same topic. You are given a list of speakers and a list of statements that they could have said, and need to match each speaker to the correct statement based on what you hear in the recording.

The exam-style questions below help you practise this type of question.

Skills required for gap-fill listening questions include:

1 listening carefully and understanding ideas, opinions and attitudes

2 understanding the connections between related ideas

3 understanding what is implied although not directly stated – for example, feelings, intentions.

REMEMBER TO...

✓ Use the pauses between the speakers in exactly the same way to review the last answer and to prepare yourself for the next part as you did for the earlier listening questions.

✓ Use your pre-reading skills. Look at the statements carefully. Make sure you really understand them to prepare yourself for the sorts of information or clues you need to listen out for.

✓ Underline any key words in the statements which might help you focus and identify the clues you need to answer the question.

✓ After you have heard the six speakers for the first time, there is a short pause. Use this time to think quickly and decide which speakers you will really want to check or consider again.

✓ In the pause after the second playing, check that you have not put the same letter down twice.

✓ Remember that two of the letters will not be used – these are an extra two to make you think hard.

✓ Never leave a gap – you can always have a guess.

Practise listening: matching speakers to statements questions

> You will hear six people talking about sport. For each of the Speakers 1 to 6, choose from the list A to H, which opinion each speaker expresses. Use each letter only once. There are two extra letters which you do not need to use.
>
> You will hear the full recording of all six speakers twice.
>
> Speaker 1 [____] [1]   Speaker 2 [____] [1]   Speaker 3 [____] [1]
>
> Speaker 4 [____] [1]   Speaker 5 [____] [1]   Speaker 6 [____] [1]
>
> **A** I enjoy sport because it keeps me fit and helps me make friends.
>
> **B** I love my sport and want to play in international competitions.
>
> **C** I am really lucky because I am earning my living doing the sport I love.
>
> **D** I have always enjoyed sport but it is definitely just a hobby for me.
>
> **E** I am sorry that I do not do as much sport now as I did when younger.
>
> **F** I used to hate sport but now I am really keen and will never stop.
>
> **G** I have never liked sport, not when I was young, and not now.
>
> **H** My parents are both professional sports people and I grew up wanting to be exactly like them.
>
> **[Total: 6 marks]**

APPROACHING LISTENING QUESTIONS ON LONGER INTERVIEWS

This type of question involves listening to a longer text between an interviewer and someone who has made a study of a particular topic. The questions test your understanding of what you have heard, and you are given a choice of options from which you need to choose the correct answer. The exam-style questions below help you practise this type of question.

Skills required for this type of question include:

1 listening carefully for details

2 understanding key words and phrases

3 understanding a speaker's ideas, opinions and attitudes

4 understanding exactly which detail you need to select to answer each question

5 5 understanding what is implied although not directly stated.

REMEMBER TO…

✓ Use the pauses in exactly the same way to prepare yourself as you did for the earlier listening questions.

✓ Use your pre-reading skills, just as you did before. Look at the questions and their three possible answers very carefully. Make sure you really understand them to prepare yourself for the sorts of information or clues you need to listen for.

✓ Underline any key words in the questions which might help you focus and identify the clues you need to answer the question.

Practise listening: longer interview questions

You will hear an interview with Liang Chen, who makes travel documentaries. For each question, choose the correct answer, A, B or C.

You will hear the interview twice.

18.5

Now look at questions 1–10.

1. How can we tell that pearl divers have been at work for at least 2000 years?

   A The divers have found 2000-year-old pearls.

   B There is a 2000-year-old book that describes pearl diving.

   C People have admired pearls for at least 2000 years.

2. What quantity of shellfish do you need to give you about four good pearls?

   A 2000 tonnes

   B 20 tonnes

   C 1 tonne

3. Why were people prepared to face death by diving down so deep?

   A They loved diving.

   B They thought the pearls were beautiful.

   C They knew the pearls were valuable.

4. In Japan, why are women thought to be better than men at diving for pearls?

   A Their bodies are able to keep warm better.

   B They are older than the men.

   C They are more active than the men.

5. How does Ms Sakai feel now about her life as a pearl diver in the old days?

   A sad

   B angry

   C proud

6. What did the divers use to help them dive down as quickly as possible?

   A a heavy basket

   B an oxygen tank

   C a big stone

7. Why do the women pearl divers in Toba dive nowadays?

    A to find pearls to sell to tourists

    B to give tourists an idea of the past

    C to show tourists how people still risk their lives

8. In the last hundred years, the number of pearl divers in Toba has

    A gone down.

    B gone up.

    C stayed about the same.

[Total: 8 marks]

19 Responding to speaking questions

SYLLABUS INFORMATION:

Paper 3
Approximately 10–15 minutes
Speaking
40 marks

The speaking component of Cambridge IGCSE English as a Second Language involves a conversation between the student and an interviewer on a particular topic. After a short warm-up conversation, there is a discussion on a given topic which includes an interview, a short talk and a further discussion.

The assessed part of the text starts with a short interview with questions on a particular topic. Then students are asked to give a short talk, for which they are given a Speaking Assessment card with a particular topic. They have up to 1 minute to prepare for the talk. They are not allowed to make any notes but can keep the card until the end of the talk. The final part of the test is a discussion using questions related to the topic. The complete test lasts between 10 and 15 minutes.

This chapter gives you step-by-step guidance on how to answer speaking questions and helps you to prepare to take speaking tests. Exam-style speaking cards are included for you to practise answering interview questions and developing a discussion. These relate to topics of contemporary interest. For example, they may cover subjects related to conservation, the environment, culture, history, science, technology, music, the arts, or human achievement.

In order to respond to speaking questions, you need to practise:

1 understanding the question on a speaking card

2 using your preparation time efficiently

3 responding to questions effectively

4 developing a discussion

5 using a variety of structures and a good range of vocabulary

TOP TIP

Practise recording yourself giving a short talk, and also practise recording a conversation between yourself and another person. Listen back to the recordings and reflect on what you did well and what you could improve.

STEP 1 Warm-up

A warm-up is a short period of time during a speaking test in which you are asked a few questions about yourself to help you relax and get used to the situation. For example, you may be asked about your family and friends, your town, your hobbies and interests or your future plans.

Interviews begin with the interviewer asking some questions about a particular topic.

Try to say as much as you can for each question; first, giving a direct answer to the question, then offering more information or developing your opinion a little more.

> **TOP TIP**
>
> Think of the conversation as a football moving between the two of you. You have to show how good you are at moving the ball onwards, with tiny pushes and kicks, or a long pass to the other person. But never let it stop. Remember, the interviewer is there to help you keep the ball rolling.

2.1 Effective responses

Look at the **transcript** below. The interviewer and the student are talking about how having more money might change a student's daily life. Remember that people do not talk in full and unbroken sentences all the time, so there may be a lot of pauses, and hesitations – eg 'er'– as the student speaks. This is quite usual. No one expects a perfectly formed paragraph and perfect sentences in a conversation.

> **GLOSSARY** **transcript** – a written record of what is said

Interviewer:	Do you think having more money might help you in your daily life?
Student:	Well... not really ... I think ... er ...I've got everything I need for my daily life actually. Er... I have money for travelling next year as well ... er ... and I think having more money wouldn't really change anything.
Interviewer:	I like that. I mean, it seems you appreciate what you have already.
Student:	Yeah, I do ... er ... and ... er ... the only thing I think I'd do with more money would be ... er ... give it to charity ... er ... I mean or just not spend it anyway.

Looking at the transcript, find one place in the conversation where the student:

- answers a question, but then goes a step further to make the conversation move on
- picks up on a point made by the interviewer and does not wait for an actual question to continue the conversation
- introduces a new idea into the conversation.

> **TOP TIP**
>
> To keep conversation flowing, you can also pick up on words, phrases or ideas and use them as a way to move forward. You can use these same techniques to keep the conversation going when you are having longer discussions or conversations.

2.2 Ineffective responses

If you are asked a question where you could just answer 'Yes' or 'No', try to find a way to briefly explain or give reasons for your answer. Avoid giving short answers that stop the conversation. Look back at the last transcript. What might a weaker response to this question have been?

STEP 3 Using preparation time for the talk effectively

3.1 Understanding the speaking card

It is very important to make the best possible use of any preparation time to understand the topic on the speaking card and to think about what you are going to say. In speaking questions you do not make any written notes but you have the topic card in front of you until the end of your short talk. You need to:

- read the card carefully. Check if there are any words, phrases or ideas you do not understand, and ask the interviewer for help with these if you need it. The title and statement is followed by two options to discuss.
- look at the statement and the options, and think silently what you could include in your response. What are the advantages and disadvantages of each option? What is your opinion or attitude to the topic?
- for each option, think about vocabulary you can use.

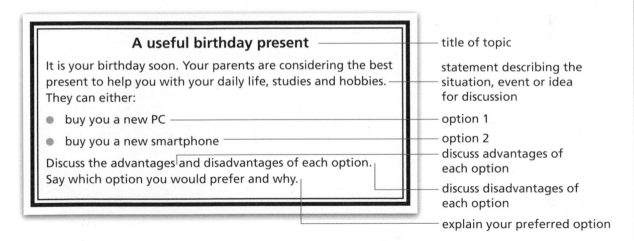

3.2 Preparing what to say

For this practice exercise you are going to make notes, just so that you can see the thought processes you need to go through when answering speaking questions. Of course, in a test, you are not allowed to write any notes and need to organise your ideas in your head.

Look again at the 'A useful birthday present' topic card above. Note down some ideas on the advantages and disadvantages of each option and your personal preference. You are being asked for your own opinions and will be expected to support these with reasons, details or examples. Remember you are not being tested on your specialist knowledge of the topic. So don't worry about stating correct facts and figures.

Copy the following chart to complete the notes under each heading and add your own ideas

Birthday present	Notes Add your own examples	Useful vocabulary. Add five other words to each list
a new PC	**Advantages:** **I use a PC to.........** do longer pieces of writing **I like them because.........** the screen is bigger **they are very good for.........** my spelling because I write more	essay, image, digital keyboard, microphone, audio apps, type, format
	Disadvantages: **I can't.........** use it everywhere I go **things I don't like about them are.........** they can be very expensive **they are not very good for.........** instantly receiving email notifications	inconvenient, impractical, store cost, space, equipment speed, time-saving, messages
a new smartphone	**Advantages:** **I use a smartphone to.........** contact people or catch up with news when I am doing something else like watching TV **I like it because.........** I can easily use it without getting out of bed **They are very good for/to.........** telling me instantly that I have received a message	instantly, multi-task, social media convenient, practical, comfortable an emergency, immediate, communication
	Disadvantages: **I can't/don't use them for.........** doing more complicated schoolwork and projects **things I don't like about them are.........** they are not as powerful as PCs **they are not very good for.........** my eyes	spreadsheet, calculation, planning software, memory, touchscreen eyestrain, quality, compose
My preference	For my birthday I would prefer to receive......... (State your preference – PC or smartphone.)	
Why	Reasons why......... (Use the above words in the vocabulary column and your own ideas.)	

LANGUAGE TIP The words noted in the 'Useful vocabulary' column are mainly **nouns** but there are also some **adjectives** and **verbs**. **Adjectives** will add interest and variety to your talk and show off your skills with vocabulary. So try to use a few of these in your conversation too.

3.3 Working without notes

Here is another topic card. This time prepare your ideas without notes.

Watching TV

You are planning a relaxing evening with your friends.
You are considering what to watch. You can either:

- watch something on live TV
- watch a film on DVD /stream from your computer

Discuss the advantages and disadvantages of each option.
Say which option you would prefer and why.

In pairs, spend about one minute looking at the card.

As you consider the situation and each option, imagine the types of things you could talk about. Remember to:
- discuss the advantages and disadvantages of each option
- finish off you talk by choosing the option that you personally prefer
- give reasons for your choice.

Tell one another what you would say about each of the prompts. If one of you is stuck for an idea, make suggestions or ask more questions to inspire ideas.

STEP 4 Giving the talk

You should make your points in a structured way. Decide whether you will first discuss the advantages and disadvantages of one option then move on to do the same for the second option, or whether you will compare and contrast the advantages of both options followed by the disadvantages. Having a good structure worked out for your talk will help you to remember what you want to say and also to avoid repeating the same point. Begin your talk by explaining how you will structure it.

Remember that in speaking tests you are given a set amount of time for your talk – for example, 3 or 4 minutes – so make sure you take this into consideration so that you neither finish too early nor run out of time to finish.

Whenever possible, vary the language that you use, trying not to repeat the words 'advantages and disadvantages' too often, for example. Instead try using the words, *benefits and drawbacks*, *pros and cons*, or *positive and negative aspects*. You could also vary the language that you use to give your opinions, for example: *in my opinion*, *I think*, *as far as I'm concerned*.

Decide whether you can bring in personal experiences to make your talk more engaging for the listener and also give you more to say on each point.

Look at the transcript below. The speaker is explaining some advantages and disadvantages of receiving a new PC for their birthday.

> So, in my opinion … er … I think that there are a few benefits to getting a new PC and not a er smartphone … er it is better for me to do homework on a PC and not on a smartphone. I can write longer … er things, for example when I have to write an essay. The screen is bigger and I can see what I write better. I think that the major disadvantage of them is that they are so big and not very er… con … practical. I can't take it everywhere that I go or use it everywhere.

Looking at the transcript, find one place where the speaker:
- adds a second advantage to the one already given
- uses an alternative word to *advantages*
- can't remember a word and so uses a different word instead.

Finishing your talk

Don't forget to finish your talk by summarising your ideas and then giving your own personal preference, explaining why this would be your choice.

Look at the following transcript. The speaker is finishing their talk.

> So, that's all that I wanted to say on the er … topic and you can see that there are both er … good things and bad things about PCs and smartphones. Personally, I would prefer to receive a new PC. The reason for that is because I can use it to do more things like make my own … music, with a better sound and er … edit my photos easier. So I would like a new PC better than a new smartphone.

Looking at the transcript, find the language that the speaker uses to:
- sum up her talk
- introduce her personal preference
- give a reason for her choice

 TOP TIP If you find yourself running out of time, signal this to the interviewer and round off your talk with your personal preference. For example, *I'm sorry I have not finished telling you all of my ideas but I have run out of time. So I will just finish by saying that I would choose a PC because….*

STEP 5 **Answering questions to develop the discussion**

The interviewer will encourage you to further develop the topic by asking you questions on that topic. They will ask a few specific questions about aspects of the topic that have not already been discussed but will also ask you additional questions throughout the discussion.

So let's look at what types of questions the interviewer may ask you in this part and how to answer them appropriately. The following examples are on the topic of daily life or daily life in the future.

5.1 Explaining and giving information

Questions could include:
- Could you talk me through..........?
- Can you explain..........?
- Could you give me some information about..........?

For instance, the interviewer might start by asking: *Could you talk me through a typical day in your life*. You could explain what you do in the morning, afternoon and evening on a school day, or at the weekend, or what time you do things or who you do them with.

5.2 Giving your opinion

You may be asked for your opinion with questions such as:
- What is your opinion of..........?
- What do you think of..........?
- How do you feel about..........?
- What's your view on that?

5.3 Discussing whether something is a good or bad idea

- Do you think that is a good or bad thing?
- In your opinion, is that good or bad?
- How important do you think it is that..........?
- Do you think this is important, and if so, why..........?

These types of questions all invite your personal opinion. The interviewer may ask: *and what do you think of having to do homework at the weekend?* You can then explain what you think about this and always remember to give a reason or reasons for your view. For example, you could develop an answer to this question by explaining what homework you usually have to do, when and where you do it, how long it takes.

5.4 Agreeeing or disagreeing and explaining why
- Do you agree and if so, why?
- Do you agree or disagree and why?
- Are you in agreement with that?
- Some people think that... do you share the same opinion?

The interviewer might say: *Many people think that daily life in the future will be easier than now – do you agree?* You could start by saying that you understand why people might think that before explaining whether you personally agree or disagree. You could then go on to explain why you agree or disagree, remembering to give more than one example if possible.

LANGUAGE TIP

Remember the functions of basic **connectives** when you respond to questions: use '*and*' before adding detail; use '*or*' when giving an alternative; use '*but*' to signal you have a different view or disagree.

5.5 Adding more detail

Questions that encourage you to develop your views with well-chosen detail include:

- Could you tell me more about..........?
- Can you give me more information about..........?
- Could you explain more about..........?

As noted in Step 2, it can be easy to answer a question with a one- or two-word answer. If this happens the interviewer might help you by asking one of the above questions For example, you might be asked what you like doing on Sundays and your answer is *playing football*. *Could you tell me more*? would invite you to explain more, such as who you play with or where.

5.6 Giving examples

Similar to adding detail, you might be asked to provide some examples to develop your view.

- Could you give me an example of that?
- Are there any other examples that you can think of?
- Can you think of a specific situation?
- Do you know a specific situation?

The interviewer may also ask you one of the above questions if you have answered their first question with just one word. Think about things that you have read about or seen on TV or heard about or situations that have happened to people you know. Try to think of more than one example again.

5.7 Using personal experience

You may be asked questions about your own experience, for example:

- Do you have any experience of that?
- Can you tell me what happened?
- What did they do about it / do next?
- Have you done / tried / experienced.........?

This might concern a hobby or travel experiences, for example. Obviously the interviewer will not ask you questions that are too personal and neither will they expect you to talk about anything you do not want to. However, do try to include appropriate personal experience that you do not mind sharing. Or you could talk about the experience of someone you know. Again, you should try to give two or three examples.

5.8 Clarifying what you have said or what you mean

The interviewer may ask you one of the following questions if they do not quite follow something you have said:

- Can you explain what you mean exactly?
- Could you just clarify what you mean by..........?
- Could you be more specific about that?

In this case, instead of repeating what you said, find a different way of saying it using different vocabulary or phrasing. Do not worry, if you are asked to clarify something, it may be a misunderstanding on the part of the interviewer or they may just be prompting you in order to keep the discussion going.

5.9 Making a suggestion

The interviewer might pick up on one of your opinions or comments, for instance if you state that something should or should not happen, by asking you to offer a suggestion.

- What would you suggest?
- What would you recommend?
- Do you have any suggestions?

For example if you expressed the view that *in the future we should find new sources of energy for our daily life*, this would be a perfect opportunity for the interviewer to respond by asking one of the above questions.

5.10 Talking about the future

The next three question types encourage you to predict, speculate or hypothesise in some way. As always, you are not expected to be a specialist on the topic or necessarily to have realistic ideas. The interviewer will not tell you that you are wrong if you give good reasons for your ideas so just use your imagination. If you simply don't have any ideas, it is also fine to say that and the interviewer will move on. For example, the interviewer might ask, *How would people's daily lives be different if they didn't have any technology?* and your answer could be, *I've never thought about that before and I really don't have any specific ideas... only that everything would be very different.*

When you practise speaking about a topic, think about how you could answer questions about the future, for example:

- What do you think will happen in the future?
- How do you think this will change in the future?
- Do you think it will be different in the future and if so, how?
- Do you think this will be the same in the future?

5.11 What if...?

You may be asked to imagine a situation and talk about what you think would happen in that situation. For example:

- How do you see the situation in 50 years from now?
- What would you do if.........?
- What would happen if.........?
- What do you think the consequences will be?
- What effect might this have on that situation?
- What do you think caused this?
- What would you have to say about that?
- How would you feel about that?

5.12 Choosing from one or more option

Be prepared for questions asking you to choose between different options. For example:

- If you had to choose between x or y, which one would you choose?
- What would your choice be?
- Which is the best/worst one in your opinion?
- If you were given the choice, would you......... or ....?

5.13 Explaining advantages and disadvantages

This type of question will give you the chance to offer more than one example and keep the discussion moving:

- What are the advantages of.........?
- What are the disadvantages of.........?
- Are there any benefits to this, in your opinion?
- Can you see any drawbacks?
- What are the pros and cons?
- What are the good and bad aspects of this?

For example, if you are asked about the good and bad things about technological progress, you could:

- give some examples of technology
- explain one or two ways in which technological progress can have good effects
- mention one or two ways in which it could have bad effects
- add your own opinion.

In pairs, take it in turns to role-play the 'interviewer' and the 'student'. Decide on a topic and then have a discussion. The person role-playing the interviewer can use some of the questions above to encourage you to say more and keep the discussion moving.

REMEMBER TO...?

✓ Read the topic card carefully.

✓ Ask about anything on the card that you don't understand.

✓ Use your time effectively.

✓ Communicate your ideas and opinions.

✓ Use a range of vocabulary.

✓ Develop responses to keep the discussion going.

✓ Think about pronunciation and intonation.

✓ Ensure that you speak. The interviewer cannot assess you if you remain silent!

PRACTISE SPEAKING QUESTIONS

Now you are ready to do a practice speaking test, using exam-style questions.

Part 1 Interview

Daily life in the future

- Can you tell me about what you do on a typical week day?
- Can you tell me something about what you enjoy doing at the weekend?
- Do you think having more money might help you in your daily life?

Part 2 Short talk

Making a better school

Your Head has been given some money to spend on the school. She is considering the best way to use the money to improve students' learning experiences both now and in the future. She can either spend it on:

- updating the school's computers and technological equipment
- buying more books and other paper resources for the library.

Discuss the advantages and disadvantages of each option. Say which option you would prefer and why.

Part 3 Discussion

- Will our daily life in the future be easier or more difficult than it is today because of modern technology? What do you think?

- Some people have a negative attitude towards the fast progress they have seen in their lives. What do you think?

- Many people think that modern progress does not always bring great happiness. Do you agree?

- Too much technological progress is dangerous for society. Do you agree?

Sample answers

This chapter contains sample answers to the questions given in Chapters 13–19. There are usually two sample answers for each question.

Read and listen to the sample answers. Then look at the marks and comments to help you understand the total mark each answer is given. Exam-style questions and sample answers have been written by the authors. In examinations, the way marks are awarded may be different.

Chapter 13

OPEN-RESPONSE READING QUESTION

For these answers, you could try covering up the last two columns, and think what mark you would have given before checking. You can do this on your own or with a partner.

Answer 1

	Mark	Comment
1. half or 50%	1	Correct answer. Both answers are correct but only one of them was necessary so the other is time wasted.
2. Beekeepers don't earn so much money	0	This is a problem but it is not 'the most concerning issue'.
3. food	1	Food is the correct answer.
4. herbicides	0	Incorrect. Insecticides is the correct answer.
5. renting (them)	1	Correct answer
6. fuel and controlling bugs	2	Only 2 out of the 3 possible answers given.

This answer got 5 out of a possible 8 marks.

Answer 2

	Mark	Comment
1. 50 million	1	Correct answer
2. threatens crop production	1	Correct answer
3. food from new plants and flowers	1	Food is the correct answer (time is wasted on unnecessary words – new plants and flowers).
4. chemicals	0	Incorrect. Insecticides is the correct answer. Not all chemicals are harmful for the bees.
5. renting (them)	1	Correct answer
6. fuel, equipment, controlling bugs, queen bees	3	All 4 answers from the text are given. The last one is correct but is ignored here as there are only 3 marks available.

This answer got 7 out of a possible 8 marks.

MULTIPLE-MATCHING READING QUESTION

For these answers, you could try covering up the second and third columns, and think what mark you would have given before checking. You can do this on your own or with a partner.

MULTIPLE-MATCHING QUESTIONS

Which person gives the following information?

Answer 1

	Mark	Comment
a) a time when they were sent clothing that was too small Answer: **A** (Joe)	0	**Incorrect. The correct answer is B.** A's top was the wrong size, but B's trousers were too small ('they didn't even fit my little sister').
b) the fact that they are not paid for their part-time job Answer: **C** (Danni)	1	**Correct answer C**'s work is **voluntary** which means he isn't paid.
c) the suggestion that going shopping is a good way to meet up with friends face-to-face Answer: **D** (Mariko)	0	**Incorrect. The correct answer is B.** A meets up online, **C** plays football with friends and goes out in the evenings, **D**, no mention of friends
d) an example of how sometimes shopping online can lead to losing money Answer: **D** (Mariko)	1	**Correct answer A** had a long delay in getting his money back, but **D** did not get a refund.
e) an explanation of why they go to a shop every day without buying anything Answer: **A** (Joe)	1	**Correct answer D** does not buy things in shops, but we don't know if she goes every day. **A** works in a shop for two hours **every morning**.
f) the idea that they have not had any problems with shopping online Answer: **C** (Danni)	1	**Correct answer** The rest of them talk about problems but **C** does not mention any.
g) the wish to be able to not spend any money on petrol and parking when shopping Answer: **B** (Alex)	0	**Incorrect. The correct answer is A.** B and C have to pay for petrol and in D it is not mentioned **A** comments: *I don't want to waste money on petrol and parking when I'm shopping.'*
h) a recommendation for how to combine buying things online and in shops Answer: **C** (Danni)	1	**Correct answer C** buys online and collects what he has bought from the shop where he can change it for something else.
i) the idea that they mainly socialise online Answer: **B** (Alex)	0	**Incorrect. The correct answer is A.** The other young people all go out with their friends. **A** contacts his friends through social media.

This answer got 5 out of 9 possible marks.

Answer 2

	Mark	Comment
a) a time when they were sent clothing that was too small? Answer: **B** (Alex)	1	**Correct answer** B's trousers were too small ('they didn't even fit my little sister').
b) the fact that they are not paid for their part-time job? **C** (Danni)	1	**Correct answer** C's work is **voluntary** which means he isn't paid.
c) the suggestion that going shopping is a good way to meet up with friends face-to-face? Answer: **B** (Alex)	1	**Correct answer** A enjoys meeting at the shops with her friends.
d) an example of how sometimes shopping online can lead to losing money? Answer: **A** (Joe)	0	**Incorrect. The correct answer is D.** D did not get a refund. A only had a long wait to get his money back.
e) an explanation of why they go to a shop every day without buying anything? Answer: **D** (Mariko)	0	**Incorrect. The correct answer is A.** A works in a shop for two hours **every morning.** D does not buy things in shops, but we don't know if she goes every day.
f) the idea that they have not had any problems with shopping online? Answer: **C** (Danni)	1	**Correct answer** The rest of them talk about problems but **C** does not mention any.
g) the wish to be able to not spend any money on petrol and parking when shopping? Answer: **A** (Joe)	1	**Correct answer** A comments: 'I don't want to waste money on petrol and parking when I'm shopping.'
h) a recommendation for how to combine buying things online and in shops? Answer: **C** (Danni)	1	**Correct answer** C buys online and collects what he has bought from the shop where he can change it for something else.
i) the idea that they mainly socialise online? Answer: **A** (Joe)	1	**Correct answer** A contacts his friends through social media. The other young people all go out with their friends.

This answer got 7 out of 9 possible marks.

Chapter 14

NOTE-TAKING QUESTION

For these answers, you could try covering up the second and third columns, and think what you would have given the answers before looking. You can do this on your own or with a partner.

Answer

	Answer	Mark	Comment
How the present way of life for the Inuits is different from the past	*use more modern weapons like guns*	1	Correct but too long as using too many words wastes time, 'use guns' would be sufficient.
	make rings and necklacez to earn a living	1	Good clear answer. Incorrect spelling does not impede or lose marks
	drive cars	1	This is a reasonable assumption from 'petrol-driven vehicles'
What will not change for many Inuits in the future	*the Inuit language*	1	Correct answer
	the Inuit values and ways of life	1	Correct answer
	the Arctic Winter Games will still be held	1	Good clear answer
	their sense of identity	1	Correct answer

This answer got 3 marks for the first part, 4 marks for the second part.

Total: 3 + 4 = 7 marks out of 7 possible marks.

Chapter 15

MULTIPLE-CHOICE READING QUESTION

Answer
Scuba diving blog

	Answer	Mark	Comment
1	C	0	**Incorrect.** Reference to 'the latter' has not been understood. **The correct answer is B.**
2	A	1	
3	B	1	
4	B	0	**Incorrect.** They paid for some of the training but not all of it. **The correct answer is A.**
5	A	0	**Incorrect.** Although she had to get a medical fitness certificate, she does not say that being fit enough is an issue for other people to consider. **The correct answer is C.**
6	B	1	

This answer got 3 marks out of a possible 6 marks.

Answer
My cat speaks sign language with her tail blog

	Answer	Mark	Comment
1	B	1	
2	A	0	**Incorrect.** It was not stated that she was surprised that such a degree was possible but it is clear that she didn't know what career this would lead to. **The correct answer is C.**
3	B	1	
4	C	1	
5	B	1	
6	A	0	**Incorrect.** She says it would be great if everyone did but thinks it's unlikely. **The correct answer is C.**

This answer got 4 marks out of a possible 6 marks.

Chapter 16

INFORMAL WRITING QUESTION

In this section there is an answer for the Practice task only.

Answer

Hello my friend,

It's a long time that we don't see us. I am very tiring now after so much exams and so I will not study more today but write to you about something funny when I went to visit my cousine last week for celebrate his birthday.

I decided to go on the train, because my cousine lives in another city, about 75 kilometres from our house so my dad said he did not have time to take me. I like travelling by train because I can watch out of the window or read my book.

We were nearly finished our journey and I got ready to get off at the station where lives my cousine, but I was very surprised because the train did not stop at that station, just carried on.

At the end, the driver made a speech to all passengers to say that the train had to take a different line because there were cows on our line. Can you belive it?

See us soon, I hope.

Your friend

Tomas

Comments
Length: 177. Slightly longer than the recommended word count of 120 to 160 words.

Content
Relevance: All three bullet points are covered. Paragraph 2 has unnecessary detail.

Style and register: Generally good sense of reader – informal tone used, appropriate for a friend, for example the opening and closing remarks, although they are not completely accurate, for example: 'See us soon'.

Development: The content is generally developed but point 3 is dealt with only briefly in 'I was surprised'.

Language
Range and accuracy: Uses a range of common vocabulary appropriately, and attempts to use some less common vocabulary ('carried on' / 'passengers'). Uses a range of simple structures, and attempts to use some complex structures ('I like travelling', 'I got ready to get off'). Generally good level of accuracy and meaning is always clear despite the errors when more complex language or verb tenses are attempted ('where lives my cousine' / 'made a speech' or 'We don't see us' / 'We were nearly finished'). Two spelling errors: 'cousine' and 'belive'.

Organisation: It is generally well organised, with effective paragraphs. Simple linking phrases and connectives are used accurately; for example, 'at the end'.

This answer got 4 marks for Content and 6 marks for Language.

Total: 10 marks out of a possible 15 marks.

Chapter 17

FORMAL WRITING QUESTION
In this section there is an answer for the Practice task only.

Answer

<u>Computer Games, should the under-16s play them?</u>

Nowadays, many children enjoy playing games on computers. Some parents, however question whether they should allow under16s to occupy their free time in this way.

To start with, young children can and do learn from playing these games. Skills like problem-solving and coordination can be developed, as well as teknical ability.

Another argument in favour of them is that they are relaxing. Today, even very young children can feel stressed, so taking time out to play encourages them to relax their minds and bodies.

On the other hand, there is no doubt that children have to do homework. Consequently, many parents prefer them to study rather than waste time on games.

In addition, other parents wish to spend more time with their children. They feel that having more conversations together would create closer family bonds.

I personally understand both sides of the arguement. Was I a parent though, I would say that having quality family time is more important. So ultimately I would agree with the idea of no computer games for under-16s.

Comments
Length: 173. Slightly longer than the recommended 160 word limit but this does not detract from the quality of the answer. Everything is relevant and it is not long-winded and flows well.

Content
Task fulfilment: Fulfils the task – covers all prompts; excellent sense of purpose – very clearly explains both sides of the argument before giving own opinion; good sense of the reader – uses formal style, tone and language throughout.

Development: The content is very well developed throughout with clear expansion of the comments in the speech bubbles.

Language
Range and accuracy: Uses a wide range of common and less common vocabulary appropriately and simple and complex structures with an extremely high level of accuracy. There are two spelling errors (technical and argument) and one error with a more complex second conditional ('Was I a parent though' instead of 'Were I...',) none of which impede communication.

Organisation: Very well organised, with effective paragraphs and good use of a wide range of appropriate linking phrases and connectives.

This answer got 6 marks for Content and 9 marks for Language.

Total: 15 out of a possible 15 marks.

Chapter 18

MULTIPLE-CHOICE LISTENING QUESTIONS WITH VISUAL PROMPTS

Answer

	Mark	Comment
1 B – a necklace	1	Correct answer
2 B – the fashion museum	1	Correct answer
3 C – the forest	1	Correct answer
4 A – the cafeteria	1	Correct answer
5 D – a boy cleaning up an untidy bedroom	0	**Incorrect. The correct answer is B.** They can't go for a drive because the car is still at the garage. Cleaning his room is mentioned but only as a result of Alan not being able to go out.
6 B – musical trio	1	Correct answer

This answer got 5 out of a possible 6 marks.

SHORTER MULTIPLE-CHOICE LISTENING QUESTIONS

Answer

	Mark	Comment
1 B – film festival	1	Correct answer
2 C – 6.00 am	1	Correct answer
3 B – biscuits	1	Correct answer
4 A – 50g	1	Correct answer
5 A – missed the bus	0	**Incorrect.** She only mentions that she might be later if she misses the bus. **The correct answer is B** – a problem with her car.
6 A – mobile phone	1	Correct answer
7 C – drinks menu	1	Correct answer
8 A – orange and mango	1	Correct answer
9 A – boring	0	**Incorrect.** She was worried that it might be boring but it wasn't. **The correct answer is B** – it made her want to travel more
10 C – get involved with charity work	1	Correct answer

This answer got 8 out of a possible 10 marks.

GAP-FILL LISTENING QUESTIONS

For these answers, you could try covering up the last two columns, and think what mark you would have given, before taking a look. You could do this on your own or with a partner.

Answers

	Answer	Mark	Comment
1	**B** Josh has been a National Champion 21 times.	1	Correct answer
2	**A** Josh first became interested in chess when he was in a park	1	Correct answer
3	**A** Josh became an International Master at the age of 16	1	Correct answer
4	**A** *How to Win at Chess* was Josh's least successful book	1	Correct answer
5	**B** The writer recommends chess fanatics to read *I am a Player not a Piece*.	0	**Incorrect. The correct answer is C.** He says he would totally recommend it to anyone, not just chess fanatics.
6	**B** Josh was attracted to Tai Chi Chuan because of his interest in eastern philosophy.	1	Correct answer
7	**B** Josh travels the world giving lectures on methods of learning, mental attitude and the psychology of competition.	1	Correct answer
8	**B** Josh believes that people have to avoid taking risks in order to be successful.	0	**Incorrect. The correct answer is A.** He suggests that people should take risks, not avoid them.

This answer got 6 out of a possible 8 marks.

LISTENING: MATCHING SPEAKERS TO STATEMENT QUESTIONS

Answers

	Answer	Statement
Speaker 1	B	I love my sport and want to play in international competitions.
Speaker 2	G	I have never liked sport, not when I was young, and not now.
Speaker 3	D	I have always enjoyed sport but it is definitely just a hobby for me.
Speaker 4	E	I am sorry that I do not do as much sport now as I did when younger.
Speaker 5	A	I enjoy sport because it keeps me fit and helps me make friends.
Speaker 6	C	I am really lucky because I am earning my living doing the sport I love.

Statements F and H should be the two left unused.

F – Not mentioned. Speaker 2 used to hate sport and still does.

H – Not mentioned.

LISTENING QUESTIONS ON LONGER INTERVIEWS

Answers

	Answer	Mark	Comment
1	**A** The divers have found 2000-year-old pearls.	0	**Incorrect. The correct answer is B.** There is a 'written account' of pearl diving from 2000 years ago but nothing mentioned about finding pearls then.
2	**C** 1 tonne	1	Correct answer
3	**C** They knew the pearls were valuable.	1	Correct answer
4	**A** Their bodies are able to keep warm better.	1	Correct answer
5	**A** sad	0	**Incorrect. The correct answer is C 'proud'.** This is implied rather than directly stated, but the other two answers can also be eliminated as not being logical.
6	**C** a big stone	1	Correct answer
7	**A** to find pearls to sell to tourists	0	**Incorrect. The correct answer is B** 'to give tourists an idea of the past'. The text states that they do it just for this reason; it does not mention diving for actual pearls.
8	**A** gone down.	1	Correct answer

This answer got 5 out of possible 8 marks.

Chapter 19

SPEAKING QUESTIONS

Listen to three recordings which show attempted answers for the topic card headed 'Daily life in the future'. The comments below show the marks these sample recordings received for each of the following: Grammar, Vocabulary, Development and Pronunciation.

Alternatively, you could listen to them and try to decide on the mark you think they should have received before you look at the comments to help you understand why they got that mark.

Answer 1 19.1

Oral assessments	Mark	Comment
Grammar (out of 10)	10	Uses an extremely wide range of both simple and complex grammar very accurately indeed; there are no errors.
Vocabulary (out of 10)	10	Uses a very wide range of vocabulary extremely accurately to discuss a variety of facts, ideas and opinions.
Development (out of 10)	10	All responses are excellent. They are relevant and always well-developed. Communication is natural and flows easily throughout the conversation.
Pronunciation (out of 10)	10	The speaker uses very clear pronunciation and uses intonation very effectively to convey intended meaning.
Total: marks (out of 40)	40	Excellent

Answer 2 19.2

Oral assessments	Mark	Comment
Grammar (out of 10)	8	Most straightforward grammar is correct and any slips or errors with more complex grammar do not impede communication.
Vocabulary (out of 10)	8	Uses a range of vocabulary mostly appropriately to discuss facts, ideas and opinions.
Development (out of 10)	10	Excellent responses. Takes ideas and develops them; offers own opinion and ideas without much support from the interviewer.
Pronunciation (out of 10)	8	Most of the time pronunciation is clear and any inaccuracies do not cause issues with understanding. Intonation is sometimes used effectively to help convey meaning.
Total: marks (out of 40)	34	Excellent

Answer 3 🎧 19.3

Oral assessments	Mark	Comment
Grammar (out of 10)	8	Occasional slips or errors with grammar but mostly when attempting more complex structures. Any inaccuracies do not impede communication.
Vocabulary (out of 10)	8	Some overuse of certain words, like '*stuff*' but demonstrates enough of a range of vocabulary to keep meaning clear and to communicate simple ideas. Does not demonstrate enough vocabulary to express more complex ideas.
Development (out of 10)	8	Responds well to questions and although they require occasional support they respond with appropriate development.
Pronunciation (out of 10)	8	Pronunciation is mostly clear and inaccuracies do not impede communication; intonation is sometimes used effectively to convey intended meaning.
Total: marks (out of 40)	32	Excellent

Acknowledgements

Text acknowledgements

The publishers gratefully acknowledge the permission granted to reproduce the copyright material in this book. Every effort has been made to trace and contact copyright holders and obtain their permission for the use of copyright material. The publishers will gladly receive any information enabling them to rectify any error or omission at the first opportunity.

We are grateful to the following for permission to reproduce copyright material:

An extract on p.11 from *A Century of Innovation: Twenty Engineering Achievements that Transformed our Lives* by George Constable, et al. 2003, Joseph Henry Press, copyright © National Academy of Sciences 2003; Origami boat diagrams on p.45 from origami-fun.com/. Reproduced with kind permission of Robyn Hondow; Extract on p.64 from 'Junk food and poor diet is blamed for blighting behaviour of Britain's teenagers' *Daily Record*, 16/03/2016, copyright © Daily Record/Reach Licensing. Reproduced with permission; An extract on p.124 adapted from 'Work in the digital era' *Sunday Times* magazine, 06/11/2011, copyright © The Sunday Times / News Licensing; Statistics on p.133 from "The top five countries emitting the most CO2 in 2018", Union of Concerned Scientist. Reproduced with permission; Extract on p.140 from 'Carbon Monoxide' from *Environmental Science in the 21st Century* – an online textbook by Robert Stewart, reproduced with kind permission of the author; Cover artwork by La Boca on p.214 from *Brave New World* by Aldous Huxley, published by Vintage Classics, copyright © Mrs Laura Huxley, 1932. Reproduced by permission of The Random House Group Limited; Extract on p.216 from *Scorpia Rising* by Anthony Horowitz, copyright © 2011 by Anthony Horowitz and Stormbreaker Productions Ltd. Covers © 2015 Walker Books Ltd; Trademarks Alex Rider™; Boy with Torch Logo™ © 2000-2021 Stormbreaker Productions Ltd. Reproduced by permission of Walker Books Ltd, London, SE11 5HJ; and Philomel, an imprint of Penguin Young Readers Group, a division of Penguin Random House LLC. All rights reserved; An extract on p.221 from "The Generation Gap in TV Consumption [Digital image]" by Felix Richter, 20/11/2020. Retrieved 11/08/2021, from https://www.statista.com. Reproduced with permission; and an extract on p.244 from 'World's oldest marathon runner completes Toronto race at age 100' by Caroline Davies, *The Guardian*, 18/10/2011, copyright © Guardian News & Media Ltd, 2021.

Image acknowledgements

p8t and 9tl shepele4ek2304/ Shutterstock, p8c and 9cl ifong/Shutterstock, p8b and 9bl Cristi Matei/ Shutterstock, p9bm william casey/Shutterstock, p9br Andrey Semenov/Shutterstock, p9tc Marietjie/ Shutterstock, p11 Martin Shields/Alamy, p13t REDPIXEL. PL/Shutterstock, p13b Kaspars Grinvalds/Shutterstock, p14br dboystudio/Shutterstock, p16b New Africa/ Shutterstock, p18 Juan Ci/Shutterstock, p19br Take A Pix Media/Shutterstock, p21b sdecoret/Shutterstock, p22bl Luis Louro/Shutterstock, p22bc Chronicle/Alamy, p22rt Shawn Hempel/Shutterstock, p22rc Claire Slingerland/ Shutterstock, p22br elena moiseeva/Shutterstock, p23b Makistock/Shutterstock, p24 Makistock/Shutterstock, p26tl Sarunyu_foto/Shutterstock, p26tc K303/ Shutterstock, p26tr kosam/Shutterstock, p28tr and 29tl Royal Geographical Society/Alamy, p28cr and 29cl Joinmepic/Shutterstock, p28br and 29 bl David Fleetham/ Alamy, p29cr Greg Epperson/Shutterstock, p29br NASA, p30br INTERFOTO/Alamy, p31 Chris Hellier/Getty, p32 astarik/Shutterstock, p32 Christopher Wood/ Shutterstock, p33 North Wind Picture Archives/Alamy, p34t NASA, p34c sripfoto/Shutterstock, p34b Dima Zel/ Shutterstock, p36 MARK GARLICK/SCIENCE PHOTO LIBRARY, p37br Vladi333/Shutterstock, p38 Collins Bartholomew Ltd, p38br Volodymyr Goinyk/Shutterstock, p38br Armin Rose/Shutterstock, p38br Alexey Seafarer/ Shutterstock, p39t Rainer Lesniewski/Shutterstock, p39b vladsilver/Shutterstock, p40br Michelle Sole/Shutterstock, p41br Hurst Photo/Shutterstock, p42 and 43 Mark Doherty/Shutterstock, p42 Mariusz S. Jurgielewicz/ Shutterstock, p43t JonMilnes/Shutterstock, p43b Vismar UK/Shutterstock, p44 littlesam/Shutterstock, p46l Pinosub/Shutterstock, p46c Mesa Studios/Shutterstock, p46r NASA, p48tr and 49tl Krakenimages.com/ Shutterstock, p48cr and 49cl Prostock-studio/ Shutterstock, p48br and 49 bl Niloo/Shutterstock, p49c YAKOBCHUK VIACHESLAV/Shutterstock, p49cr Syda Productions/Shutterstock, p49br Stefan Holm/ Shutterstock, p51 Paul Cowan/Shutterstock, p52 Levent Konuk/Shutterstock, p53br Netfalls - Remy Musser/ Shutterstock, p54 Micheko Productions, Inh. Michele Vitucci/Alamy Stock Photo, p56 Jose Gil/Shutterstock, p56 and 57 Flystock/Shutterstock, p58l Kletr/ Shutterstock, p58r M_Agency/Shutterstock, p59br Alena Brozova/Shutterstock, p60tr Wutthichai/Shutterstock, p62 javi_indy/Shutterstock, p63lt Elena Elisseeva/ Shutterstock, p63bl Piotr Rzeszutek/Shutterstock, p63rt Nikola Bilic/Shutterstock, p63rb Matt Antonino/ Shutterstock, p66tl Fotokostic/Shutterstock, p66tc Pressmaster/Shutterstock, p66tr Farknot Architect/ Shutterstock, p68tr and 69tl Black Rock Digital/ Shutterstock, p68cr and 69cl Rohit Seth/Shutterstock, p68br and 69bl Zurijeta/Shutterstock, p69cr Design Pics/ SuperStock, p69br Tom Wang/Shutterstock, p70 YAKOBCHUK VASYL/Shutterstock, p74 chippix/ Shutterstock, p75 Ivan Soto Cobos/Shutterstock, p76 The Stapleton Collection/Bridgeman Images, p77 Sergey Nivens/Shutterstock, p79 MEHAU KULYK/SCIENCE PHOTO LIBRARY, p80 Monkey Business Images/Shutterstock, p82l michaeljung/Shutterstock, p82r Rehan Qureshi/ Shutterstock, p84 REUTERS/Jo Yong-Hak/Alamy, p86tl Phovoir/Shutterstock, p86tc Hunter Bliss Images/ Shutterstock, p86tr Gorodenkoff/Shutterstock, p88rt and 89lt 000 Words/Shutterstock, p88rc and 89lc pirita/ Shutterstock, p88rb and 89lb Rocksweeper/Shutterstock, p89cr fotosparrow/Shutterstock, p89br Ollyy/ Shutterstock, p90l All Canada Photos/Alamy, p90c Gerrit_de_Vries/Shutterstock, p90r NATTANAN KLOENPRATHOM/Shutterstock, p91l Jim Agronick/ Shutterstock, p91r Stefan Pircher/Shutterstock, p93l Christian Musat/Shutterstock, p93tr Tory Kallman/ Shutterstock, p93tr Tory Kallman/Shutterstock, p93cr Dudarev Mikhail/Shutterstock, p93br Russell Watkins/ Shutterstock, p94tr Pand P Studio/Shutterstock, p94br Alex Kravtsov/Shutterstock, p94l ESB Professional/ Shutterstock, p95 360b/Shutterstock, p96 Hemis/Alamy, p97 NumenaStudios/Shutterstock, p101br Wirestock Creators/Shutterstock, p104br netopaek/Shutterstock, p106tl Petrychenko Anton/Shutterstock, p108rt and 109lt nikkytok/Shutterstock, p108rc and 109lc Photoroyalty/Shutterstock, p108rb and 109lb Golden Pixels LLC/Shutterstock, p109cr Vasily Smirnov/ Shutterstock, p109br Johnny Habell/Shutterstock, p110br mykeyruna/Shutterstock, p114bl michaeljung/

Shutterstock, p118 Monkey Business Images/Shutterstock, p120 GaudiLab/Shutterstock, p122tr dboystudio/Shutterstock, p122l ESB Professional/Shutterstock, p122c ESB Professional /Shutterstock, p122r Africa Studio/Shutterstock, p123l Hank Morgan/Rainbow/Science Faction/SuperStock, p123c Gunter Marx/AE/Alamy, p123r Todd Shoemake/Shutterstock, p125 Monkey Business Images/Shutterstock, p126 Franck Boston/Shutterstock, p128tr and 129tl NASA, p128cr and 129cl Rich Carey/Shutterstock, p128br and 129bl Bilanol/Shutterstock, p129cr NadyGinzburg/Shutterstock , p129br erwinf/Shutterstock, p129bc Wild Carpathians/Shutterstock, p131 VectorMine/Shutterstock , p134 Patrick Poendl/Shutterstock, p136 and 137 Bryon Palmer/Shutterstock, p137 badboydt7/Shutterstock, p138br Lycia W/Shutterstock, p139bl BlueRingMedia/Shutterstock, p140 grynold/Shutterstock, p141 Serg64/Shutterstock, p144br Prerna Bindra, p145bl Ondrej Prosicky/Shutterstock, p146tr sarayut_sy/Shutterstock, p148tr Heritage Image Partnership Ltd/Alamy, p148cr Vladimir Melnik/Shutterstock, p148br Prisma by Dukas Presseagentur GmbH/Alamy, p149tl wong yu liang/Shutterstock, p149cr gary yim/Shutterstock, p149br Chayathorn Lertpanyaroj/Shutterstock, p151 Santiago Nunez/Shutterstock, p152tr chaoss/Shutterstock, p153 JingAiping/Shutterstock, p154t Cora Reed/Shutterstock, p154b VN Stock/Shutterstock, p156 Carsten Reisinger/Shutterstock, p157 Pres Panayotov/Shutterstock, p158 CImage Source/Alamy, p159tr Studio.G photography/Shutterstock, p161 Ohishiapply/Shutterstock, p162t Seleznev Oleg/Shutterstock, p162b Mohammed younos/Shutterstock, p163t Tayvay/Shutterstock, p163b Hung Chung Chih/Shutterstock, p165tr Zzvet/Shutterstock, p165b Nicram Sabod/Shutterstock, p168tr Pichugin Dmitry/Shutterstock, p168cr WorldStock/Shutterstock, p168br Fernando Jose Vasconcelos Soares/Shutterstock, p169cr pixbox77/Shutterstock, p169br Thomas Nord/Shutterstock, p170 Joko SL/Shutterstock, p171 HelloRF Zcool/Shutterstock, p172 C.Snooprock/Shutterstock, p172bl Alexandr Shevchenko/ Shutterstock, p172br chipix/Shutterstock, p173 V Kuzmishchev/Shutterstock, p175t T.W. van Urk/Shutterstock, p175c DesiDrewPhotography/Shutterstock, p175b travelview/Shutterstock, p176bl travelwild/Shutterstock, p176tr Jaromir Chalabala/Shutterstock, p176tbr Iryna Rasko/Shutterstock, p178 Vitalii Nesterchuk/Shutterstock, p179 Claudiu Paizan/Shutterstock, p180 Macklin Holloway/Shutterstock, p182 andrey_l/Shutterstock, p182 ©Volocopter, p182 © TIAGO BARROS STUDIO, p184 Shutterstock, p184 Ajiro Bicycle image reproduced by kind permission of Alexander Vittouris, p184 Cal Craven, p186 andrey_l/Shutterstock, p186 Pavel Chagochkin/Shutterstock, p186 chuyuss chungking/Shutterstock, p188tr and 189tl Anna Omelchenko/Shutterstock, p188cr and 189cl dpa picture alliance/Alamy, p188br and 189bl Pete Niesen/Shutterstock, p189c Gino Santa Maria/Shutterstock, p189cr Beauty Style/Shutterstock, p189bc ViDI Studios/Shutterstock, p189br crystalfoto/Shutterstock, p192 Miguel Caibarien/Mauritius Images/Shutterstock, p193tr photoBeard/Shutterstock, p193l Prisma by Dukas Presseagentur GmbH/Alamy, p193r Victor Jiang/Shutterstock, p194_1 NBC/NBCUniversal/Getty Images, p194_2 Neale Cousland/Shutterstock, p194_3 IndianFaces/Shutterstock, p194_4 CREATISTA/Shutterstock, p194_5 Foxytail/Shutterstock, p194_6 Rick's Photography/Shutterstock, p194_7 Alena Ozerova/Shutterstock, p194_8 Dennis Albert Richardson/Shutterstock, p195 Victoria Chudinova/Shutterstock,

p196br shevtsovy/Shutterstock, p197br David Bergman/Sports Illustrated/Getty Images, p198_1 jivan child/Shutterstock, p198_2 Michele Burgess/Alamy, p198_3 John Messingham/Shutterstock, p198_4 takayuki/Shutterstock, p198_5 swissmacky/Shutterstock, p199tr Tukaram.Karve/Shutterstock, p199tr Tetra Images, LLC/Alamy, p199br agefotostock/Alamy, p200br cristovao/Shutterstock, p201tr RTimages/Shutterstock, p201br Sergey Peterman/Shutterstock, p202cr Srdjan Randjelovic/Shutterstock, p202bl oneinchpunh/Shutterstock, p204br humphrey/Shutterstock, p208tr and 209tl Media Union/Shutterstock, p208cr and 209cl Nolte Lourens/Shutterstock, p208br and 209bl Odua Images/Shutterstock, p209c Anna Jurkovska. Shutterstock, p209bc Pixel-Shot/Shutterstock, p209br Steven Markham/Speed Media/Alamy, p210 Sebastian Gauret/Westend61 on Offset/Shutterstock, p211tr Just Life/Shutterstock, p212tr Mario Cales/Shutterstock, p212cr sharpner/Shutterstock, p213bl Dmitry Molchanov/Shutterstock, p214cr Sebastian Crocker/Shutterstock, p214tl Michael Barajas/Shutterstock, p214tr stockfour/Shutterstock, p214br parkerphotgraphy/Alamy, p216tr Ben Molyneux/Shutterstock, p217tr Rawpixel.com/Shutterstock, p218r Anton27/Shutterstock, p222r Allies Interactive/Shutterstock, p223 CHRISTINA ALDEHUELA/Getty, p224r OmMishra/Shutterstock, p226tr Dejan Dundjerski/Shutterstock, p228tr and 228tl Pressmaster/Shutterstock, p228cr and 229cl Asia Images Group, p228br and 229bl takayuki/Shutterstock, p229c Lucian Coman/Shutterstock, p229br ivazousky/Shutterstock, p231br Ms Jane Campbell/Shutterstock, p233r Monkey Business Images/Shutterstock, p235br Paul Maguire/Shutterstock, p237tr fizkes/ Shutterstock, p238bl CREATISTA/Shutterstock, p238bc AlenD/Shutterstock, p238br Phil Date/Shutterstock, p239tr robertharding/Alamy, p239bl Ryan M. Bolton/Shutterstock, p239br Herve Collart/Sygma/Getty Images, p240br Monkey Business Images/Shutterstock, p241l zhu difeng/Shutterstock, p242bl Action Plus Sports Images/Alamy, p243l Hyoung Chang/The Denver Post via Getty Images, p243c Action Plus Sports Images / Alamy Stock Photo, p243r Zuri Swimmer/Alamy, p244r PA Images/Alamy, p289 George Rudy/Shutterstock.

Audio Acknowledgements

Track 3.2: Extract from NHS Long Term Plan, Crown Copyright © 2021, Open Government Licence v3; Track 4.2: Extracts adapted from 'How to make a Mindmap – the Basics'. Reproduced by kind permission of Susan Gregory, bestworkyet.com; and 'Rules for mindmapping'. Mind Map is a registered trademark of Tony Buzan. Information on how to mind map is taken from the website ayoa.com. Reproduced by permission; Track 6.7: Extract adapted from 'Work in the digital era' Sunday Times magazine, 06/11/2011, copyright © The Sunday Times / News Licensing; Track 7.2: Extract adapted from 'The Plight of Endangered Species/Endangered Earth' by Craig Kasnoff. EndangeredEarth.com. Reproduced with kind permission of the author; Tracks 7.3, 7.4: Extracts by Prerna Bindra. Reproduced with kind permission; Track 12.6: Extract from 'World's oldest marathon runner completes Toronto race at age 100' by Caroline Davies, The Guardian, 18/10/2011, copyright © Guardian News & Media Ltd 2021.

In some instances we have been unable to trace the owners of copyright material, and we would appreciate any information that would enable us to do so.